The Hispanic Journey

One Golden Nugget

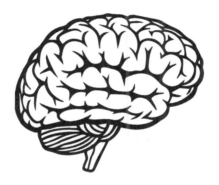

Rocío Pérez

Inclusion and Diversity Thought Leader and Trainer

Cover Design - Gerardo Garcia-Jurado & David Torres Mora
Content Design - David Torres Mora

Registered office
7-8 Church St, Wimborne BH21 1JH

Published by One Golden Nugget
ISBN: 978-1-4478-3232-4

About This Book

What an incredible journey the making of this book has been. The co-authors have truly each shared their Hispanic Journey with the reader. It has moments of sorrow and despair, and moments of great joys and achievements. It demonstrates the leadership, tenacity and grit that the title reflects.

Perhaps one of the things to come through in this book is the willingness to change to make the Hispanic community a greater and more widely visible community in the USA. On every level we are shown throughout these pages what can be done to help and improve the lives of others and we hope it will be read and shared by younger Hispanics who wish to make the climb to the top of their chosen paths.

We were also very lucky to have some retrospective history in the extended chapter with Adrianna Abarca that we hope can shed a light on the Hispanic culture often not seen today in schools.

One Golden Nugget would like to thank each and every co-author for their time and patience in the creation of this nearly 100,000-word epic. We hope you will enjoy sharing the experiences of the other co-authors with friends and family alike.

Thank you.

The contents and chapters of this book are taken from video interviews conducted with Rocío Pérez and One Golden Nugget with each co-author in 2022. The stories, places and people mentioned are as recalled and verified by the contributors. Every effort has been made ensure the spelling of people's names, titles and company names are correct. Some chapters contain different versions of acceptable word usage or capitalizations according to the preferences supplied following the proof readings by each co-author. Where photographs have been used these have been supplied by the co-authors. Every effort has been made to retain the 'voice' of each co-author and their sentence styling so that the character of each comes through to the reader including personal changes to grammar on final proofing. If there are any errors or omissions in this first edition and we are made aware of them, the print on demand file will be updated accordingly in due course. The publisher is not currently affiliated to or has ever been affiliated to the people or companies named in this book and expresses no opinion or bias with regard to the contents of the recordings or information supplied to it by the co-authors for this publication. E&OE

DISCLAIMER

In Memoriam

R.I.P.
Eduardo Ibacache Rodriguez

During the creation of this book,
we all sadly lost a very dear friend,
'EduardoX'
An energetic Hispanic mentor &
Founder member No.2 at OGN

We miss his passion, and his legacy serves to remind
us all of the importance of our mental health

Contents

One Golden Nugget - The Hispanic Journey

Introduction

I have often been asked why I wrote this book; my response is simple.

I wanted to share stories from the ground up, including the trials and tribulations that both myself and my fellow co-authors, as Hispanics, overcame along the way.

This book shares previously untold stories of how people got to where they are today, often from very humble beginnings. On my journey, I often meet successful people, such as CEO's and others in corporate leadership roles. It appeared to me that some of the people I met were hesitant to talk about where they came from, as if sharing that information would negate their accomplishments.

I wanted to know: Where did they come from? What inspired them? How did they get there? What lessons did they learn along the way? Why is it wrong to show and tell others the path from humble or poor to successful, and how do we allow that brilliance to inspire our young?

Learning the stories of these individuals, initially shared in private and now here for you, only after I got to know them, inspired me to keep moving forward because I thought it had been only me who had experienced these trials and tribulations. My co-authors and I share our stories here with the wider world, and the Hispanic community, to inspire them to take the bold actions required to become who they choose to be.

Success does not have a set path; it is not a straight line to reach your end goal. It takes work for sure; it actually takes 'leadership, tenacity, and grit'. The stories you will read can serve as a roadmap, a guide and an aspiration, regardless of where you are on your journey.

Once you have read this book, perhaps you would like to pass it on to someone else or order them a copy as a gift. I would like to think that people will enjoy reading the heartfelt and often brutally honest texts and understand the true purpose of this book. I hope the messages it contains make people want to share it with others - their team members, children, people in their organization, or any other group who could benefit.

We are all on various journeys, and this one we will share together.

It takes work to get where we want to be, and part of that work is being authentic, vulnerable, and courageous; that is our fastest way to success.

I want to bring communities together to tell the stories of *nuestra gente*. We are people who have grit. We have tenacity. We have been leaders and will continue that leadership role. We are hard workers.

Before I sign off and introduce our amazing co-authors to you, I have one last story to tell. Not too long ago, a gentleman served my meal at a local Mexican restaurant here in the US. I learned that he had come from Mexico and for the last year, his wife had working alongside him at the restaurant. I found out, to improve his family's lot in life, a sacrifice had been made and that he had not seen his son for six years; that his son was now six and a half years old. He shared with me how he and his wife left Mexico in search of a better life, and later this year, they will finally be able to reunite with their children here in the United States.

These are the types of stories I want to highlight: stories of hardship and triumph told from the heart. We as a *gente* have felt shame and criticism in each of our lives' stories. Let us now change that narrative and transform the shame and criticism into pride and wisdom. The first time I shared my story, it was with a mentor over lunch; he said I should never share it in public. "Why not?" His comment lacked humanity.

Modern technology and globalization have made it possible to connect socially with our deeper humanity. We are human beings first and foremost. It is time to be more empathetic, compassionate, vulnerable, and authentic. As we open up to our humanity, we have the opportunity to touch, move, and inspire others to do the same.

As a culture that values humility, at times we do not exercise our *ganas,* which can be perceived as lacking grit. The opposite is true. As a Latina entrepreneur, I am seen as an enigma by some people. I graduated with a dual master's degree even though my own mother told me to never pursue a college education. I also started a few companies when I was told it couldn't be done. Also of note, most of the Latinas in this book were told that young girls do not need an education. Some of them still carry the pain of those experiences with them.

How do we move beyond what has kept our culture and successes a secret? The answer is simple - inspire and speak belief to every man, woman, and child. What better way to inspire than to share real-life stories of people who were able to overcome their circumstances?

I selected the people featured in this book carefully because of their story and their generosity in wanting to help others by sharing their hardships and successes. We have people like José Hernández, the first Mexican American astronaut; Jasmine Diaz, who has created her own opportunities; Joanne Siracusa, the first Community Manager for *The MindShift Game*; James Pérez Foster, a Latino venture capitalist; and many others. Every person in the book has brought their own magic to it - people from all walks of life, who made their own way.

When I started this book and began telling my own story, it was nothing like the one you are reading now. I talked about my life as if it were perfect, highlighting my accomplishments. It was only through listening to the authentic stories of my fellow co-authors that I realized that there was so much more to my own. I decided to be vulnerable and to write my entry authentically. My own confidence has been boosted through listening to my co-authors' journeys and by telling my reality. As a result, I now have many more 'items' in my toolkit.

Throughout this book-writing journey, I learned that:

- People in our multifaceted culture are all different from one another, and their differences extend beyond their points of origin.
- What unites us is our belief in what is possible in our cities, in our neighborhoods, and in *nuestras familias,* and the limitations of that belief in our individual dreams for our lives.

- Some people want to help others, and they are willing to be vulnerable and connect with people.
- Some people feel more confident and worthy, so they share their authentic story.

There is not another book that I currently know of that is so authentic in its nature, that talks about grit, the journey, the things we love and our successes. Here you can learn from the experiences of more than twenty people who are, in many ways, just like you; their stories from the heart will move you. Laugh, cry, and celebrate with them as you acknowledge yourself for the progress you are making on your own journey.

The co-authors and I have come together on a mission that is greater than us, it is about our current and future generations, who are on their journey to live life to its fullest potential. Our greatest desire is for this book to get out in the world and make the impact we know it can make.

To accompany this book, we have created an inclusive online community that unites people from all walks of life. *"The Hispanic Journey"* brings people together to share their collective wisdom, support, and inspire each other.

There is no benefit to keeping your story to yourself. Our goal is for you to learn from our mistakes, trials, tribulations and successes and then create your own dream outcome.

Thank you for becoming a part of *"The Hispanic Journey."*

Rocío Pérez

HISPANIC JOURNEY

Chief Leadership Officer

I wish my story was not needed to be told. That it was bizarre, one that was so unique that it stood so far out of the historical rhetoric of Hispanic folk lore and that I did not need to shout loud as a Latina for the world to hear every word. As you will read throughout this book, one created with many, often-emotional, hours spent with others as they recounted similar experiences and, also ridiculous successes despite the odds, my story is only one of many.

I have learned many things about our people and myself during what has proved to be an intense and emotionally charged journey to create this shared text. Working with others who were not from our background has taught me to look at things from other perspectives and to question the questions we ask ourselves. There are uncomfortable moments to follow and amazing successes too.

I started this process with an interview with the team that I had to completely re-write knowing what I know now. I realized I had delved deeply into the lives of others to make this book and, as such, I too needed to speak candidly. That was tough. Really tough. I appreciate now the gifts and honest replies the contributors gave to this project. Thank you all. As such, I start this book with no punches pulled, no stones left unturned and my story.

I am of Mexican American descent. My parents emigrated from Mexico to the United States. I was born in the border town of Laredo, Texas as the middle child and only female, in a family of five children and lived in my grandfather's house for a few years. Laredo was locally known as 'The Devil's Belly Button', because it would get so hot that you could fry an egg on the sidewalk. It was a small town with few opportunities and high poverty.

My mother was a housewife, and my father was the sole provider. His job sometimes required him to work and live in different cities; I do not remember him being around much. As a result of my father's job insecurity and lack of financial safety, our family relied on government assistance to put food on the table.

To our detriment, my parents repeated the patterns of abuse and poor life choices taken by their family of origin. These patterns restricted them to a similar life of poverty - something that went unquestioned - and negatively impacted the rest of the family. They disconnected from their humanity and brutally abused their children physically, mentally, and emotionally, especially when they experienced great desperation or hardship. The moments I remember most vividly, those of being beaten, far outnumber the nurturing and happy times that childhood memories should include.

Some of my first memories of my father were of him coming home bloody and intoxicated in the middle of the night after being in another bar fight. I clearly remember my mother doing her very best to clean and disinfect his wounds. Sometimes, I was abruptly awoken by the distressing sounds of my father physically beating my mother while my older brother, only five years old at the time, did his best to stop him.

We moved around often and were mainly raised in secluded areas, isolated from the wider community. Even when we could have connected with other people, my father did not allow it. We did not have friends and could not have guests in our home.

We had to change location many times, usually without much notice. When my father's jobs ended or he got fired for not showing up for work, he would come home and announce that we were moving

"As a result of my father's job insecurity and lack of financial safety, our family relied on government assistance to put food on the table."

again. My parents, more often than not my mother, would pack the car with a few essential items of clothing for each person and the family possessions; as children, we did not have much of a say in what we could take with us. The little space in the car had to be used to pack necessary things like our one-burner electric tabletop stove, a tortilla press, a *comal* (griddle), and a 'makeup caboodle' my mom used to store all of our important documents such as birth certificates, immunization records and photographs. Then, lightly packed, we would head on to the next city, the next house, the next school and so on.

As a result of moving so much we did not have an opportunity to create a sense of belonging to any community – we remained outsiders.

As horrendous as it would seem now, when I was only five years old, I had a plan to commit suicide. I was mentally and emotionally depleted and could not imagine continuing to live in my horrific nightmare. It was in that moment, as I prepared myself to run in front of a semi-truck and end my life, that something stopped me. Call it God, a higher power, the Universe, or what you will, but from that moment I remember being filled with a new desire: a love and passion of becoming a teacher.

Looking back to that time, I first remember seeing a teacher talking with her students and helping them learn and grow on a television show. I wanted to be her and teach children in a school. After that, and probably for most of my free-thinking time as a young girl, I fantasized about school and learning, especially when I was left home alone for hours at a time as a child; I was still only five years old, but I had had the vision that was to shape me.

My Tío Sergio was one of a few family members who would come over to our house and often found me home alone. I would be running around carrying tattered books and chatting about how I was going to become a teacher. He would ask about the rest of the family, and I would ignore him and continue talking about teaching others when I grew up. He was caring, listened, and would take me to his home to keep me safe; not surprisingly, having done this, he would get in trouble with my parents for doing so.

I lived in my fantasy world, a place where I was safe, happy, and teaching others. My imagination kept me alive; in my state of helplessness, I somehow always found a way to focus on my vision of becoming a teacher and helping others. This inspiration occupied my mind and let me travel to my future even in the midst of my then-horrific daily reality.

As I was growing up, moving from city to city, home to home, and school to school, I remember having conversations with my older brother, telling him I would become a teacher, and sharing what my life was going to look like. I also inspired him to share his dreams, yet I never felt safe enough to have a conversation with my parents, much less share my own dreams with them. It simply was not a conversation to be had let alone acknowledged at that time.

By the age of ten, I had lived with my parents for maybe seven years of my life in total. The rest of the time I also lived with my Tía Maruca, my Uncle Pete, and my elderly Tía Lorenza. After my Tía Lorenza needed to be placed in assisted living, I moved back in with my parents. That summer, we moved to Colorado for the second time, starting all over again and leaving the extended family I had met and respected behind. The greatest thing I did in Colorado was to question the destructive behaviors of my family of origin and to realize what would happen if I were to stay in this toxic environment.

When I was twelve years old, my daily routine was not conducive to my dreams: I was woken up around three o'clock in the morning to help cook my father's lunch, went back to bed, and got up again at 5 am to get my younger brothers ready for school. I ironed their clothes, showered them, fed them and took them to school.

Personally, I did not own many clothes, so I would borrow and wear my older brother's clothes. At night, I washed his clothes in the bathtub and hung them to drip-dry on the shower rod; if I had time in the morning, I would do my best to iron-dry those shared clothes before putting them on. As a female it was my place to make these 'sacrifices' and in the middle of winter, I walked to school with half-frozen pants that felt like ice cubes on my legs.

Throughout this turbulent time in my life, the physical, mental, and emotional abuse escalated. Still only 12 years old and doing my best, my parents took turns beating me; when one got tired, they would toss me to the other one. Sometimes the beatings were so severe that even the feel and weight of the clothing on my body were unbearable.

TIME TO TAKE CONTROL.
(Or so I thought)

At the age of thirteen, I made the life-or-death choice to run away from home. Our family was getting ready to move back to Texas, where I knew I would be at greater risk because I would no longer have the protection of my grandparents.

My window of time for taking action was a brief one. That particular morning, while my parents were downstairs preparing their things for our move that night, I desperately darted into my grandmother's (Tita) and uncle Jesús' room. I looked my grandma in the eyes pleaded with her, and said, "You know, they are going to kill me!" She agreed quietly, "I know." Heartbroken and defeated, I begged her, "Please help me!" As she stood there in shock, searching for a response, my uncle Jesús agreed to help me. He had witnessed much of the abuse directed at me and was the only one who had ever confronted my mother about it. Thankfully, my grandmother also then agreed to help me.

As soon as my parents left to gas up the car on that frigid evening, I saw the opportunity I was looking for and darted out the front door to escape the nightmare, wearing only a thin windbreaker jacket.

My parents left Colorado without me, and I moved in with my grandparents to begin my new life. It was not all I had hoped it would be. Unbeknown to those around me, I struggled with the memories of physical, mental, and emotional abuse at the hands of my parents. I started smoking, drinking, and partying to simply numb the pain of the abuse that I had lived through. As I look back now the one thing that kept me moving forward was that overriding vision of becoming a teacher.

I had lived with my grandparents for a little over a year before things got out of control in their home. I was not easy on them. They felt it was best for me to go back to living with my parents. The awful thought of returning to the same abusive environment I had already left once was not an option for me; I decided to take my chances elsewhere and ran away with my twenty-two-year-old boyfriend.

I was only 14 years old, and he was a guy I barely knew, yet I figured

"At the age of thirteen, I made the life-or-death choice to run away from home."

that life could not be any worse. Nevertheless, I had unknowingly entered into another mentally, physically, and emotionally abusive relationship. It probably comes as no surprise as to what happened next: I soon became pregnant and found myself feeling trapped all over again.

All I knew was that I was going to keep my baby – my child became my WHY and ultimately, later on, my saving grace.

I was now forced to live with, a man I no longer wanted in my life. I was constantly threatened by him, and he said that he would take our son away from me if I left. I believed him for a very long time. He told me that my family did not care about me, in fact, that nobody cared about me. He was right on some levels, BUT he was also wrong! I cared and knew that our son Victor did not stand a chance in life without my presence; I had to set the foundation for his future and break the cycle of abuse, poverty, and ignorance in my family.

SOMEONE TO LOOK UP TO.
ANN: A PERSON WHO BELIEVED IN ME.

I met my first mentor, Ann, when I was fifteen years old, and my son was only fifteen days old. Although she had lived a variety of life experiences, we often miscommunicated due to our cultural, generational, and socio-economic differences - she was white, I was a Latina. She would often give me parenting and life tips, yet sometimes those tips were unable to serve me as intended because of my limited resources.

I vividly remember her saying to me, "Rocío, you have to go to high school!" And I replied that I did not belong in high school; I belonged in university. After all that had recently happened, I did not see the benefit of high school anymore - a place where I saw people my age smoking, drinking, and partying. I knew instinctively that I could not go back there if I was going to lead a better life.

As a Latina, uneducated and a teenage mother in an abusive relationship and working in menial labor, I knew, that without a big change, my son did not stand a chance in the world. I had to create opportunities for him. It was something so vital for his future, that I did all I could. And I worked hard to achieve that outcome.

At the age of 15 and with only a sixth-grade education, I effectively 'divorced' and emancipated my parents to attend university. Lacking a solid foundation in reading, writing, and math, attending this level of education very nearly insurmountable. In addition, my son's father made it more difficult to go to university by denying me every resource I had available, including the use of his spare vehicle; thankfully my tuition included a bus pass.

I gave the opportunity of a proper education everything I had. I went to bed at midnight and woke up at three in the morning to get my son and me ready for the day. By 4 am, I set off on my four-hour journey to school, which involved dropping off my infant son at my maternal grandma's house and taking two or sometimes three buses to get to the campus. I would eat my only meal of the day, consisting of a burrito that I had prepared when I awoke, as I walked to my first class at eight in the morning.

I only had $10 a day to pay for Victor's daycare; on campus daycare was charged $16 a day. I often paid family members to watch my son. When Victor was sick, I would take him to class with me. Sometimes I took exams with my two-year-old running around all over the place.

"As a Latina, uneducated and a teenage mother in an abusive relationship and working in menial labor, I knew, that without a big change, my son did not stand a chance in the world. I had to create opportunities for him."

I attended classes, and to improve my chances, I asked a lot of questions. I did my homework in the lab every day. At times, I felt like an impostor and feared someone would find out that I did not even know what I needed to learn. To overcome this, I spent a lot of time in the library researching what I did not understand in class.

THE NEXT CHALLENGE: HOMELESS, STUDY, WORK AND A GROWING SON.

At the age of 19, after many failed attempts, I finally escaped the abusive relationship with my boyfriend.

Victor and I were thankfully free. We had nothing; we were homeless. I worked 130 hours a month in exchange for a temporary furnished apartment. Our first 'real apartment' was in a two-year transitional housing program.

The odds were against me. My family repeatedly told me that they wanted me to fail. My son's father made life difficult for me in many ways and went as far as preventing his own family, Victor's relatives by birth, from helping me out. Even the people in the program were not very optimistic. However, this was the break, the renewed determination that I needed to earn my first degree. Every night, I made my son a makeshift bed in the corner of the living room with blankets so he could sleep. I'd get up in the morning and get ready for the day, drop Victor off at daycare and take a number of buses to my two jobs and school. To get through, I cleaned houses two or three days a week, mentored students three or four days a week, and went to class in between.

At the same time, I had created a safe, supportive environment at home where Victor could thrive. His father, unfortunately, continued to stalk and threaten us. During this time, I was even threatened with a knife if I did not stop pursuing child support; I complied.

My personal journey proved to be very different from the one chosen by my family; I chose to intentionally parent my son. I worked two jobs, made it home on a bus to pick him up from daycare and always found the time to take him to his doctor's appointments across town.

There was a particularly difficult moment that I will never forget; Victor asking me, at the age of five, carrying him up the hill while I was so exhausted and thinking that to carry him was impossible. I could not tell him I was too tired; my lack of energy was *not* his fault. I wanted to make this difficult moment positive and asked myself, "what can I do to help him right now?" I started telling him the story of *'The Little Engine That Could'*, the tale of perseverance, with the engine going up the hill and saying, "I think I can, I think I can," as we continued step by step to move up our hill. With this motivation, Victor and I made it without him having to be carried. I had turned a negative into a positive by choosing to tell him a story that captivated and inspired him to continue moving forward, and to do something he did not think he could do for himself.

HARD WORK AND DETERMINATION AT ANY AGE WINS THE DAY.

I earned my associate degree at the age 21 and my bachelor's degree at the age of 24. When I could not find opportunities, I created them. I mentored and coached students at varying levels of education; some of them already had high school diplomas, were working on a second degree, or were already in a new career. Some of the students I helped were also many years my senior.

"On my 34th birthday, I ended up in the emergency department. Thirteen days later, I was diagnosed with a brain tumor."

After graduating from university, I persuaded a regional manager to give me a job opportunity in retail by visiting his corporate office numerous times until he said yes. I had zero experience in this area at the time, but with tenacity, I landed myself a 10-week paid internship in the retail sector. The job only paid $10 an hour, so I asked the regional manager to allow me to work two shifts. He agreed. On my first day at the job, I showed up at 5 am and by the time he arrived, I was running the cash register and the customer service desk. By eight o'clock, he looked over at me and informed me I was going to management school. That's how I received my first promotion over others who had been waiting up to thirteen years for that opportunity.

That led to my attending management school in Arkansas for three months. As you can imagine, it was hard to be separated from my 10-year-old son in Colorado, so every week or two, as my training allowed, I flew back to visit.

Following my time at management school, everything seemed to be working out great. There were challenges, of course. I experienced long hours, employee insubordination, and having to run the entire store from the early hours to sundown on my own. I did the work, and when another job opportunity came up, I took it.

For the next two years, I created my own opportunities, volunteered in the community, got myself introduced to the media, and built my own professional network. In addition, I discovered my passion, which was helping people live a better life. I was now able to bring my experience, skills, and abilities together to serve the community. I had the privilege and opportunity to share my findings with well-educated people in particular fields. To this day, the programs we developed then are still going strong.

By my early 30's, I had become a full-time entrepreneur providing marketing services. I was also an 'empty nester' by then as well; I had a car, a house, an education, a business and more than I could ever have imagined when I was a little girl – I thought I had it all. Then, life, as so often it does, decided I needed a shake up!

On my 34th birthday, I ended up in the emergency department. Thirteen days later, I was diagnosed with a brain tumor. That brought on some deep thinking, but all I could think of saying was, "Thank you, God. Thank you for the blessing and privilege to raise my son and watch him become a man." Now, after much research into the condition and self-care, that brain tumor thankfully remains in remission, and I can tell you that raising my son has been and continues to be my greatest achievement in life to this day.

I had achieved multiple educational degrees and had also always wanted my son to get a college degree. However, after my diagnosis, I realized his happiness was more important than any degree and decided to stop worrying about my plans for him. My focus changed, and I helped prepare my son in a different way: to be responsible for himself.

CHANGE OF CLIMATE - CHANGE OF THINKING

I sold my house and moved to downtown Denver. Shortly after my move, six months later, I relocated to San Diego, California, to be in a better climate for my own recovery and wellbeing.

I still had numerous people that I had coached previously who continued to call me and ask for support. They were all apparently doing very well. I started to question how this could be. I was upset and thought, "How could the very people I am coaching be more successful than me?" After all, I was the one who guided them to their success so why didn't I have what I wanted? It was not education, achievement, or accolades. After much soul searching it became clear that what I really wanted, what I had truly missed, was my mother's love.

Knowing that I could not have that particular love led me on a journey of self-discovery that changed my life forever. Nobody had ever guided ME! Consequently, I decided to take up coaching myself. On this new journey, I discovered that I needed to love myself and acknowledge my own successes. That the only love that mattered was my own. The greatest gift that the brain tumor gave me was the message, "Wake up and live; you haven't lived. You've been denying yourself beautiful things and experiences all this time; you've been pretending that everything is perfect, yet it's not."

From that point on, I started learning from as many different people from all over the world as I could. I attended and volunteered at numerous conferences. I traveled from city to city and from state to state and discovered that the more I gave, the more I received. I danced with my pain, I consoled my sorrows, I made peace with my past, I acknowledged my successes, I opened up my heart and I let go of the shame. I put in the work to transform myself into the woman that I knew I was capable of being, the woman I knew was hiding inside.

One day, I was unrecognizable. I had become the person I came here to be, not who I was as a result of my life experiences. Now, all around the world, I can be open and proud to stand in front of an audience and say, *"I have been to Hell and back; – I have suffered physical, emotional, and mental abuse, and that those experiences have all made me who I am today."*

*"I danced with my pain, I consoled my
sorrows, I made peace with my past, I
acknowledged my successes, I opened
up my heart and I let go of the shame."*

*"Raising my son has been
and continues to be my
greatest achievement in life."*

"I believe leadership is not determined by title or authority. Leadership is about being someone who can influence, inspire and help others see their potential."

Today, I 'own' my story, I share all my vulnerabilities, and I am authentic and empathetic to myself. I do what makes my heart sing. I use my creativity, life experience, and education to help others achieve the life they also desire. I teach them to use *visualizations, affirmations,* and *bold actions* to believe in themselves and create their own opportunities.

This is how my companies, Veertuous and Inventíva, came to be. These are global companies that level the leadership playing field by providing services to people from all walks of life. Leadership is not a commodity limited to those who have financial resources; it is for all, every single one of us.

We all have the capacity to transform our lives into who we choose to be.

Rocío X

Jazmin Diaz

HISPANIC JOURNEY

Mother, Chief of Staff, Thought Leader and Mentor

Jazmin Diaz is a bright light in our community and a real fighter. She has worked diligently and reached a senior position with a tech software giant as a Chief of Staff. Jazmin closely partners with a Chief Executive as a trusted partner and advisor. She leads executive business operations and communications, strategic planning and coordination, employee success and engagement programs, and DEI initiatives. Jazmin is a born 'people person' and absolutely dedicated to pursuing a culture of inclusion in the workplace. I admire her very much as a woman of integrity, one who is incredibly relatable, whose influence is being felt, day by day, in our community.

Our conversation was enlightening, and I think there is something relatable to us all in Jazmin's story. Here is how she started her journey, in her own words.

My mother was 15 years old when she had me, I was born in Mountain View, California. Because of various life circumstances, my grandparents legally adopted me and raised me as their daughter. For most of my early childhood, I was raised in Mexico, Degollado, Jalisco, where I attended grade school and, during that time, I absorbed and embraced the Mexican culture.

At the age of eight or nine, I moved back to California. At that time, I had many self-doubts and low confidence because my first years of schooling had been predominantly in Mexico, and in Spanish. Suddenly, I was at an American elementary school having to re-learn proper English, grammar, and vocabulary. I had insecurities about the way I spoke, and sometimes I used words that I couldn't fully comprehend.

I struggled during those first couple of years back in the States, but with time I progressed and blossomed. I made many friends and had a social life. I attended schools that were diverse and rich with many cultures and backgrounds, Hispanic and Latinos were the majority.

When I got to high school, my environment and social life changed. Because of where I lived, my assigned high school was predominantly white. I could truly count on two hands how many Hispanic or Latinos were at my school. We, Hispanic and Latinos, stuck out like a sore thumb, we were the minority, and often felt excluded from the rest of the student body.

I found myself struggling, again. I started skipping school and getting into trouble. I ended up finishing high school through an alternative learning program. This program worked for me because I was in a 'one-on-one' setting, off campus, with a dedicated teacher every day. I succeeded this way because I didn't have any distractions to keep me from focusing on what I had to do. The program and teaching staff made me want to thrive. I was engaged with my learning and as such, I graduated with my high school diploma. Later that year, I married my husband, Gabriel, a young man that I had met years before at middle school, at the age of twelve. God brought us back into each other's lives, He had a plan for us.

Fast forward, and twenty-five years later, I am very proud to share that Gabriel and I are happily married and have four amazing kids together, Alejandra, Gabriel Jr, Isaac and Isaiah. Our journey was not without hardship or adversity.

My husband and I are, to this day, both very determined, and totally committed, to the mindset that '*failure is not an option*'. Since the beginning of our life together, we knew that we were going to do whatever it took to ensure our babies were taken care of and that they would have better opportunities than we had. We both worked hard to uphold our commitment and promise to our family.

"It was my fear of failing manifesting itself, but my husband reminded me that I had nothing to lose, that I was never going to know who I could become or where this opportunity would take me unless I gave it a shot."

Early in my career, as a young mother, I worked for my local school district, at a middle school. The job paid the bills, had good benefits and the work was extremely rewarding and fulfilling to me personally. I had school holidays and summers off, which gifted me the opportunity to have that bonding time with our children.

I kept that position for 13 years, and by that time, as the children were getting older, I began feeling like my career had flatlined and I wanted to try something new. I was great at my job, and I loved it, but I had reached the point where I was no longer being challenged. I knew I had potential, and I felt there was so much more I could do with my life.

I took a good look around me and started to think about what I wanted to do next. I would often see other mothers come to pick up their children from school and I would notice their polished and professional attire and think how 'chingona' they must be in their careers. They were corporate professionals and executives, and it was impressive to hear them talk about their roles and experiences in Corporate America - things that sounded exciting, yet foreign to me because I had primarily been in education in the public sector. I was intrigued and inspired. I wanted to be like them. It awakened something inside me. I knew I had to pursue a different career to see who I could become, and what that could do for our family.

With my husband's support and encouragement, I explored ways of forging a career in the tech industry. I considered the skills that I already had in accounting, planning, purchasing, communication, and event management, and how they might translate to executive support and operations. There were so many roles I had performed over the years – I had developed a wealth of experience that I was sure would be transferable.

I started applying for jobs.

But, as many people know, the frequent rejection becomes disheartening. I was turned down many times, a dozen at least. I began to think I was in over my head and that, perhaps, my skills did not belong in Corporate America.

Around this time, I had a conversation with a woman I love and trust, a friend of my mother's, someone I respect and admire. She was a single parent, crushing it in the tech industry, and an executive at a well-known company. I shared my career aspirations with her and told her what I was trying to do for my family and myself.

This family friend suggested I try a slightly different approach to change my career path. I should aim for an entry-level position, instead of a lateral move, and concentrate on simply getting my foot in the door. She was confident that once I got in the door, there would be no stopping me and I would advance in my career quickly. Her advice intrigued me, this strategy made sense. I thought she was probably right - it was time for me to take a step backward, in order to move forward.

On her advice, I applied for a receptionist role, and sure enough, I received an offer. Just like that, my life was about to change... and I was terrified!

Fear took over, I started listing all the reasons I should decline this job offer and stay where I was, in my comfortable and safe role at the middle school. This was crazy, right?!

It was my fear of failing manifesting itself, but my husband reminded me that I had nothing to lose, that I was never going to know who I could become or where this opportunity would take me unless I gave it a shot. And he pointed out that I was leaving the school district on good terms and with great rapport. I could always go back if things didn't work out or try something elsewhere.

I knew he was right. I had nothing to lose. I went for it! And months later, having joined as a receptionist, I was energized and challenged. I was working with the Corporate Facilities and Real Estate team. I got involved with as many aspects of the business as I could.

I was working cross-functionally, supporting company executives, executive assistants, and running the executive briefing center and collaborating with security operations, facilities, space planning, events and finance teams. I was determined to succeed. I was eager to help with anything I could. I took on special projects, and asked a lot of questions, and got out of my comfort zone. This was a special time for me.

I remember frequently having to look up acronyms because the new environment I was in was foreign to me. I would hear acronyms such as EBC, QBR, TAC, GTM, and I didn't know what any of them meant. I spent time researching and asking colleagues questions so I could understand the verbiage and business fundamentals better. And, because I was in an environment with people that made me feel comfortable and safe enough to ask those questions, I never felt dumb or ignorant, I embraced the learning path. I am grateful for the many teachers and coaches who helped me along the way.

In a short span of time, I became familiar with the business models, language, and structure of the company. As a result, I transitioned into an Executive Admin role to support the Head of Global Customer Success and Services. The strategy to get my foot in the door and hard work paid off.

I was at a pivotal moment in my career. The Executive I worked for, my boss, was an incredible teacher and mentor to me. It took time to build rapport and trust with him, as with any new manager, but once I hit that mark, he saw my potential and empowered me to take on more responsibility. He involved me in business planning, reporting, and strategy sessions, and before I knew it, I felt confident and capable. I was making big strides in my personal growth and career journey. At that moment, the voice of doubt that had limited me for so long finally quieted.

Those pivotal moments are really special.

Was there a time in your life where you wished someone could have just said: 'You can do this?'

I previously shared that I dealt with many insecurities growing up, due to the language and cultural barriers which affected me as I entered adulthood. I wish someone had encouraged me to take risks and pursue my goals, despite my fear of failing.

There is a quote by Zig Ziglar that resonates with me, and Mr Worldwide, aka Pitbull speaks it often: "F-E-A-R has two meanings: 'Forget Everything And Run' or 'Face Everything And Rise.' The choice is yours."

What were some of the roadblocks, or bottlenecks, you encountered on your journey?

In hindsight, I realize that I was often my own worst enemy. I allowed fear and doubt to limit me, and I did not have the self-confidence to make bold decisions for myself.

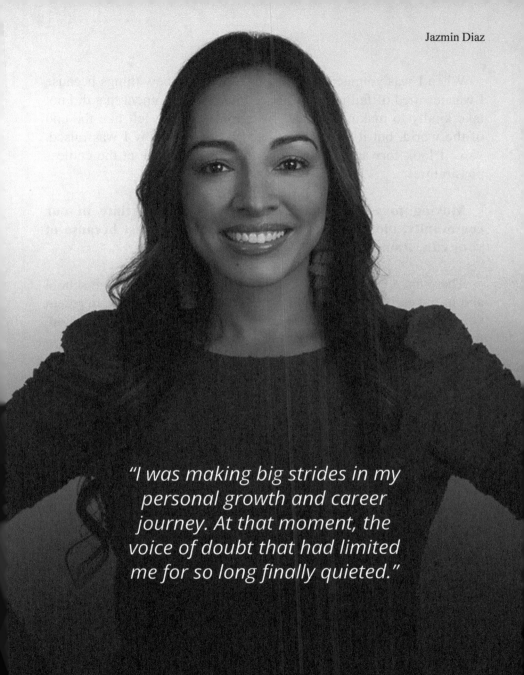

"*I was making big strides in my personal growth and career journey. At that moment, the voice of doubt that had limited me for so long finally quieted.*"

When I was younger, I refrained from trying new things because I was terrified of failing. I was raised in an environment that did not take kindly to making mistakes or errors. Failing felt like the end of the world, but it was self-inflicted because of how I was raised. Now, I look forward to new opportunities and smile at the endless possibilities.

Moving to something that comes up all the time in our community, did you ever feel discriminated against because of your education or culture?

There have been moments, especially when I was in high school and in my early career, when I experienced discrimination. In recent years, I experienced some dark and difficult times, and that was more to do with being a woman, not my education or ethnicity.

Like many women, I've experienced disrespectful and dismissive comments in the workplace. I have been degraded and demeaned by male counterparts. In the past I have brushed off these behaviors, however, because of those experiences, I made the decision to stand up for who I am, uphold my values as a person, and address these behaviors accordingly.

You would be amazed at how many young women I have spoken to who have been in similar environments or situations. They have experienced dismissive or unpleasant behaviors and do nothing out of fear of retribution. In other cases, they also think it's the norm and that they need to deal with it.

I'd be remiss if I didn't give a shout-out to the incredible men who have been allies to women, me included, and continue to uplift and champion us. Thank you to those individuals, you know who you are.

"Failing felt like the end of the world, but it was self-inflicted because of how I was raised. Now, I look forward to new opportunities and smile at the endless possibilities."

Who showed you the ropes? Who mentored you?

There have been many phenomenal people in my life who have taught and mentored me over the years, and still do today.

Of course, my mother's friend, whose advice helped me get that first interview and job at a well-known cybersecurity company, continues to be a bright light in my life today. The Executive I worked for when I first joined Corporate America helped me develop and grow professionally in many ways. I am forever grateful for the opportunity I had to work with him and for the many lessons and skills I learned under his guidance and leadership. Also, the people who saw something in me, and continue to believe in me. They took the time to teach and enable me so that I could be successful in my journey, and they still play an active role in my life.

I am a huge believer that we can't do it alone, and that we all need help along the way. It's a wonderful gift to have people in your life who you can connect with on a human level and know they truly care about you, your happiness, and your success.

What do you want people to remember you for?

I would most like to be remembered for my caring spirit and willingness to help others.

How do you define leadership?

I believe leadership is not determined by title or authority. Leadership is about being someone who can influence, inspire and help others see and activate their potential.

A true leader is someone with humility, and courage, and who genuinely wants others to succeed as much as they want success for themselves.

What is the largest obstacle to the career advancement of Hispanics and Latinos?

In my opinion, mindset is the largest obstacle. Many of us think like victims instead of victors. We often allow ourselves to be labeled, pigeonholed, and limited by a narrative that does not reflect who we are.

Our heritage, background, and upbringing should empower us; but generations of traditional norms, gender roles, and cultural nuances have kept many of us from advancing or tapping into new possibilities.

Additionally, I think we can all do a better job by showing up and supporting each other to reach our career aspirations. While progressing through my career, I've both experienced and witnessed a lack of support from some of my own gente which was disappointing. On the flip side, due to that lack of support, avenues opened up for me to be vulnerable, rebrand myself, and tap into ecosystems of people that have empowered me to believe in myself.

On the family front, if the goals and aspirations are to break the status quo and enter the Tech space, I believe changes are required at home. For instance, I know many Mexican American families who prioritized a Quinceañera fund for their daughters. Why not plan for both a party and a college fund instead? While at the dinner table and at family gatherings, start discussing topics such as higher education, investing, careers in STEM, and financial literacy.

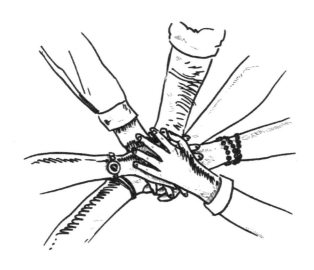

*"I am a huge believer that we can't
do it alone, and that we all need
help along the way."*

At the end of the day, we are all in charge of our path and how we walk it.

I chose to shake things up and do things differently, and since then, opportunities I never foresaw have continuously surfaced.

What's your approach when pursuing or creating new opportunities for yourself?

From my point of view, there are opportunities everywhere. For starters, I think we have to ask ourselves "what do I want?" Once you find that answer, dive right into setting your goals. There's no one size fits all or cookie-cutter approach for this, your plan needs to be specifically tailored to you. This plan deserves thoughtfulness, intention, timelines, and a pragmatic approach. Now, surround yourself with people who will push you to tap into your potential to be your best.

A few guiding principles I recommend adhering to are:

Be yourself. No opportunity should require you to compromise your personal values or betray who you are. You have something to contribute and offer, it would be a disservice to alter who you are or hold yourself back to meet the agendas or expectations of others.

Foster your relationships. Get out there and build new relationships while continuing to nurture those that already exist. For me, this gives me a sense of fulfillment and gratitude that keeps me motivated to continue growing.

Practice self-awareness. Any negative demeanor and how we interact with others can be career-limiting. The ability to self-reflect is crucial for growth, it will support us to change and develop into better people. We all have habits and behaviors to improve; find those traits and put in the work to grow and be better than you are today.

Be patient. Progress takes time to develop and play out, don't rush the process. Avoid the urge to be frustrated and enjoy the journey-there is beauty in adversity and struggle.

Ask Questions. To learn and amplify our knowledge, we need to research and ask questions. Informational interviews are a good method to gather new and insightful information. Whether you are curious about a potential role you may want to pursue, investment opportunities, entrepreneurship, or getting into something completely new.

If you had to give three keys of success to people reading your story, what would they be?

First, don't overreact. That applies both professionally and personally. I have learned in life that we don't control anything, so, give yourself time to process whatever is happening and think it through. Take a view from afar, and see a situation from more than just your own personal perspective.

Second, don't be afraid to get out of your comfort zone, if you're comfortable, you're not learning. Comfort feels nice because it brings a sense of familiarity and calm, but it hinders curiosity and the ability to try new things. You will learn a lot about yourself and will adapt to change. To grow, we must step out of our comfort zone and embrace the journey.

Lastly, take initiative. In life, things don't just magically happen. You have to put in the work. If it is your aspiration to grow or do something new, then go for it. You have nothing to lose and everything to gain. I don't see mistakes as failures, they are lessons - fail fast, learn from them and move on.

How do we step into our power and embrace the present moment?

We all have a set of powerful gifts and qualities. Whatever they are, those gifts are useless if our mental health is not prioritized. Along with everything else I've shared as advice and guidance; mental health should be front and center. Keep your balance and peace. If your emotional and mental state is not well, your immune system will deteriorate, creativity will dwindle, energy will decline, and you won't be able to care for others or live a joyful and fulfilled life. We must take care of ourselves, physically and mentally, to step into our power and achieve our goals.

Be present. Appreciate each day and be grateful for the blessings in your life. And choose how you spend your time wisely. Time is the one thing we don't get back, so be choosy with it. There was a time in my life when I would say yes to everything and everyone, and over-commit myself. I've since learned that being more selective with how I spend my time is necessary to manage my priorities. The key is not to spread yourself too thin for the sake of everyone else; do the things that are important to you, your well-being, and with the people who truly matter.

Finally, what is your Nugget of wisdom for when things aren't working?

I love that you asked me that question. This is something I am constantly reminding myself and my family about. Each of us is in charge of our circumstances and our environment. If something is not going to your liking, or you don't like the way something is going in your life, change it, that includes who you surround yourself with.

In my opinion there's nothing worse than being unhappy, doing nothing to change your circumstances, and complaining about it. You have the power to make a change.

You must change the things that you don't like or don't bring value to your life. No one else will do it for you.

Dedication

I dedicate this to my best friend, husband, confidant, ride or die, Gabriel Luis Diaz, Sr. To my incredibly strong, hermosa, poderosa, and chingona daughter, Alejandra Jazmin. My son Gabriel Jr whose focus and discipline are like no other. My loving and thoughtful son, Isaiah, who is beautiful inside and out. And to my dear son, Isaac, who has a big heart, the strength of a superhero, and inspires me every day. I love you all con todo mi corazón, por siempre. May God bless you and keep you safe always.

And to my beautiful and talented Goddaughters, Lay Lay, Aaliyah, Brianna, and Trinity, I love you with all my heart. Always be yourself and keep shining bright like the stars that you are.

OGN INTERACTIVE
Gloria Jazmin Diaz
Scan here
to visit my profile

Guillermo Diaz, Jr.

HISPANIC JOURNEY

Founder / CEO – Conectado Inc.
Chairman - HITEC

As the Chairman of the Hispanic Technology Executive Council (HITEC), the premier global tech executive leadership organization, Guillermo Diaz, Jr. is a transformative business leader and long-standing champion of diversity, equity and inclusion. Throughout his career he has a track record of getting the most out of people, process and technology, securing a fine reputation for making a positive impact on the wider community by leading education, study and scholarship programs.

I started by asking Guillermo what makes his heart sing.

I have this notion of a compass called the G Compass. On the G Compass, there is a North Star, and there is a South Pole which is the foundation. There is, an East and West too.

The North Star represents my purpose, which is how we raise people and develop their potential. Because of that, what makes my heart sing first is my family, and then others in the generation that are underrepresented. I want to help people in the areas where I grew up get the opportunities, promotions, and results they deserve because I know what it's like to be in so many of these people's shoes. That is what my North Star represents: how we build the next generation knowing that family is behind them, helping to drive the opportunities that they deserve.

I am just a 'patch in the quilt' on their journey, a helping hand, all related to my North Star which is *the purpose*.

The foundation, my South Pole, is *the platform*, which has three main elements, primarily technology, secondly, diversity and thirdly community. I have been very intentional about inclusion, diversity and equity. I make sure that the lessons and experiences that I have

The G Compass

Purpose

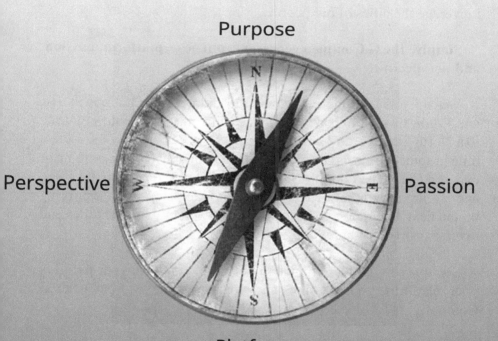

Perspective

Passion

Platform
(Technology, Diversity and Community)

learned from being Latino and being under-represented are woven into everything I do, not only in my CIO or tech roles.

The East which represents passion, to always remember where I came from and inspire where I am going.

The West represents perspective, which is about making sure that I leverage the allies of our people.

Simply, the G Compass represents purpose, platform, passion, and perspective.

When I was growing in my career, I did not have Latinos to ask, and I didn't have anybody that looked like me who could point me to a North Star. I didn't have that perspective of being able to walk a mile in someone else's shoes and understanding that not everything or everyone has to be Latino! Now I know that we are all here together, and we are all human beings. I want to make sure that I can bring up the next generation with opportunity, leveraging all the allies and diverse people that are willing to help us.

So, applying all these things to your life, you have your purpose, your platform, your passion, and your perspective. That's the G Compass.

A beautiful outlook on life. I will never see a map again without thinking of my own G Compass. Guillermo's journey and ideas are worthy of a whole book itself.

I asked how it was for him growing up.

I was born and raised in Pueblo, Colorado. My dad was from

Mexico City and my mom, and her siblings, were born in the Mexican camps in southern Colorado. There happened to be a lot of work on the railroads there so that's where my grandfather ended up. I knew that, that I needed to make a better life because my grandma used to say that I had to leave there, I had something that was different, that I was going to change the world.

I was brought up to think that if someone is going to change the world, why not me? That thought was always in my head so when I finished high school, I went to the US Navy so that I could get money, go to a new school, and gain further education to make a difference. I was accomplishing that while doing my job in the Navy as a technologist, a technology specialist. I learned and executed technology, telecommunications and security, all of which were not that big a thing in civilian life back then but are now key.

Growing up in Pueblo, it was mostly Hispanic, I was around people like me. When I went to the Navy, it was 90% other backgrounds, there were not very many Hispanics in the Navy. There were a lot of blacks, a lot of whites and many Asians who were largely Filipino, and there were a couple that were Mexican American or Mexican of Mexican descent. I learned about the power of diversity and technology, and those two things, intertwined, were the foundation for everything after that, although I didn't really understand it at the time.

Now I want to get to know people and the background that drives them. That conversation sparks my interest and being around people and having allies who are different than you is really important. This is the power of diversity.

Interestingly, when I left the Navy, I was quite alone, there were not many Latinos, if any, to build with and all of the people that supported me and helped me were not Latino. And this is why it's really important for me to talk about this. The power of allies. The people that supported me along the way and took me under their wing were people like John Chambers, who was the CEO of Cisco. Then there was David L. Steward, the Founder of WorldWide Technology from St Louis, Missouri, and Rebecca Jacoby, one of the most powerful leaders I know, from Hayward, California. All these people were there to be my shield, and after their help I used the power of who I was, my culture and my technical competence to pave my path and hopefully for others like me.

I held key roles at companies like Alza Corporation and Silicon Graphics, where I ran the worldwide networks, and then ultimately most of my career at Cisco Systems, where I was the first Latino CIO. It wasn't just about the tech; it was about how I connected with the people around me.

I was also the founder, or the catalyst, for Conexión, the Latino Hispanic Employee Resource Group (ERG) at Cisco. That organization is now one of the most powerful ERG's anywhere. It wasn't about me being the CIO, it was about being the guy who was ready, willing and able.

The good news is that I was able to support the communities that I came from: the Latino community and the veterans. Those things are really important to me, they were foundational, especially the Navy, which drove a lot of discipline and built a lot of resilience. Being out on ships for months at a time was not easy.

In the Navy you have to do whatever it takes to get things done. My job was tech, but no one else is going to clean the bathrooms for you, clean the floors, or do the laundry, so you've got to do things

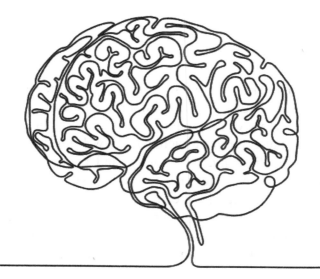

"You've got to do whatever it takes to make it happen."

yourself. I guess, in some interesting way, these experiences gave me scale, a spirit of entrepreneurship.

A One Golden Nugget is, *"You got to do whatever it takes to make it happen."*

I grew up in Pueblo, Colorado; I grew up in the Navy; And I grew up at Cisco. Those were the important times in my life that changed the trajectory of everything that I do, everything that I am, and everything that I am yet to achieve. Now I am taking all those pieces - the tech, diversity, community, and people - and pulling them together as I move into what I do next, which is being a tech entrepreneur. By showing that it can be done, showing people that it is possible, I'm using all the tools that I have garnered along the way in my toolkit to build a platform that will accelerate opportunities for those who are where I came from, the under-represented.

I had to put this to Guillermo: Considering that you're one of the few Latinos in tech, what allowed you to jump? What inspired you to jump into the tech field as an entrepreneur and make a difference? What was that launching point, the tools, knowledge, skills, abilities that enabled you to do this?

I think that the reality is, when I started this journey, I was one of the few Latinos in tech. Since then, I don't think that is the case anymore, even though the numbers are still very low, but if you are ever at a HITEC conference, you will wonder where all these Latino executives came from. They're at C- level, executive level roles, in some of the biggest corporations in the world. They are the best of the best!

I think that I had something to do with that as I go back to the quilt analogy and being probably a bigger patch than some in the quilt of Latinos in technology.

What has inspired me since day one, when I was just out of the Navy and starting a tech job in Silicon Valley, was that when I looked around, no-one looked like me. No-one was Latino, and no-one was a veteran. But there was this one gentleman named Al Cresta. I remember him so clearly. He was a phone and network technician who took me under his wing and showed me the business side. He really helped me because I was wired to the military side of tech.

At that time, I used to get upset because people couldn't say my name, so Al said: "You know what? I'm so tired of everybody butchering your name. I'm just going to call you G. Right?"

That is how the 'G' came to be. By the time I got to Cisco I was just G to everyone. That man inspired me in a lot of ways because he made me feel accepted. He wasn't Latino, but he made me feel good, like it's okay to be Latino, to be who I am, even though there's nobody like me. It was as if he was telling me that grandma was right – *"If somebody is going to change the world, why not me?"* I just happen to be brown, and I should be proud of who I am. He simply inspired me to live my life accordingly.

He said "I don't see too many people like you in any race. You are a tech guy, a veteran, outgoing etc. There's something special about you" Now I share that and say, "Don't let anybody tell you what you can't do." That is my purpose for the next generation.

We have all talents, and we just happen to be brown. And that's a beautiful thing. Having vocalized that G was right back with...

And Black. And White. Latinos and Latinas come in all colors.

"*I was brought up to think that if someone is going to* **change the world**, *why not me?*"

What I tell people about when we launched Conexión at Cisco, is that our mantra was that we would connect Latinos. We wanted to be a place where Latinos came and connected and became inspired.

However, after about two years as the president, I changed the mantra to 'connecting people.' I had to explain that at Cisco we should be leaders first, that should be our first mindset. The fact that we happen to be Latino is a benefit, but we don't want to be known by our color, but because we are leaders. Our color gives us a cultural relevance and so we put the two things together.

Initially it was let's just do this for Latinos because at Cisco Latinos were only 5% of the company demographic, but why would we not embrace the other 95%? When we did that, we started getting much more relevance and way more support and talked about it in terms of the business value that we were driving. No longer we were talking Taco Tuesdays or Corona Thursdays, we were leaders, and we were Latino.

It was inspiring to see Guillermo's level of detail and generosity. That is a huge thing. As we all continue to have this conversation, these are the details that are going to help people. There was a journey and then a considered choice. Expecting to make this huge leap in a large corporation is unrealistic if it does not have this humanity. There is a process.

It is true, a lot of folks I mentor now approach and label me a genius because I have broken through 'The Barrier'. The first question is always how I did it and my answer is that when they asked what I wanted to do in my job I replied that I wanted to be them. I told them I wanted to be in their chair. And they offered to help me - ask, and after that comes sponsorship.

If somebody is going to be a sponsor for you It is a major responsibility on your part too. If, I'm going to put my badge on the table for you, you had better deliver what is required or why would I be doing that in the first place? You have to understand that I am betting my chips on you, and I have a lot of trust in you. I believe in you. But you also need to make sure that what you say is what you are going to do and that you will do it.

Sponsorship is great but it is not a free ticket that you have been gifted, you have a responsibility in that transaction. Fulfilling your agreed obligations or the mutual gift of sponsorship and the benefits it contains are manifested by your actions.

The truth, that it is not a one-way street, but a give-and-take across races, is a process that we need to embrace. It is a value that many in this book, including our friends at One Golden Nugget bring. I personally know the value of a mentorship, or a sponsorship champion, and that we have that opportunity to grow if we ask and deliver.

I have, what I like to call, the C's of Success – Competence, Confidence, Courage, Communications, Connections and of course our Culture.

I grew up doing martial arts. When you have white belts, you don't know much: you don't know much about the skill; you don't know much about the taxonomy; you don't know much about the vocabulary, and you don't have a lot of confidence. But as you go, you learn this discipline, and you learn the skill set.

By the time I was 12 maybe 13 years old, I was already teaching adults. To take that on I had to have the courage, the confidence and the communication to teach them. I mean, these people are looking at you for guidance and saying Yes Sir! and you're only 12 years old!

So, how do you go from white belt to black belt? You do it by building the skill and the courage, confidence and communication. Once you get to black belt, you know you are an expert, and people are looking at you, expecting something very profound to come out of your mouth - they believe what you say because you know it.

But if you have the skill and you do not share or are unable to communicate it well, you will not inspire anyone. I know that there is a great opportunity to be able to develop and mold ourselves in any field, but it is not just the competency, or that we know what we're talking about, we must be able to communicate effectively and get the concepts across.

How did your Familia (Family) help you be who you have become?

My father died when I was a year and three months old, and my brother was four months old. I knew my mother had to work hard to raise us. I knew her resiliency and her background. She would always keep us connected to my father's family in Mexico City. So, I saw all of that, and that is why I say, "Always remember where you came from," to inspire where you are going.

The other piece of my childhood was my grandmother who lived with us as my mother worked to support us. My grandma was my biggest champion and my biggest cheerleader. I was going to the nationals tournament in martial arts. I was so scared, and I doubted whether I should even be there at the tournament. She said, "Of course you should be there. Not only are you going to be there, you are going to win! You are going to come home with a trophy." Fast forward: I won and was national champion. I brought home a huge trophy that barely fit in the house!

My grandma told me when I came back, "I knew that was going to happen." She would tell me, "You are going to change the world. You have something different; you have to go from here. Someone's going to change the world. Why not you?" That's why I always say, "Why not you?"

I also had a step-dad that helped keep us going. He helped shelter us and helped put food on the table. He was not my biological dad, but he was the only dad I knew. I never called him "dad," but that was my dad.

My mom and grandma were my main drivers. My mother had twenty-one siblings; I had a large family. The oldest four aunts and uncles were closest to me. I had a lot of cousins which I learned from. They all showed me what I *should do* and what I *shouldn't do*! That was my foundation.

It was time to reflect on a very important topic for Guillermo. - How the Hispanic community moves from being consumers to makers?

The cool thing is, there are more entrepreneurs that are Latino than any other demographic. If you look at the digital natives, Latinos are the most digital and use the most digital tools and services, far more than any other demographic. We only need to look at our kids to see the future.

When I see my young nephew, he tells me what to do to get onto the network. He says: "You are the CIO but you don't know!" And he's right, I don't always know! Our kids are more tech savvy than at any other time in history. I strongly believe that every job will become technology powered and as we are also the youngest demographic, the people doing my job are getting younger, we are well placed to play an important role moving forward.

If you look at the top four skills that are going to be required in the future, especially in the IT industry or the software industry is looking for: First is software developer; second is cyber security specialist, third is data scientist, and fourth is infrastructure or cloud automation. And where are those skills needed the most? In the US. And where in the US? Mainly in the top five states. So, those four skills, in the top two states, California and Texas, are needed, and the population are already majority Latino – If you look at K-12 grades in California, 55% of students are Latino - These jobs are already required in these states and wouldn't that be a nice pipeline as the need spreads to others. My question is how do we build that pipeline?

The Web 3.0 world that we are growing is going to be very different. We had a Web 1.0 World, which was the first Internet and Web 2.0 World, the second Internet, which is approximately what we live in today. But now we have this new world of Web 3.0, which is this new experiential Metaverse, blockchains, NFTs and other exciting new technologies.

In my opinion, Latinos are in a perfect space for that, because they are the entrepreneurs that are building companies around these technologies. And, if you think about STEM, and you go one step further to STEAM (which includes art), who better than the Latino community to bring artistic value and the digital world together? We see it all over in our murals and creative talents. What if we can create NFTs out of Latino art, and have those artists make millions of dollars?

Latinos are skilled where the skills are required. What's more, with the future of Web 3.0, Latinos are going to be the majority of the population. We are in a perfect spot, given this set of coincidences, to plan this kind of roadmap.

We are in a great place for our community to continue to grow and impact those industries. I am delighted we can start that conversation here with so many wonderful collaborators, connections and all of those reading this book too. It will also take the sponsorships and open mindedness we discussed earlier to work with others.

Now I wanted a hint that can help us inspire each other, because I know sometimes, and it is not everyone, we 'take the sun and breathe the air' and we don't always share that success in our community. How can we help inspire each other?

This is a great question. I believe that Latinos are, unfortunately, very segmented still. One of the reasons I even launched Conectado Inc. was to properly use technology to bring things together to reduce that segmentation.

We want to be able to look at those who have done it and tell their stories, see the roadmap for getting to those positions and open it up to others to follow. I mean, it may not be exactly like Rocío, for example, someone might have a different path, but by sharing how you did it maybe you can guide others a little bit along the way.

We have all know those barriers and it seems to be madness to me not to share our story and talents and include all who come baring gifts of benefit, brown or not.

My Last question was now appropriate, and what was the

greatest barrier G had to overcome in his career and how did he accomplish it?

"The greatest barrier any of us has is believing that we can do it - overcoming the Imposter Syndrome."

Understanding the whole notion of Imposter Syndrome is not only about should I be in this room, but why am I in this room? The reason why I am in the room is because I always had to be the one that raised my hand. I always felt like I was going to be number one at anything I do, or I was going to try my best to be that.

Then I had to ask myself if there was an underlying reason why I felt I had to push myself that way. Part of it was my own fear of not being relevant, so it was almost the inverse of Impostor Syndrome from a different angle - I'm going to make sure I'm in that room because I work hard and deserve to be and hopefully serve as an example to others like me.

That's another form of this fear. There was always a fear, even when I came prepared, nobody was able to say that I hadn't. I didn't interview for the CIO job because I did many of the roles in the IT organization. When John Chambers, Chuck Robins and Rebecca Jacoby called me and asked if I was ready. I echoed, "Are YOU ready!?" Finally, I said "I AM READY!", and they informed me I was the next CIO of Cisco.

That was the moment where I saw my life flash before my eyes. I was in my hotel room in Cincinnati, Ohio, at a STEM summit and that night I just sat there thinking: 'Holy shit. I'm the CIO of the biggest network communications company in the world.'

I was frozen. I was scared shitless. I was thinking: 'How am I going to do this?' And then I called Traci, still my assistant after 23 years. It was one o'clock in the morning, and after telling her the news and how I felt she said: "What do you mean, you don't know what to do? This is a human thing: you've done everything to prepare for this. Nobody knows this better than you. Remember what you always tell people, G. someone's got to do this job, why not you?"

This was my assistant telling me my own words. I have not looked back since that moment.

> "*The Biggest barrier*
> is you.
> **DON'T LET YOURSELF**
> get in the way of the
> *Opportunities*"
>
> Guillermo Diaz, Jr.

OGN INTERACTIVE
Guillermo Diaz, Jr.
Scan here
to visit my profile

Joanne Siracusa

HISPANIC JOURNEY

Community Manager | *The MindShift Game*
Veertuous, LLC

I am delighted to introduce you to my dear friend Joanne Siracusa in this chapter. She is extraordinary. When I decided to collaborate on this project, I thought about Joanne and how she must be in the book.

Joanne and I met years ago, and we became best friends instantly. She is amazing. She is a real mover and a shaker. She hosts events across the country and brings people together that normally don't come together. She is a phenomenal individual, and she offers extraordinary insights into the world of female Hispanic leadership.

Having trained, taught, and worked in Early Childhood Education and worked as a director level in Child Care for the YMCA. Joanne brings a unique perspective to her work as an Executive Administrator working in the Diversity department and now Community Manager in a highly competitive sector that supports people in becoming more courageous, confident, visionary, powerful, and energetic. For that reason alone, I was excited to hear her insights on leadership, tenacity, and grit.

This is what Joanne told me about her journey...

Each journey is unique, and every story deserves to be told. There's beauty and power in choosing to be vulnerable enough to share it with others. When most people think of the "Hispanic Journey" they think about how some people left their country for a "better life" the American dream which is more opportunities. or at least the concept of it. And, while some do, many do not.

Like many others my parents came to the US in search of that dream, with the support of the families they worked hard and made that dream a reality.

When I reflect on my upbringing and culture... It's a great reminder of just how important a role it played in my life. At home, it was imperative to learn Spanish first. Read, write and speak it fluently. And if I'm honest to this day I still get a kick from people's reaction when I speak Spanish.

Here are just a few examples of what I recall hearing as a child. You don't interrupt adult conversations, you greet everyone when you enter a room, and you don't speak unless you are spoken to. After some reflection, I believe that those lessons were valuable, particularly in terms of leadership.

"I am naturally candid, direct and decisive."

In my home, you were to fly under the radar - which was quite challenging for me given my spunky attitude and God-given disposition. A constant battle between who I was born to be and who I became. Some of us weren't created to blend in. "I am naturally candid, direct, and decisive." As a result of that, I limited myself as I was growing up. Leadership is a gift that some people are born with. They don't require a title or a position; others learn to lead, and few simply become "bosses." People naturally gravitate towards leaders and follow their lead. These people are also trendsetters. I am a trendsetter.

Since I was young, people have followed my lead and I achieved a leadership role very early in my education career. I missed out on a sponsorship opportunity after high school because it was crucial for me to be close to my family. I had to choose a different route. Due to my late college enrollment, the majority of the classes were already full.

"Let me start by saying each journey is unique. Each story is important to tell."

I didn't know what path I was going to take. God knew how it was going to work out, so He got me into the classes that I needed to get me on the path He had designed for me. My counselor and I worked out my career plan, and I discovered that I needed a diversity class.. At the time, the only class available was Childcare Diversity. So I enrolled, and that was the first of my four classes, I started the course - and I loved it! In fact, that one course revolutionized my career trajectory.

That was the beginning of my career in education. The teacher of that diversity class was the director of the Child Development Center. Best of all, she really liked me, and before the semester ended, she asked me to present her with my resume. I took what I had without thinking much about it, thinking she was going to help me reformat it; instead, she offered me a job. This opportunity changed my life.

That simple request to see my resume led to a position as a student teacher at the Childcare Development Center. My first leadership job. What an amazing opportunity to mentor student teachers. Looking back, if you had asked me, then if I knew that would happen, I would have said, "No!" There was no way I could have known, that early break, that experience would change my life. This experience opened so many doors.

Now, most Hispanic households are accustomed to having more than one job. So going to school full-time and working two jobs was quite normal for me. My second job was as an after-school childcare director.

Most of my staff were older than me, so when the parents of the children walked into the room, they usually all walked right past me! Since leadership requires action, I quickly gained their trust and respect. In a very short time, they all supported me because of my willingness to learn from and grow with them. Many times, they even asked me if I would like to come home with them to help them there too.

"I was taught that you greet the janitor with the same respect and courtesy that you would the principal or president." Good things to learn when you're young!"

My family instilled the value of attentive listening when told not to interrupt adult conversations. For that reason, I became a skillful listener - a skill that has always helped me excel in leadership roles. I learned to listen to understand.

Being taught to greet everyone when entering a room taught me to greet everyone warmly and with compassion, to greet everyone equally. Later, that became part of my success; these lessons from my childhood served me well."

"Glory and thanks be to God." He created me, and when I forgot my purpose, He put the right people on my path to remind me of who I was meant to be." There's purpose in pain." growth in the process. Fulfillment is in progress. Power in perseverance.

Another very influential part of my journey is religion. From the very start, it has played a huge role in my life. My mother took me to church when I was two years old because she went, and I stayed because of my personal relationship with God. Leaders I admired taught me the kind of leader I should be. And when I was in leadership roles, I believe that was what made me different. Faith kept me optimistic. I prayed and trusted. Matthew 20:26 says, "But among you it will be different." "Whoever wants to become great among you must be your servant,". Good leaders serve others. To achieve true significance, one must serve.

"Faith kept me optimistic. I prayed and trusted!

God put me in the places and positions that I needed to be in order to teach me something valuable. And, without doubt, it did. My Hispanic background and knowing the language and culture helped me in so many ways. It is a gift. Even when traveling to other countries, people automatically connect to me because of it. Beautiful! Now I am empowered!

Adversity is a part of life. Adversities are a reminder to stay humble. To depend on my faith, resilience, and gratitude. The nudge to let go of my ego and pride that prevent growth. It appears in a variety of settings, and in all aspects of our hectic lives. It can be as simple as not seeing eye-to-eye with someone, discrimination, or people simply not liking you. Whatever it is, different personalities, opinions, or beliefs can all create conflict; none of us is exempt from it, but I learned that constructive criticism is not always a bad thing when you see the gifts within it.

When constructive criticism arrives, I reflect on what it's meant to teach me. What can I learn from it? In retrospect, those are all the things that kept me humble and grounded and were able to help me excel in each role. I think because of that trait, even in the role that I am in now, people still gravitate toward me. It is important to remember that just because you don't have a title, it doesn't mean you're not a leader. And that's it! You don't need a leadership title to lead. You can do it anytime.

When dealing with adversity in the form of people. I remind myself that we're human. We all know what pain feels like. Even if we all deal with it differently. My journey is still ongoing... I'm still evolving.

I began to ask Joanne some questions, starting with the one I love: What makes your heart sing?

Helping others. It doesn't matter in what capacity I assist someone; it just makes me happy. I feel joy when I see their smiles of appreciation, or their faces light up.

That's it, I thought. That is really exciting! That someone can find a passion and do something that excites them enough to do something that is making a difference. Joanne has worked in both education and the construction industry.

Having worked in the for-profit and non-profit worlds, how does a person make the leap from one to the other? It is not traditional to go from education into the construction industry. How did she make the leap to working for an international company?

Well, it wasn't planned. Joshua 1:9 says, 'Be strong and courageous." Don't be afraid or discouraged because the Lord, your God, is always with you. I had no idea where I was going, I simply trusted God would guide me.

I began in a non-profit sector because it was in line with my interests. I knew exactly what I was going to do; it's straightforward. So, when you go from that to the private sector, an international construction company, as I'm trying to rebuild my own life... I didn't know what to expect; I just knew to dive in fearlessly because God was with me.

I quit my job in education without having anything lined up. That was a first for me. It wasn't an easy decision, but in my heart, I just knew it was what I needed to do. It was time for something new. I wasn't sure what, so I looked through the college course catalog; Human Resources Assistant stood out right away. I figured I had learned the administrative role of it as a director, and this was a great opportunity to learn the investigative side and more of training and development, which I later discovered I loved.

The teacher told me I was made for training and development. So, my Community Manager role now is perfect. We'll come back to that. When I finished the course, I hadn't worked for a year! I had to pay bills. So, I got a job through a temp agency. Luckily, it was a temporary assignment because it wasn't where I was supposed to be.

When I interviewed for this private sector job, it just felt right. After the interview, I called my sister to tell her I loved it and went out with a friend to celebrate. I just knew; I felt in my heart, "This is it!" I was there for about eight months, when I stumbled upon the diversity department, which is where I felt it even more. Lit a fire in me.

How do you define success?

For me, success is defined by people. It comes down to this: Yes, success is exceeding goals, budgets, and personal goals that you set for yourself. Whatever you accomplish is powerful. That is success. However, as leaders, we do have the opportunity to change someone's life every day. Leadership is all about people, the little things make a huge difference, and the leaders that understand that are the ones that ultimately succeed.

Being successful is an extraordinary achievement - how does she balance her work and personal life to ensure wellbeing?

I became a Director and a leader young, and I was in school so I would work and study 10, 12, and 14 hours a day. I was young so I still wanted to live my life to the fullest and I had the energy, so I intentionally planned school, work and my life. Times are different now. Now, I have to occasionally disconnect. I begin and end my daytime in prayer and meditation. Connect with people and things that give me joy and peace and disconnect from anything or anyone that disturbs that. Our body needs rest. Our mind needs peace. Our soul needs happiness. It's important to me to rest, recharge and restore my mind, spirit and body.

I had decided to move to those things that Joanne thought were the significant factors that have been contributing to her success now, and what she said next sits perfectly with the title of this book.

My personality and passion. I think great passion makes big things happen. I think you come with the abilities and the skills. At the same time, it's your personality, your heart, your tenacity, your grit - all of those are things that keep you there. I mentioned early on in my story that there are leaders and bosses; if you have the desire to lead, you can be a leader, and if you don't, you just become a 'boss', simply a boss. I made sure in the process that I kept mindful of this, which

Joanne Siracusa

"I think great **passion** *makes big things happen."*

helped me and opened doors as I continue to be a leader. It was really my passion and my willingness to grow.

Joanne and I had talked about knowledge, skills and abilities. I asked her what she was doing, in terms of that, to set the foundation for an even more extraordinary future.

Constantly learn and consistently grow. By deep and meaningful conversations, by taking classes, listening to podcasts, and reading books and for me, attending church and serving. I believe that we get back what we give. It is essential for me just to stay aligned with that. A huge part of it is simply putting myself out there and serving others. This book is about leadership, tenacity and grit and since we're talking about a more extraordinary future, now is a good time to come back to my current role at *The MindShift Game* (TMSG). The first self-coaching game system in the world. It's revolutionary. It is a great leadership training tool. Tenacity is the bridge to success. TMSG is bridging and filling the gaps both personally and professionally. It supports your individual growth. Our goal is to serve millions of people from all walks of life to achieve their version of success, build determination, feel more empowered, act with intention, tap into their power, elevate their energy. One in which I get to work together.

There is a personal story I want to share with you about Joanne. When I was launching my first solo book, I had several things that I needed to complete. Joanne flew in, and she'll tell you her story in a moment, but once, we spent a whole weekend looking at things together. 'What else do I need for the book?' I asked her. Later, she flew up a second time when I launched the book. That was so humbling, and I was very excited. She had come straight out of South Africa to come into town to be there. Just for me. That was my feeling of Hermana, Sister to Sister. That is family.

Here is Joanne's side of that special time.

For me, it was exciting. I felt grateful and blessed to be a part of the process and a part of her book launch. I remember staying all weekend in the apartment and going through things. When Rocío told me she was launching the book on the date I was still on vacation, I thought: 'Can I change my return?' Then she asked me when I was due to come back, and it was two days after the planned launch. 'OK,' she said, 'then I'm going make it two days later.' Perfect, I'll be there, So I got off a plane, unpacked and 24 hours later, was on a plane again for the book launch. I was, to say the least, a little jet lagged and excited to support and be there for my friend. What a privilege.

Joanne has the only author copy there is of the book. That night, after the launch, we celebrated in her hotel room. She said: 'I want that copy.' At the time, it was my only copy, the first copy, the one copy from the book presentation... and it's autographed to Joanne! Joanne and I had done a great job preparing the final items for the book launch... and it was well worth it!

Joanne had already answered my questions on career advice in general, so I asked her what One Golden Nugget she would give other Hispanic leaders, as an influential Hispanic leader herself.

Things often get lost in translation. I think because we speak another language, and although it's not just for Hispanics, it is crucial to have clear communication - to ensure that your message is concise and understood. And vice versa, that you understand the message that you are given because I've seen many things get lost in translation. It's important to listen to understand rather than to respond.

Next, build each other up. Life is competitive, and people are

*"I believe that we get back
what we give."*

constantly putting people down. There is no need; for that we all have a place in the world. Once we all understand that everything changes. You don't inspire people by showing them how amazing you are. You inspire them by showing them how amazing they are.

Joanne and I had talked about business for a while, and I wanted to ask her a lighter question - what makes you smile? A big grin arrived with her reply.

Anything! I smile at anything; a grateful heart is a happy heart so I think you always have to look for that something to be grateful for. When I wake up, I smile because I was gifted another day. I mean, there's always something to smile about.

And my reason to smile is always going to be the fact that I'm in a good place and making a difference one way or another. I think energy is contagious, so I'll always find something to smile about even if I don't feel like smiling. Sometimes, even force a smile, fake the funk, you know they say - fake it till you make it—same concept. I smile even when I don't feel like it and you just keep going, and then God gives me plenty of reasons to smile.

Which book would you recommend that is a must-read for Latina businesswomen?

There are so many. I like Finding Your Why. Right now, I've taken a break from leadership books, and it's been more self-help books. One of my favorites is The Purpose Driven Life: What on Earth Am I Here For? Currently I'm reading What Happened to You. Another book I read continuously is The Bible; Basic Instructions Before Leaving Earth. It covers everything.

In one word, which quality do you want to be remembered for?

Kindness. I want to be remembered for being kind. I think that's the best description and the best word. In a world full of critics, I want to encourage people and be kind.

Which piece of software or specialized technology has assisted you the most in making significant change happen?

I love Microsoft. I use it for everything. When I started my career, it was blank papers and pens, markers or a typewriter. Microsoft was a game changer. I use Outlook, Excel, Word, and PowerPoint a lot!

I continued this theme and asked Joanne about her ultimate joy.

Giving joy, making a difference, giving people shining light, giving people purpose and helping people, and supporting people. I genuinely believe we were made for the community, and that truly gives me joy.

"Lead with your heart."

*"Give what you feel
the world lacks."*

*"Look for the good in people
and focus on that."*

OGN INTERACTIVE
Joanne Siracusa
Scan here
to visit my profile

Carlos Quezada

HISPANIC JOURNEY

Global Vice President of Customer Experience Strategy

Speaker & Mentor

Carlos is a technologist and a diversity, equity and inclusion leader at heart. In his over 20-year career, he has helped both start-ups and large enterprise companies create greater opportunities to improve efficiencies, grow service revenue and drive digital transformation leveraging scalable, and digital 1st data-driven framework.

Named top 100 Customer Success Strategists by Success Coaching and named Top 100 'Most Influential Latino in Tech' by the Hispanic IT Executive Council (HITEC) he is much in demand as a public speaker, motivator and mentor because of his non-traditional path to career success and his passion to uplift everyone around him.

We originally met online and have connected in person since. We are both continually looking to help people succeed, knowing that it's not just people who have the knowledge, skills, abilities, money, resources, or even the facility of language that can succeed; it is everybody. I felt that few were really targeting the Hispanic audience from a mindset perspective, and that is what I love about the work that Carlos is doing.

I started by asking him his side of the story about how we met.

Rocío and I met around two years ago on a panel, speaking about the challenges we face as Latinos in tech during Hispanic Heritage Month. Some of the subjects that resonated most with me revolved around our cultural virtues that we carry with us as part of the workforce like, work ethic, and loyalty to the job. While we have that work ethic, we also have certain downfalls.

Culturally, we are taught to not stand out, to go with the flow, to keep our heads down, and to simply assume that our work will speak for itself. Unfortunately, in business, and especially in the high-tech world, it's cutthroat. If we don't celebrate our victories and don't promote and elevate ourselves, we won't achieve the success we're looking for.

I love watching Carlos make an impact on the world; - he is an extraordinary leader. Whenever he takes people with him on the journey - no one is left behind. We must bring others with us and be that beacon of hope, that person who connects people.

It's funny, because I've heard people say that it's very lonely at the top and that the more success you get, the more you have to be shedding members of your community and building new communities on the way up. I agree that the top can be lonely, but only if you don't bring anyone with you.

I asked Carlos my favorite question - what makes your heart sing?

I find joy in seeing other people grow, seeing other people unlock potential they either didn't realize they had or were too afraid to explore. I run into many situations where people feel they're not supposed to dream.

One of the things that I write about in my own book, 'The Immigrant Survival Guide to Silicon Valley' is what I call the immigrant evolution journey and the differences between first-generation immigrants and second-generation immigrants. What I find is that typically the first generation, especially the immigrant adults, do not feel like they can have dreams, they feel like they have to come here to survive, and they put that burden on their kids to carry that torch.

But when you talk to first-generation immigrants that came here as kids, like me, they don't carry that same responsibility that their parents do, and they absolutely have the ability to dream and the ability to fulfill the dreams of those before them. So, what really motivates me is being able to work with people to help them shed the 'imposter syndrome' and help them flourish.

I've been blessed; I've had a lot of amazing coincidences, circumstances, or experiences, and they all have taken me on this non-linear and non-traditional route to career success. I feel like I have been blessed with what I have been given, and my purpose is to elevate others and share a lot of the experiences and lessons that I've learned. If I can reduce the time it takes between when families arrive in the country without knowing English and when their first child graduates from college, I will have succeeded in accelerating the success evolution of immigrant families. This is my passion and how I feel I can give back to the community that I am still very much a part of.

We will discover more about what Carlos does to help later. We all have aspirations to be better, and I asked him what inspired him to be the man he is today.

I am inspired by the opportunities given to me thanks to all the blessings I have received throughout my professional career. Inspired by the fact that I can help shorten the path to success for others by sharing my story and lessons learned along what has not been a linear path to success.

I am also inspired and motivated by the stories of those around me. For example, when our friend, NASA astronaut José Hernández, witnessed the landing on the moon and decided he wanted to be an astronaut he demonstrated tenacity and grit to make it happen, that is true inspiration.

I am also inspired and motivated by the opportunity to help our people break generational cycles. When I was in high school, I used to work in the walnut orchards in the summers and a Mexican grocery store during my entire high school career as a butcher, cashier, and warehouseman.

My family didn't have high expectations. To them, I was supposed to finish high school, and work in construction and maybe have my own construction company someday. There's nothing wrong with that, but it really leaned into the cultural bias of a Mexican in California. I would end up being a gardener or construction worker, like many other Latinos.

For me, I felt like there had to be more. I've always been very curious, different, and non-traditional, and I like to do things I'm not supposed to do. I always live by the motto "Ask for forgiveness not permission."

We should always drive ourselves to try different things and not necessarily abide by things that we know. I've always been motivated to prove that we can do and be things that we are not necessarily brought up to think we can do. In my life and in my career, I have tried everything from scuba diving and DJ'ing to flying all over the world as a self-taught engineer. Traditionally, those things are not typical of a first-generation immigrant Mexican.

My true inspiration? I'm inspired by the opportunity to ensure my kids do not start from zero, by the opportunity to help others grow and by the legacy I leave behind. I feel like I have a responsibility not only to my kids, but also to my people. It's my purpose to demonstrate everywhere I go that as a Mexican, I can be in the boardroom, I can be scuba diving on the coast in the Caribbean, and many more things.

"Culturally, we are taught to not stand out, to go with the flow, to keep our heads down, and to simply assume that our work will speak for itself. Unfortunately, in business, and especially in the high-tech world, it's cutthroat. If we don't celebrate our victories and don't promote and elevate ourselves, we won't achieve the success we're looking for."

As my good friend Guillermo Diaz, Jr. always says, "Why not me?" That is what motivates me to continue to grow, change the narrative and break generational cycles.

Carlos has taken power in positions where others have wanted to overshadow him. I asked him what happened and how he stepped into his power to do whatever it takes.

I've been in tech for over 22 years. I started my career in a start-up as a NOC technician, followed that role as a presales engineer for Latin America and the Caribbean. This role had me traveling about 85% of the time to Latin America. I had no education as a wireless engineer, it was all ‹on the job training.'

After almost 3 years of travel and learning a lot about wireless communications and networking, I decided it was time for a change. I was tired of traveling, so I changed careers and became a tech support engineer at the same company.

As a support engineer, I was always stay on top of new technologies and protocols. In my earlier years, I was a sponge and very much enjoyed learning. However, after a while, I realized this was not sustainable, for me. I made the decision that I really enjoyed coaching and growing people.

As part of the technical support organization, I was able to accelerate my career and get into leadership as a Tech Support Manager. Some years, many companies, and many promotions later, I have achieved my current role as a VP at the company that is recognized as the birthplace of Silicon Valley. In my current role, I get to leverage every job experience I've had throughout my life and bring it all together. I've worked as a butcher (customer service), DJ (public speaking), machinist (assembly line workflows), and at start-ups doing big data analytics, machine learning, and tech support.

I am currently Global Vice President of Customer Experience Strategy. It is a very transformational role that engages cross-functionally across the entire company, helping drive the company's adoption and revenue from the new subscription model. Moving from a traditional transaction business to helping them drive what we now recognize as a new "As-A-Service" model, or a subscription business.

My team has done an amazing job establishing itself as a thought leader within the company and has gained a lot of industry recognition.

I've always led by being bold and unafraid to take risks. However, to me, the most important thing is to ensure that no matter what you're doing, you treat everyone with respect and lead from the heart. One thing that I will never tolerate is professional bullying. I recall one situation where a more senior-level employee thought that because of their role and title, they could assume leadership over what my team and I had built over the previous years.

I have coached and mentored many people over the years. One of the things I always say is to stand up for what is right and be the voice of others who are afraid to speak.

I was now in a situation where I needed to take my own advice. It got to the point where this leader started to take the work my team and I had labored so hard on and demonstrate it as their own, essentially taking the credit and placing my team in the shadows.

Going back to my roots and understanding the importance of

honesty and a solid work ethic, I couldn't just sit by and let them take credit for my team's hard work. It wasn't about me at that point; I needed to make sure that my team felt they were heard and that I was going to stand up for them.

I heard there was going to be a meeting of some of the company's most senior leadership at our headquarters and that my work would be presented without me. I had a decision to make: either allow it to happen and see what came of it or do one of the boldest things I've ever done in my career and show up at the meeting uninvited.

This is a meeting with all the GMs of the company. Without telling anyone, I flew there and invited myself to that meeting.

I'll never forget that morning. I showed up at the office and walked to the large conference room where the meeting was being held. There was a table with name badges, for every invited senior leader, it was intimidating. There was someone handing the badges out as people walked up to the room.

I have two rules in situations like this: 1) 'Fake it till you make it,' and 2) 'Seek forgiveness rather than ask permission.' I confidently walked to the table, laptop bag on my shoulder, coffee in hand, and asked, "Is this where this meeting is supposed to take place?" She answered, "Yes," I continued, "Okay, great. It seems like my badge isn't here."

Because I approached her with such confidence, she was very apologetic. She handed me a Post-it note and asked me to write my first and last names and job title on it and said, "Let me make you one quickly." then she opened the door while letting me know that breakfast was on the right, and the meeting would start in 20 minutes. And so, I walked in.

I found a couple of folks in that room that I already knew and used them as anchor points, started to chat and made myself at home. I ended up spending the next two days with some of the most senior leaders in the company. Essentially learning the company's overall strategy for the next couple of years and walking away owning three initiatives that report directly to the CEO.

More importantly, I ended up presenting the work that my team had done for the last couple of years, and the entire committee acknowledged the work, and even asked us to expand on it to the rest of the company.

That trip established our team as a thought leader across the entire organization. I had evaded a situation where my team was going to be consumed by another group that had already started making moves to take them over. Because of the work my team had accomplished, the connections we had made, and the transparency of the entire situation, a number of the leaders actually applauded me for being there and made comments about how happy they were to see me at the event.

I was very honest with them and explained the situation, saying that I wasn't supposed to be there and had invited myself because I couldn't let it happen. Now, because of that, I have very strong allies at the most senior leadership levels of the company who didn't allow the hostile takeover because they recognized the value that I brought.

To be clear, I made it very apparent that I would resign if my team and their work were consumed in this way. I had already accepted the possibility I could be fired.

The two-day workshop was a success. I was able to elevate my team's work at the most senior levels of the company and be rewarded

I always live by the motto

"Ask for forgiveness not permission."
Carlos Quezada

for it. We were asked to expand what we currently do to the rest of the company.

It was a very emotional moment for me. I was reminded of all the advice and lessons from my parents and grandparents about always standing up for what you believe in and doing what's right. I was willing to lose my job over this. I am reminded of a famous quote from Emiliano Zapata: "It is better to die on your feet than live on your knees."

I was so emotional about what happened that, immediately after the meeting, I went outside and recorded a video giving my team the news. They didn't know I had made the trip, and I felt it was important to let them know the company had recognized their work and how proud I was of what we had accomplished.

Carlos really had gone all out to step into his power and allow others to see the vulnerability, the connection with the team. It was obvious he was passionate about his team, so I asked him what principles he lives by?

I was born and raised in a very small town in Mexico, where chivalry isn't dead, and you're taught to be a man of your word. I was brought up with certain manners and a different type of ethical and moral education. My mother's father was a blue-collar worker known as an extremely hard worker, and he was a man of law, a man of conviction, and a man of his word. I take that with me everywhere I go.

My father's father was a little better off. He was a businessman and had his own hog farm business. Although he was very successful, he was always very humble, and he always gave back. He was very, very ethical and well-loved by everyone that knew him.

Having learned these great values from both my grandfathers, I am very conscious of how I behave and how I treat people. I will never ask anybody to do something I'm not willing to do myself. When times are difficult, I've learned to stay true to myself, stay honest, and do what's right.

A man or woman is nothing without their word. I will never commit to something unless I know I can do it. If there is a chance that I cannot deliver, I will not commit. My word is something very important to me and something I feel holds a lot of weight.

Regardless of the outcome, at least you know that you didn't have to cheat, lie, or steal to get to where you are. It comes down to work ethic, to being a person of your word, and to being a person of good faith. I also feel like I'm very blessed, and it's my responsibility to give back a bit of what God's given me.

We all know that life can be a little messy at times, so I asked Carlos what is his driving force in the midst of chaos?

One of the things that I share with José Hernández, also a co-author of this book, is that during my early years and during my adolescence, change was constant. I was moving back and forth between the US and Mexico constantly, and that obviously impacts one's education and stability. It also makes you very accustomed to change.

I feel that one of my best virtues is that I thrive in chaos. I don't easily get frazzled, which is probably why I ended up in a job like tech support. A job where I am supposed to pick up the phone without having a clue what's waiting for me on the other end. However, I need to ensure the customer feels confident that I am the right person to help them either solve their problem or get them the help they need to solve their issue. You constantly look at the chaos and put it in order, chipping away at it little by little. What motivates me and helps me thrive in chaos is the sense of accomplishment when you have been able to solve a problem and provide relief or a solution to a customer.

This is going to sound a little weird, but I look forward to chaos; I look forward to the challenge because I feel like that is my purpose - To dive deep and unravel that rat's nest. I'm a very curious person and like to solve problems, so anytime there's disruption, I try to be methodical about it and work through it.

How does Carlos embrace his culture and prepare his children for even greater success?

I embrace my culture largely because of the work ethic that my grandfathers instilled in me. I also recognize what's happening right now in the United States with regards to the political climate and the opportunity that Latinos have, the economic power that we bring now and, in the future, and the power that the Latino vote will have.

I feel I have a larger purpose. I feel I was born in just the right era to be a flag bearer for our people and to demonstrate, "Si Se Puede" (Yes We Can). The way that I embrace my culture is by never forgetting where I came from and what I stand for. Understanding my heritage and my roots. From the pride I get from knowing I come from indigenous warriors such as the 'Mexicas' and 'Aztecs' to the role Catholicism and faith played in my upbringing. My culture is driven by work ethic, family and faith.

We hear a lot in discussions around Hispanic Heritage Month about bringing your whole self to work and taking off the mask. I feel that I do that a lot. It's important for people to recognize me

"I've always led by being bold and unafraid to take risks. However, to me, the most important thing is to ensure that no matter what you're doing, you treat everyone with respect and lead from the heart."

as a Hispanic male, a father an immigrant, and everything else that I stand for and represent, because I don't think we are always well represented. People are not used to seeing a Hispanic or Mexican man gain some of the positions that I have had the opportunity to hold. Often, people assume that I am an Arab because there's no way that I could possibly be Hispanic. I must embrace that and recognize the responsibility and opportunity I have to represent my people.

The way I prepare my children for success starts by making sure they know where they come from and embrace their culture. I have four kids, and I have taken all of them at one point or another to the office and to conferences with me so they can see what I do and see others like them at the office or Latino leadership conferences. They know they're not alone, and I make sure that they recognize the responsibility that they must pick up the torch and move that forward as well. I try to instill in them those values that my grandfathers instilled in me. Now, when my kids are presented with situations, they can lean on those values, have a clear conscience, and make informed decisions going forward.

Our trials in life often make us stronger and I wondered which moment of adversity has become his greatest gift in his career.

I look for opportunities where I'm not supposed to be. I never went to a four-year university. I am surrounded by people with double MBAs from prestigious institutions such as Harvard, Stanford, or Yale, amongst many others. Early on, I thought that I would not get very far in my career because I didn't have an MBA, or that I would only get so far because I only held a bachelor's degree from a school no-one had ever heard of (a local trade school that doesn't exist anymore).

Not going to a 'real' university used to be my reason why I couldn't succeed. I used it as a crutch. Now it has become the reason why I did succeed. Because I didn't go to university, I have probably had every job from entry-level to where I am now in my business, so when I sit at the table making decisions, I feel I can do so comfortably knowing that I know what it takes to do what is required. Had I gone to a formal university, I may not have had the work experience that I have.

Therefore, what I thought was my Achilles' heel is now my virtue. I feel that I have to remind everybody that I didn't get here by the most traditional educational route, but I wouldn't have it any other way.

That is powerful - our young can reach the top without the Harvard paperwork, but education can smooth the path to the top jobs, and we should aim for better education for all because without it, you need the extraordinary determination of Carlos!

Next, I asked him what he wished people knew about him.

I wish people knew where I came from, a small town in Mexico named Degollado in the state of Jalisco, and the situation that I was in when we first came to the US, going into a high school of 2,000 students, not knowing anybody, and being pushed to graduate from high school while still learning the language.

After going through all of that, I think it's easy to judge people based on where you see them now, but I want people to know the real Carlos, the Mexican farm boy who never says no to anything and doesn't back down from anything. I think a lot of immigrants share that passion for survival and grit. We need to recognize that it is what makes us powerful. When you have had that experience and come from that background, you take that passion and direct it towards something that can be very, very successful.

I often have conversations about the skills that Hispanics have that are not exploited enough in corporate America, and my chat with Carlos had to include this topic.

In general, immigrants have that survivalist instinct because we got up and moved, learned a new language, and had to immerse ourselves in the new culture to find our identity. There is a lot of 're-birthing' that happens during that period, a Phoenix concept if you like, but Latinos specifically always think beyond what is asked. If you ask us to do something, we will do that and more.

I feel we don't give ourselves enough credit in this space. We are natural problem solvers. We are givers. And putting those two things together is insanely good because we take pride in our work and always make sure that people walk away feeling good about whatever we deliver.

As a person of impact, I asked Carlos what he thought his legacy would be?

I think my kids will be my legacy. Throughout my career, I have had the opportunity to coach and mentor many people from different walks of life at different levels in their careers. It has been amazing to see them grow, but what's even more amazing is having my kids watch me do it.

When I first came to the US, my family's expectation for me was to get a high school diploma and work in construction. As long as I did those two things, in their eyes, I was successful, and I would have delivered on my parents' dreams.

Well, things have changed for my kids. I have three stepchildren and a nine-year-old son, and they have grown up seeing me travel. In the past four or five years, they have seen me on stage giving talks. They see it as something very normal, so much so that my 18-year-old daughter just returned from a trip to Italy after graduating high school. That is something that I would have never even considered.

For me, it's all about expanding my kids' horizons and having them witness what is possible and what they can accomplish.

That is so powerful, for empowering the next generation. I had been so intrigued to ask Carlos all the questions on my list, so I had to return to the basics and ask about his immigrant journey and early years.

I was born and raised in a very small farming community in Jalisco, Mexico. It borders the state of Michigan. My father was a migrant farm worker. He first came to Chicago, then moved to Salinas, California, and worked in the lettuce fields, then over in Santa Barbara picking strawberries, before eventually moving to Modesto where he was picking peaches and almonds.

While my father was in the US, my mom was in Mexico. My older sister, Angélica, and I would get tourist visas to come to the United States occasionally. My first recollection of a visit to the US was when I was in kindergarten. I was here for about a year and a half and then went back to Mexico. I had the opportunity to study both in the US and in Mexico, so it did give me at least a little bit of a foundation each time I went back and forth, but it also created some weirdness because what you learn in Mexico and what you learn in the US are not necessarily the same.

Growing up in Mexico, I used to work in the hog farms, and I would help my uncles who had brick ovens. It was all manual labor, loading up trucks, and after an hour of it, you literally lost your fingerprints.

After we came to the US, I had all sorts of jobs, working in a Mexican grocery store as a butcher and including working in a warehouse. I didn't actually get to graduate high school in time, and that was one of the defining moments of my life. At the time, my father was working as a manager, and he came to me and said many of his employees were asking about days off, because their kids were graduating high school. He asked when he was going to need to ask for the day off and I couldn't look him in the eyes, because I knew that I had messed up.

The look of disappointment in my father's eyes when I told him that I was not graduating was very, very emotional for me. I remember that what ran through my mind was that this was what my father was looking for when he came to the US and brought us over. He wanted me to complete this task, and I failed.

So, being a man of my word, I looked him in the face, and said: "Dad, I apologize, but I am going to make it up to you." I knew that I had to pursue some level of education after high school, but I didn't have the grades to go to a formal university, and I didn't know about junior college back then - nobody in my family had ever been to college before - so I enrolled in a 13-month trade school program where I learned systems administration and networking.

I got an associate degree from that, and I invited my parents to my graduation. After that, I attained a bachelor's degree and invited my parents to that too. Now, whenever I can, on the occasions when I get recognition or an award, I always invite my father. I feel I owe him that.

I always talk about the importance of being bilingual. One of the first jobs I had when I finished trade school was working for a start-up based in San Jose, California. That company started doing business with a company in Mexico. Coincidentally, after about six months of me working there, I came to find there was a very important meeting happening in Mexico City, and I was going to be in Mexico, so I asked, half-jokingly, if they needed anybody to translate. I was literally the only person in the company who spoke Spanish, and they took me up on the offer.

I was scared because I was just kidding but I ended up going with them to Mexico City for that business meeting. I was about 18 years old at the time, and I didn't know the difference between a business suit and a party suit, so I had the shiny black lapel, black pants, white socks, and my dress shoes that I was planning to wear at my sisters quinceañera at this meeting. Also, I went into the meeting forgetting I was supposed to translate and actually took over the meeting. I ended up landing a nationwide contract with Telcel, the largest cell phone provider in Mexico.

Because of the success I had in that meeting, they actually made me a full-time employee, and for the next two years, I led the project with Telcel that essentially brought text messaging to Mexico. So, at about 18-and-a-half years old, I worked on a project that introduced wireless data over cellular technology to Mexico.

That's when my career took off, and all because I spoke Spanish.

*"A man or woman is nothing without their **word.**"*

I had no prior experience as an engineer that qualified me for what was going on and what was about to happen, but I had a little bit of technical aptitude, so I could consume what was being thrown at me, process it, and make decisions. The important thing was that I spoke Spanish and could act as a liaison between the engineers in Mexico City and those in the United States. For two years, I went to Mexico City every month for a week.

From there, my career has been a whirlwind of working at a number of start-ups. The next company I went to was as a presales engineer for Latin America and the Caribbean, designing point-to-point microwave antenna systems - again, not something that I had experience in, but I spoke Spanish and I could learn very quickly.

I became an RF engineer by trade and was setting up 20 or 30-kilometer point-to-point microwave links over Latin America and the Caribbean, bringing voice and Internet to little towns in Mexico, Brazil, and Argentina that previously had not had Internet. I feel like there is still a huge opportunity to help bring our people forward by giving them that digital equity that first-world countries.

Eventually I moved into leadership roles at the start-ups, making it all the way to VP. I knew that because of my level of education, it would be hard for me to come in off the street as an executive for such a large company, so my goal was to accelerate my career in the start-up world, and then move to bigger companies later, and that is what I did to reach VP at a company start-up, now at HPE as a director.

Carlos is doing something that we should all be so proud of - his journey has been extraordinary. Surely, he had Nuggets of advice that he could give to people in his closing thoughts.

I am going to give the same advice that my 9 year old son gave in an interview that he did not too long ago, which is to never give up. He was at a social media convention where he was interviewed by NBC because he has 36,000 followers on TikTok.

I echo my son's sentiment: "Never give up", even if you get hate comments. Throughout my entire journey, there have been many cases where people have questioned my way of thinking and my way of working. My response was that I'm a very non-traditional executive; I like to have fun, and I build a concept of family within all my teams.

I feel that in some cases, some teams don't take me seriously because of the way that I am. The results, however, speak very, very loudly, so I don't let that get to me. The good news is that there Latino representation now in all these industries - not enough, but those that are there recognize the role that they have. We need to increase our numbers to let them know we are the target demographic and to increase those numbers - to be that mentor, coach, or sponsor who can help our brothers and sisters get to where they want to be. We are out here, looking for volunteers to come and join us.

I asked Carlos to tell me the story of what would happen if he was invited to make a presentation to motivate others now.

After 22 years of building my career, I recently had the opportunity to go in and build a team in Guadalajara, Jalisco (The capital city of the state in Mexico where I was born).

It was an amazing feeling, a surreal experience. I felt it was my opportunity to make sure that they knew that I was proud of where I came from, and in the end, they walked away feeling like I was one of them. One of the traits of a good leader is not being afraid to be vulnerable, so in my presentation, I included images of myself, my mom, and my older sister when we were living in Mexico together. I shared pictures of me in school in Mexico. More importantly, I had a slide that showed what LinkedIn says about me - in my current role - and then, the really important bit, a slide that talked about what LinkedIn *doesn't* say about me, or the jobs that didn't make it to LinkedIn.

I shared my true career progression. That I used to work in the hog farm shoveling pig crap. I used to be a brick loader; I worked as a butcher in a Mexican grocery store; I used to be a DJ for weddings; I used to be a machinist, fabricating the metal chassis that computers are built on, never knowing that I was working for one of the largest computer manufacturing companies in the world.

The reason it was important to share that is because every single job that I had, up until this point prepared me for the role that I have now. The level of customer service training that you get from working in a Mexican grocery store as a cashier is something that you can't pay for because people in Mexican grocery stores are very raw, very real, and very impatient. When I was a machinist, if any part of that line gets a kink, everything slows down, and I learned that at 17 years old. All the jobs I have had have given me some type of perspective and played a part in many of the decisions that I make today.

That is so powerful, a way to show our truths, because when Hispanic people make it, we don't talk about where we came from, nor do we talk about those jobs. I used to build waterbeds when I was a teenager. I was 16 years old and in a factory of 144 men with only six women, four of them in the office.

"I just feel it takes too much effort to be fake - it is just so much easier to be real."

Everything leads us to where we are now. Is Carlos the only one to present like this? His generosity, and sharing are extraordinary. I love the fact that he brings this level of authenticity and vulnerability - that connection to what humanity looks like.

His response to my thanks was simple.

I just feel it takes too much effort to be fake - it is just so much easier to be real, right?

OGN INTERACTIVE
Carlos Quezada
Scan here
to visit my profile

Agnes Medina

HISPANIC JOURNEY

Financial Professional
Educator and Trainer

I knew about Agnes long before I met her. For more than 20 years she has been making an impact in the Hispanic community, as well as in the lives of hundreds of people from all walks of life and cultures, specifically in the financial sector – educating, training, and creating security for clients and agents at every stage of their lives and careers.

And then it happened. We met. Unplanned, we found ourselves at a private party with friends, and just hit it off. It was amazing. We connected around her message of helping women and what it takes to build financial security, peace of mind and ultimately, lasting wealth.

Agnes helps people grow their knowledge around finances, enabling them to take control of their financial futures with confidence. Our first event, titled "Women of Prosperity", was specifically for women, however, many men attended because the concepts around money are universal, and they wanted to learn more. There is something compelling about the word 'prosperity'.

I love Agnes' story of how she found and followed her professional path, but I wanted to start by asking her about her private self.

Agnes, what makes your heart sing?

Music makes my heart sing, especially soothing piano and guitar music. It's magical how music calms my soul, helps me focus, and makes me happy. It has always been a dream of mine to play the piano, so when I was in my mid 30's, I started taking lessons, not necessarily to perform but mainly for the joy it brings me. I love sitting at my piano and making beautiful music.

Second, I love spending time with children and teens. They always make me smile, and they remind me to be curious, to have fun and most importantly, to live in the moment.

Agnes, you have achieved so much, but tell me about the journey that brought you here.

My parents and grandparents were from New Mexico, so I often say my background is New Mexican. I was born and raised in Denver, Colorado, and lived there most of my life. I grew up in a lower-middle class home with my parents and four beautiful younger sisters. Life was never boring. In 2021, I made a major move to North Texas to shake things up and create a new chapter in my life.

I am proud of my Hispanic heritage and culture for many reasons. I love our food, our music, and the way we build our lives around family and traditions. It's just part of our lives to spend special days together. I have wonderful memories of gatherings throughout my life. In my earlier years, we spent many Sundays and holidays with grandparents, aunts, uncles, and cousins, sharing meals and playing fun games. When our grandparents passed away, then our parents were the hosts. Now that my parents are gone, my sisters and I have the privilege of carrying on the family traditions.

Throughout my life, I loved learning, and going to school. I attended middle school and high school in the inner city of Denver. When I was in the 8th grade, I was selected to attend a private school in New Hampshire for the entire summer, all expenses paid. It was an adventure that changed the trajectory of my life forever! I was literally taken from the inner city of Denver and flown to the beautiful New England campus of the Phillips Exeter Academy. Along with crash courses in reading, writing, math, and history, I experienced travel, and a bigger world of learning and prosperity.

When I came back, I immersed myself in school even more. I loved it and I loved my teachers. To this day, I am grateful to the teachers that made an impact on my life, and always encouraged me to learn more and be more.

My senior year in high school was eventful, to say the least. I had a baby

"I am proud of my Hispanic heritage and culture for many reasons. I love our food, our music, and the way we build our lives around family and traditions."

"I was determined to never settle for a life of mediocrity, and I wanted desperately to change our environment."

girl, graduated early, and got married - in that order. Life was very, very emotional and tough during that time. Three days after my 18th birthday, I married my high school sweetheart. Many years later, I asked my mother, "Why didn't anyone try to stop me?" She replied, "We did, and you did not want to hear it!" My little family and I moved into a small apartment next door to his parents in the five Points/Curtis Park area, one of the most dangerous places to live in Denver. For five years, we were surrounded by crime, drugs, and negativity.

I worked retail while I decided what to do next. I was determined to never settle for a life of mediocrity, and I wanted desperately to change our environment.

With the guidance of my amazing high school teachers, I was able to attend Colorado Women's College, a private school in Denver, with a full-ride scholarship. The campus was beautiful, and most of the women that attended came from wealthy families from all over the world.

Without skipping a beat, I would take public transportation, with my baby in my arms, drop her off at the campus day care, then head straight to class. I did that for four long years. I'm proud to say, at the end of it all, I earned a Bachelor's Degree in Business and Economics. I was the first in my family to graduate from college. I would not have been able to do it without the encouragement of my professors, and the support of my family.

My first job out of college was as a computer programmer for Dakin5, a start-up accounting software company, writing code for the Apple II, one of the first generations of personal computers. Being a computer programmer and good at accounting and math, I became very detail oriented, which serves me well to this day.

Finally, we had enough income to move to a better part of town. With the help and mentorship of my boss, Eugene Carr, I was able to move up the ranks quickly, from programmer to management, supervising the customer service and quality assurance teams.

The next step on my journey was working as the accountant for a small, mining and investment company, Geo. W. Parfet Estate, Inc., in the mountain town of Golden, Colorado. In addition to the clay mining operation, the company owned multiple properties including a US Bank building, a day care building, a mobile home park, and a housing development. I was Chip Parfet's right hand (wo)man, with many responsibilities including property valuations, record keeping and financial statement preparation. It was a great job. I worked many years for Chip Parfet, and I am forever grateful for his wonderful example of generosity and caring for others.

When my first daughter was 10 years old, we were blessed with our second beautiful baby girl. I wanted to spend more time with my family, and I needed more flexibility. With the encouragement of Chip Parfet, who became my first client, I started my own accounting and bookkeeping practice, Diverse Financial Ltd. I made many new friends, and my professional knowledge grew as I worked with businesses in different industries including construction, gambling, and gold mining.

In the year 2000, there were two major events in my life. I divorced my husband and my life was turned upside down. I was also at a major crossroads in my career. Even though my income was good, and I enjoyed the clients I worked with, I did not feel like I was growing and living up to my potential. I knew in my heart that I was created for so much more.

Then I met Chris Felton, my current business coach and mentor, who introduced me to the financial services industry. I did not hesitate one minute to try something new and I'm glad I did not pass on the opportunity. It has been a fun and challenging ride on a fast train of personal development, meeting new people, and being surrounded by amazing clients and teammates. I also have had the privilege to work with world class leaders throughout the industry.

The Denver Hispanic Chamber of Commerce was instrumental in the launch of my financial services business. I participated in leadership groups, networking events, and many celebrations. My circle of friends grew, and to this day I am reaping the benefits of my associations created during that time. Thank you, Denver Hispanic Chamber.

Now, 20 years later, I am still making an impact on the lives of others by sharing knowledge and helping them build and preserve wealth for themselves and future generations. It's an honorable profession that I am grateful to be part of. What I love most is teaching and training our agents to go out into the world and do the same thing. People have never been more open for financial education and guidance.

I believe that the challenges and adversities I have faced have contributed to who I am today. I would not change a thing. It's my hopes and dreams that give me strength. My personal mission is to live my life in health, freedom, joy, prosperity, and significance.

"For God has not given us a spirit of fear and timidity, but of power, love, and a sound mind." 2 Timothy 1:7 NKJV

Who has made the greatest impact in your life?

My two beautiful daughters and two granddaughters have inspired me to live my best life. How I live is my legacy and my greatest example. My oldest daughter, Tyra, is a strong successful businesswoman, a wonderful wife to her husband, and a loving mother to their daughter, Ainsley. My other daughter, Audra, is an amazing, supportive, and loving mother to my granddaughter, Mia. In 2021, with courage and determination, Audra stepped out into entrepreneurship and launched her business, Reliant Accounting & Tax Services Solutions. I am very proud of my girls, and it makes me happy to say that they are my best friends.

*"The very first step is to take a
serious look at your money habits.
Creating better habits starts with
awareness. Make a conscious effort
to know what money you have
coming in, and where ALL of it goes."*

As a woman in finance, what do you recommend other women can do to create financial security?

First, women need to start having conversations about money. Most people don't talk about money, more so in the Hispanic culture. It's private. It's uncomfortable. I feel we need to find the courage to have those difficult conversations with our friends and loved ones. Many women need to be more involved in their finances. It is much too important to leave entirely to someone else.

Women need to seek out financial education. Financial illiteracy is the #1 economic crisis in the world. It's important to learn the basic concepts of how money works.

Here are some important questions to think about:

- How is my family protected if something happens to me, my spouse, or my partner?
- Do I have enough cash saved to cover an emergency or economic crisis?
- What downside protection do I have in place for my retirement assets? Can I afford to lose 30, 40, or even 50%?
- Are the beneficiaries up to date on all my accounts?
- What is my plan for future income?
- What is my long-term care plan?
- Would I want to leave anything to my children or a charity? How much?
- Should I create a trust?
- Is my will up to date?

Find a financial professional that you trust to guide you and help you set your financial goals and implement a clearly defined plan of action.

What would you say to people who believe they don't have money to invest?

The very first step is to take a serious look at your money habits. Creating better habits starts with awareness. Make a conscious effort to know what money you have coming in, and where ALL of it goes.

There is an activity called the 'Finding Money Exercise.' People often get wealthy or stay broke from the small dollars that leak out of their lives daily.

Step 1: Calculate how much you spend on a typical weekday, lunch, dinner, snacks, and multiply that by 20 days.

Step 2: Calculate how much you typically spend on weekends, food, entertainment, and multiply that by 4 weekends.

Step 3: Add your monthly weekday spending to your monthly weekend spending.

What did you discover? Could you save one third, or even half of this without dramatically changing your lifestyle? Save whatever you can, it doesn't matter how little the amount. Start somewhere. Imagine that what you save represents the seeds of your wealth. Seeds grow and multiply!

We need to be wise how we appropriate our income. As in all areas of life, there are consequences for every decision.

If you were to recommend one business book, what would that be?

In my opinion, one of the best business books ever written is 'The ONE Thing: by Gary Keller and Jay Pappasan, with nearly 2.5 million copies sold. It provides a method to help you get clarity on what your priorities in life are, and what is the most important thing you can do today to achieve your goals and dreams.

Success is found in doing what matters most and not just about getting things checked off your to-do list. Everything does not matter equally. Get the most important things done early in the day, while your willpower is high. Think of your willpower like your cell phone battery. As the day goes on, your battery loses charge and at night you get to re-charge. This book is a must read!

"This is not a dress rehearsal.
Live your dreams. Take risks. "

"There is much joy in purpose
and accomplishment. "

And finally, what one piece of technology has changed your life?

I cannot imagine functioning, let alone running a business, without my smart phone! In addition to helping me stay connected to others, it's my calendar, my camera, and a life saver in case of an emergency. It's a storehouse of knowledge and it's even a source of entertainment. Technology has sure come a long way!

"It's okay to want more out of life and still be extremely grateful for all you have."

"Your best investment is in yourself, your personal development, your health, and sharpening the skills of your trade."

"Never underestimate the impact you can have on the lives of others."

OGN INTERACTIVE
Agnes Medina
Scan here
to visit my profile

Gerardo Garcia-Jurado

HISPANIC JOURNEY

Creative Marketer

I met Gerardo a few years ago when I was running my marketing company. At the time people kept advising me to connect with him, saying he was amazing at what he does and, as I found out, indeed he was!

We both fell in love with the work that each of us was doing, but during COVID in 2020 I recognized Gerardo was someone who really understood my work, so I decided to invite him to become my business partner. We've been together ever since.

He is amazing at what he does. He brings a great wealth of knowledge and has committed his life's work from this point forward to helping create products and services that support people and elevate them. That's why he joined me in the Mind Shift Game and all the products that we're creating, as well as being part of a new company, Virtuous.

For his perspective on the Hispanic journey, I asked Gerardo to share his story in his own words.

"You will never be able to work at a general market advertising agency in the USA", Andrea, an account director from a Hispanic ad agency, told me when we went out for a coffee. Spoiler alert: She was wrong.

I had been in the United States for less than two weeks when someone introduced me to Andrea. I asked her for advice on getting my first job, which she gave me, but among other things she implied that we, Hispanics living in the USA, were considered second-class citizens. I got to learn she was right.

Gaby, my beautiful and intelligent wife, was commissioned to work at one of the many offices of the Mexican Foreign Trade Bank in the US, promoting Mexican exports and foreign investment. That was the reason we came to the USA. Honestly, I would never have otherwise thought about leaving Mexico in the first place.

We arrived in the Big Apple in April 2000. Being in the city that never sleeps was exciting and new, but it was meant to be a short adventure. Initially, my wife's assignment was supposed to last no less than two and no more than five years. Instead, we ended up staying there for more than eight years.

I must admit that the thought of living in NYC was as exciting as it was overwhelming. It is the most competitive market in the world, and I was afraid I was not at that level. After finishing college, I decided not to work for anyone other than myself, so in 1993 I started my own design firm, TOP MIND Visual Communications. It took a long time and a lot of arduous work until it took off. By 1996, I was creating campaigns for IBM and lesser-known companies.

By 2000, I had a profitable company with employees and great clients, so when we moved to NYC, I had to start all over again. Even worse, I had to have a job offer in order to apply for a work permit. Consider this: no one would hire someone without a job permit, or so I thought.

For many months I struggled to understand the American way to of getting a job. I had no idea how things worked in this country. For example, I had to learn how to write a resume, which is very different from how we used to do it in Mexico. It also did not help that nobody had ever hired me before. I'd never had a boss and did not know the right or wrong way to behave in a company environment. All I knew was *my* way.

"One of the things that struck me most was seeing how many Hispanic people were not taught Spanish, even though it might have been their parents' native language."

Here's a story to illustrate the cultural differences. Back then, the Internet was just starting and no one other than big corporations had a website. Designers had to carry an oversized physical portfolio containing their entire work life: printed samples of their best projects.

One day, I received a call from PepsiCo requesting me to send my portfolio for review. I said I would love to present it in person, but they insisted I send it via the postal service, and they would return it once they had reviewed it. Postal service? Are they crazy? I thought it would not even arrive at the PepsiCo offices because that had been my experience dealing with the Mexican postal service. Down there, the postal service is entirely unreliable, and I was not going to risk losing my entire life's work that lived inside my black, larger-than-life portfolio.

That's how I missed a great opportunity due to cultural differences and I have dozens of stories like that.

Another thing I had to learn when I moved to the US was to see how many different 'kinds' of people lived in this great country. Once again, where I came from, we were not Hispanics, Asians, or Blacks; we were all Mexicans, some whiter, some darker, but all Mexicans. Learning about diversity is one of the many things I owe to the melting pot that is the United States. And with that, I learned about racism and discrimination as well.

In the US, there are Hispanics from any Latin American country who, to many not well-educated people, are just called Mexicans, even though they might have arrived from Honduras, Cuba, or Venezuela. There are Puerto Ricans, even though some are Dominicans that arrived in the US through Puerto Rico. (Fun fact: There are more Puerto Ricans in New York City than in the entire island of Puerto Rico. That fact blew my mind.)

There are Cubans who have their own story, and a few that I have met don't even consider themselves Hispanics; they say they are Latinos, but I am not going to get into the nuances of this never-ending discussion. And there are also the Native Hispanics, who have been in the US way before any Americans, that were part of Mexico before the border moved south.

Let me stop here to make an acknowledgment: I know that my comments sound oversimplified, and I understand the limitations of generalizing, but I want to make a point that will allow me to tell the many stories I want to tell.

A caveat is that even though I am Mexican, born and raised, I am considered one of the 'white' Mexicans. There is even a term nowadays in Mexico that is trying to define pale skinned people like us: 'Whitexicans'. My skin is paler than many of my white American friends to the extent that at first some people don't believe I am Mexican, at least until I start speaking. I am conscious of my heavy accent.

One day, while chatting with someone, I mentioned I had emigrated from Mexico. Immediately he said that he believed Mexicans are the most hard-working, honest, and caring people in the world. I was new in the US, and I thought his comment was very peculiar. The Mexican stereotype I understood is a short, lazy, dark-skinned guy always sleeping under his sombrero next to a cactus and his burro. This made me realize that the 'Mexican' (or whatever immigrant for that matter) who is willing to risk their life crossing the border (or borders), looking for a better life, does not come here to be lazy or commit crimes. They are here because they want their families, to have a better life. They will work hard, harder than anyone else. So many are under the shadows, just making money to send back home.

He was right; these are the most hard-working, honest, and caring people in the US.

I was living in New York City when 9/11 happened. It is a story I will leave for another book, but as we know, on that day 2,977 people perished. Officially. These people's faces were part of heartbreaking, never ending murals of missing people's posts on subway station walls. But the reality is that many more people died that day.

Hundreds of illegal immigrants were at work cleaning the offices, preparing food at restaurants, arranging shelves in the stores - just like they were (and still are) every other day - but their photos were nowhere to be found. Many did not have families and were frightened to say something because they were afraid of being noticed by the government.

Has anybody seen a memorial filled with their names? Me neither.

The United States is a country built by immigrants and all minorities have always struggled - the Irish, the Italians, the Blacks, the Native Americans, and the Hispanics. They all have found roadblocks at some point. However, when I see the Hispanic community today, mostly those illegal immigrants, I think of them as these faceless warriors fighting against life every day, expecting to win a war that can never be won.

It is like all the extras in war movies, the soldiers fighting in the background while the hero defeats the enemy. They are needed because without them the scene makes no sense, but no one knows their names, they are irrelevantly relevant.

Iván was a young, intelligent kid who used to clean the offices where I worked in Manhattan. He always came to me to chat. I was the only one that could speak his language and understand, up to a point, what he was going through. He told me the scary story of how he crossed the border and how his mom had to get a loan from someone for 'el pollero' (the people smuggler) that brought him all the way from Mexico to NYC. Back in the early 2000s she paid $5000. He was working to help her pay that loan.

His story was only one of the hundreds of stories I have heard since I moved to the United States. I remember he always dreamed about becoming a tattoo artist and opening his own studio. He was passionate and had dreams, and I encouraged him to follow them. He used to say: "Un día, Gerardo, vas a ver." I really hope he has achieved his dream.

One night, coming back from clubbing in Manhattan, really late at night (or very early morning), my wife and I stopped at the only open place, a McDonald's. We had French Fries instead of Tacos Al Pastor, our go-to selection if we had been in Mexico. While sitting at the upper level, I saw this guy mopping the floors. He was clearly Hispanic, so I started talking to him. He came and sat down with me. He asked me what I did for a living, and, in those days, I was still looking for my first job in the US.

I told him I was unemployed, and he kindly offered to introduce me to his 'guy', the one that got his social security card, in case I needed one. I did not, I needed a job offer, but I appreciated his gesture. He told me he had two full-time jobs in two different McDonald's. He also mentioned he made more money than his 'compas' because he spoke some English. He lived in Queens in a rented two-bedroom apartment with nine other immigrants from Mexico.

One thing that is great to see is how Hispanics (or basically any immigrant group) support each other in this country.

Another thing I remember from my days in NYC was going to a deli. Deli owners are usually Korean, but all the workers are Mexican, at least the ones I met. I always spoke Spanish to them, and they were always so friendly; they always gave me my 'pilón', a term we use in Mexico that means 'a little extra'. Being Mexican has its perks too!

When I was the head of creative services at a branding firm in California, Victor, the cleaning guy, who happened to be a Mexican immigrant, approached me one night while I was working late and asked me what my role was at the agency. I told him that I oversaw all the creative team and the creative outcome. He looked at me and asked: "So, are you the boss of all these *güeritos*?" I said "yes". Then he said: "Wow, a Mexican can actually be the boss."

I have many other similar stories. It has been humbling to believe that I have been able to inspire others, even though I am fully aware my circumstances are very different.

This is the part where I have to state that I consider myself extremely lucky. I was born under favored circumstances. I have never felt hunger. My life has never been at risk. I cannot say I have been discriminated against for my skin color. I was able to finish college and study for a Master's degree. I grew up in a loving family. I migrated to the US legally. However, I never understood my privileged circumstances until I moved to the US and met all these brave people. Hearing from them and seeing how difficult their lives have been allowed me to be grateful for all the opportunities I have had and fueled me to be active in the community.

Since then, I have always tried to be as helpful to these communities as possible, working hand-in-hand with the local Mexican Consulates, the non-profit community and grassroots organizations; empowering the younger immigrants to fight for their rights, get educated and become whatever they want to be, but mostly someone who will make this world a better place.

While working at The Integer Group, I learned about an organization the agency supported called The Gold Crown Field House. It is a great organization founded in 2003 that accepts underprivileged kids, primarily Hispanic and Black, to offer after-school programs. They learn different trades, to be off the streets, while their parents work. It was so rewarding to see the intellect and passion.

I remember one girl, Michel (yes, that is how it is spelled). When she was very young, her parents brought her from Michoacán, Mexico. I worked with her for a few weeks, and she asked me to teach her Photoshop so she could design her own Quinceañera invitation.

So far, I have only told stories about one kind of Hispanics, the undocumented immigrants, which are clearly the most fragile group of all - we all need to protect the weakest, right?

But now let's talk about all the Hispanic people born north of the border, as well as their parents and their parents' parents. None of them actually speak Spanish and many have never even been outside the USA, yet many of them are discriminated against just by their skin color or last name.

I have met many of them during my time in this great country and I admit that I envy their love for their culture. They know more about Latin American culture than I do. For example, Heather is a

*"Allow me to be vulnerable
and say I fell into a profound
depression - something I had
never experienced before."*

super talented creative with whom I had the pleasure to work. She is also married to one of my best Mexican-American friends. She does not speak Spanish. However, she dances Native Mexican dances and knows the pre-Columbian cultures way better than I do. Her love for the Mexican culture is admirable. I learned a lot from her, and I will always be grateful.

One of the things that struck me most was seeing how many Hispanic people were not taught Spanish, even though it might have been their parents' native language. As I was told by a few of them, they did not want their kids to be rejected for speaking Spanish. It seems that was a significant stigma back in the day, and they do not want their kids to suffer in this Anglo society. I am glad to see that that perception has changed, and now speaking another language, any other language, is actually praised.

Then there are the 'corporate' Hispanic immigrants, as I call them. They are usually not part of the conversation. These immigrants, like many others, came to the United States from their country legally for different reasons. This is not particular to Hispanics; there are Indians, Asians and many others who have come to make this country a better place. Some were hired by American corporations and were brought here; others were entrepreneurs looking for business opportunities that only the number one world economy can bring.

I think that might be my case, in part, too.

We lived in the Tristate Area for eight years and while Gaby worked for the same bank, I had my share of experiences.

Allow me to be vulnerable and say I fell into a profound depression - something I had never experienced before. It took me over a year-

and-a-half to find my first job. I applied for anything and everything, but ultimately, I thought I was not good enough, and that no one would ever hire me. The few times I went to an interview, it always ended when the answer to the question "Do you have a work permit?" was "No, but..."

During that time, I worked at a few trade shows, managing booths for Mexican companies. I also did some cross-cultural presentations for ex-pats sent to live in Mexico or Mexican professionals sent to live in the USA. My job was to explain, as much as possible, the cultural differences between the two worlds. That was as much as I could aspire to without a work permit.

One day in June 2001, I went for an interview at a sales company in Midtown Manhattan - a hair accessory distributor looking for a Design Manager. An Asian lady interviewed me and never asked 'that' question. She ended up hiring me. When I started, as I was filling out the forms, I told her I would give her my work permit in a matter of weeks. She looked at me and her eyes opened wider and wider as her face turned redder and redder. Then she started yelling at me, saying I had lied to her. I corrected her and told her that she never asked, and I never told her. What's more, I said, I was willing to work for free until the permit arrived. Fortunately, she agreed and in a matter of two weeks, I was legit.

I was there for over two years, working for this wonderful Jewish family, and between them and many of the salespeople there that were also Jewish, I learned a lot about their incredible culture. There were a few Puerto Rican people, and I met Kristian L, a really good friend who had an Austrian background and married a wonderful Mexican lady. This was the start of the enlightenment of learning about diversity and other cultures.

Needless to say, that changed my life. Finally, I was able to work legally, and I was going to explore the opportunities!

After that I worked as a freelancer for AOL. Then I was hired as a remote creative director for a Tampa Bay-based marketing agency where I was in charge of developing in-store displays for Nokia exclusively for Latin American markets. I quit when I was required to move to Tampa.

In 2004, Fernando Garcia-Jurado was born, our first and only son and one of our best legacies to this world. He was born at Greenwich Hospital in Connecticut.

By the end of that year, I was hired as an art director at a promotional agency in Darien, CT. They had just acquired the Cuauhtémoc Moctezuma beer account in the US. Cuauhtémoc Moctezuma was the second largest Mexican brewery and its portfolio of beers was very relevant. For almost four years, I was responsible for developing visual communication strategies for Tecate, Dos Equis, Bohemia, Sol, and Carta Blanca.

It seemed that what Andrea told me was true and I would only work for the Hispanic market. A caveat though, I had the opportunity to be part of Dos Equis' 'The Most Interesting Man in the World' campaign targeting the general market.

Unfortunately, 2008 arrived with the news that Gaby would be sent back to Mexico. I should have mentioned that we were considered diplomats during that eight-year stay, so once again, we were relocated to our original place. It was tough for us. However, it was more challenging for Fernando, our son. Even though he spoke Spanish, he had a bit of an accent, as much as a four-year-old bilingual kid could have, and he was bullied at school in the city where Gaby and I were born. It was heartbreaking. I was witnessing discrimination in my own country by my own people.

In general, it was very hard for us to adapt. My wife was robbed at gunpoint, and it was tough for me to find a well-paid job. We were both able to recognize all the differences between the two countries. We did not fit in anymore; we felt we no longer belonged. It was unfortunate, so I started looking to return to the US. It took me a while, but at last, I was hired by the largest shopper marketing agency in the world, whose HQ happened to be in Lakewood, CO.

I was initially hired to oversee the creative development of all Kellogg's Hispanic (yes, again) promotions. We all moved to Denver, CO, in late 2010. The agency was terrific, the team was incredible, and the people were intelligent and friendly. By 2011, I was in charge of all Kellogg's Hispanic promotions and shopper marketing creative development. I was over the moon. In 2013 I was asked to switch teams and lead the creative team in charge of developing all regional promotions for all MillerCoors' portfolio of beers.

This is where I was exposed to this incredible country's different regions. I could learn first-hand all the differences between races, cultures and traits, depending on the geography. To give you an example, I realized that Texas is a universe on its own. In Texas, they are Texans first, Americans second, and Hispanics, Whites, or Blacks last. Therefore, we had to tailor every promotion to the different demographics.

But there is always a beginning and an end, and in 2016 the company laid off more than 200 people. It happens when you lose a big account - in this case, MillerCoors.

NATAS – HEARTLAND REGIONAL
EMMY° AWARDS 2017

"I am proud to be a Hispanic living in the US. I am a firm believer that our culture has made America better. Our family values, hard work, optimism, and friendliness have been essential in building this great nation."

I was unemployed and lost my working visa, which is the only way to work legally in this country as a non-permanent resident. Usually, a working visa has to be arranged through a company willing to sponsor it and, in this case, I lost my sponsorship. Fortunately, my wife was already working for a restaurant group, so they transferred my visa to be her dependant. That meant I could stay but was not allowed to work.

To keep myself busy while I was looking for a company willing to sponsor me, I was able to help a Hispanidad agency in Denver create a PSA-based campaign for the Colorado Department of Transportation. This 'Don't Drive Under The Influence' campaign was recognized with an Emmy® for the team and me in 2017. I have other marketing and creative-related awards for other campaigns, a few Effies for Kellogg's and Dos Equis, but Emmys are unique, maybe because they are more widely recognizable.

Finally, a branding company in the Bay Area hired me, so we moved here in late 2017. I oversaw the agency's entire creative development. Thankfully, the lawyer who helped me get my working visa back told me I could apply for my Green Card under self-petition status, arguing I had extraordinary abilities. I did, and considering my experience and professional trajectory, I was granted it. It was a game-changer. For a while, we were suffering, thinking we would have to leave again, but our future here is secure now, and we will apply for citizenship soon.

I have recently started my own practice again, focusing on helping mission-minded brands and organizations, developing community and environmental-driven campaigns for non-profits. At the same time, I had the privilege of becoming the President of the American Marketing Association in San Francisco, trying to help the Bay Area community and supporting the new generations of marketers, always keeping an eye on diversity, equity and inclusion.

I am proud to be a Hispanic living in the US. I am a firm believer that our culture has made America better. Our family values, hard work, optimism, and friendliness have been essential in building this great nation.

Supporting each other while respecting all different cultures and religions, fighting for our rights, and making ourselves better by studying and helping our communities are things that we have to do every day to keep demonstrating our value. Something that is clearly often overlooked.

I feel honored to be part of this project along with all these amazing people, community leaders and entrepreneurs, who have been at the center of the cultural revolution of modern America and that has shown, day in and day out, that Hispanics are essential for our society and our economy.

OGN INTERACTIVE
Gerardo Garcia-Jurado
Scan here
to visit my profile

Martha Niño

HISPANIC JOURNEY

Senior Marketer / Diversity Advocate
Adobe

A Senior Marketing Manager at Adobe and self-styled diversity and inclusion advocate, Martha Niño embodies the American Dream.

She was born in a shack in Mexico where her parents picked cotton to feed the family. She was handed to a stranger to make her way to the USA, undocumented. Martha grew up in California, in Silicon Valley in fact, and today is one of just three percent of Latinos that have had a career in tech for more than 20 years.

Through all the ups and downs, she has retained her passion not only for helping innovative companies achieve goals, but for helping people be better people.

We met online, connecting through LinkedIn during the pandemic. I started learning about her journey and fell in love with what she does to help touch, move, and inspire people to see their greatness.

I began, as I usually do, by asking Martha what makes her heart sing.

So many things make my heart sing. First, trying to be a good mom and seeing my kids thrive makes my heart sing. The second thing is seeing others succeed, those who maybe didn't think they could. I have been on a quest to inspire people whenever I get the opportunity to help somebody be better than they thought they could, that feels pretty good.

My next question to Martha was this: What do you think is the biggest misconception of immigrants in the US?

That is a deep question. I am an immigrant. First, I think we all need to remember that.

We might have come a year ago, maybe we came 100 years ago, but many of us have been adopted by this country, and some of us are still hoping to be adopted by this country. So, the biggest misconception, I think, is that we are all in the same place of our immigration journey.

From my perspective as a previously undocumented immigrant, there are different flavors of immigrants. There are some that come to this country with a lot of money, they have been educated in their native countries, and they can be doctors, they can run high tech companies, they can do all kinds of things. And then there are immigrants in this country that just want to do a basic job and have a room to sleep in with electricity.

Those extremes need to be talked about more because they are important. Understanding that there are many extremes to being an immigrant in this country, and so many things that go into the middle of it – for some, a lack of education and for others fully educated journeys. Nonetheless, we are all humans; the background is irrelevant. I feel like we just need to be kind and to learn from each story. That is why I am so passionate about being in this book, to have my story heard, because I come from the extreme, I come from the side that comes from nothing.

I was born in a shack with no electricity and no water, and I have made it to a place where I'm working with many people that come from very educated backgrounds. How the heck did this girl, me, do that?

That is why I am speaking so passionately about the many different lives an immigrant can encounter in this country, the many different paths that we can take. In my case, as an undocumented immigrant at one time, I know that the undocumented immigrant is scared, afraid to talk to anybody because we might have an accent, because we are afraid of being kicked out of the USA. We live in fear. Fear that the dream we risked everything for can be taken away.

I don't think people understand how scary it is to be in a country where you're not wanted. We come out of necessity and need because in our own country, we might not have the basic necessities: running water, electricity, education. We might not have anything, so risking everything to come to this country means just that - everything.

Hearing Martha say that gave me chills from head to toe because there are many different types of immigrants, and we emigrate for many different reasons. It brings me back to the day in university when I started at the age of 17 and met our janitor, an engineer in his own country, and it reminded me that people in our circle were doctors. They had no opportunities to use those skills here in the USA other than to start from fresh, despite qualifications. Since then, I have met doctors who have attempted to help here for many years so that they can become certified in this country and be able to practice, each having to start from scratch over and over again.

I returned to Martha's journey and asked where she came from.

Who am I? I'm just like everybody else. I am also a business professional from Silicon Valley.

I am a very lucky human; I am very fortunate. I came from absolutely nothing, my parents picked cotton in Mexico, so I have very, very humble beginnings.

"I feel like we just need to be kind and to learn from each story. That is why I am so passionate about being in this book, to have my story heard, because I come from the extreme, I come from the side that comes from nothing."

I was handed to a stranger to pass across the Mexican border in the hope of a better life. My parents were not with me, they could only hope we would be reunited. There is much of this talk about this practice, and you know, sometimes it works out and the risks pay off. I grew up in a very humble environment. I didn't have electricity, running water or anything like that.

When we came here, our first little American home was a duplex with one bedroom. We had walls, we had electricity and we had water - we were already 'making it' from the moment we got here. To have only those essentials was a joy; I was already having a better life because I had a roof over my head that was a little warmer than a shack.

Until I spoke for the first time, I didn't realize how important speaking up would be. I'm almost 50 years old and I just recently started speaking about this story. As a matter of fact, if you tried to talk to other immigrants, they might sugar coat their story, but sugar coating is not how we learn. We can't sugar coat reality.

I didn't even know I was in poverty; I was just a kid. Unless your parents tell you, or other kids start teasing you, and that did start happening when I was a little older, you don't know you've gone without until others point it out. Then you start realizing other kids have Ataris, they have Cabbage Patch Dolls, and they have Reebok shoes. I didn't have any of that, I grew up in the 80s and I knew I was a little bit different, but I wasn't the only one. There were other kids who didn't have Cabbage Patch Dolls, Ataris or Reeboks either, so I wasn't alone in that situation. We were taught to believe those things were not for us.

At that time my parents worked any job they could - my mom

sewed clothes, she babysat, she did whatever she could, she even worked in factories back in the early days of Silicon Valley. That is where I grew up, before it was even the Valley as we know it. There were cherry and apricot orchards - my mom even worked at one of the cherry orchard canneries. She stood on her feet for hours on end - that was a tough job.

At the same time my dad was working hard in construction type jobs.

Throughout all this, there was never any talk about education. The poorer Mexicans like me don't have educated parents, so there wasn't much talk about school, it was all work. My parents didn't know the educational system either, I think they sent me to school because they needed a babysitter. It was simply functional, they had to go to work, and Martha was safe at school. They were not worried about a college future. They didn't know it.

I started work at a very young age, I was 10 and delivering newspapers daily. I did this for four years. I was earning money to buy my own clothes and pay a bill or two. Then I went into high school and had a very tough time to be honest. I didn't know why I was there, and I still had to work. At the age of 14, I ended up working with my mom at a factory. I showed up every day after school. No one at my school knew I worked daily.

Factory work is hard, trust me. That factory was cold too. However, I wanted to continue earning money. At that time, I was earning the minimum wage of $3.35 an hour. That was a big deal back then. Mom was my supervisor, and I was terrible at the job.

In that factory, the owner, who was this beautiful blonde woman with blue eyes, pearls, and fancy shoes, spotted me and told me that she knew I was not cut out for factory work and told me to help her in the office. That was a pivotal moment for me, because had she not seen something in me, and given me another option, maybe I would still be in a factory. The office was a whole new world for me.

Like Cabbage Patch dolls, Ataris and Reeboks that we thought were not for us being in an office was no different. It just does not happen to people like me. We're usually tucked away in the back of these companies; my entering the front of the business got me hooked on the office setting. It was warm and there were doughnuts, I could even get a free drink. Not bad, at 14, having an office job was absolutely a big deal.

During that time, I was working so much that I didn't focus on school at all. On the first day of my senior year, the principal informed me that I was getting kicked out. He said I was a 'bad' influence. At that point, I didn't even realize what was happening and within days, I was at a continuation school. Looking back, that continuation school, was another thing that shaped me.

I was now feeling like a complete loser. I looked around and noticed a lot of my relatives were there, which was interesting! There were also a lot of gang members, many girls had babies, so many in fact that there was even a day care center at the school.

There were also kids that were homeless. There were kids that had parents hooked on drugs. There were some whose parents were in prison. It was a completely new environment to me. It was a school where they sent the "bad" kids. I wasn't a bad kid, it's just that the principal never asked me why I had to work so much.

At the time, my father had cancer and my mom had to work two shifts, so I had to help. Had that principal just dug a little deeper they would have realized I was living a whole other life and it was the same for many of the others at the continuation school. Nobody asked them why they were there, or what was happening at home, and that is my point. These were all good kids who had simply got stuck in bad situations that were not their fault at all.

I was in awe of that part of our conversation. It was such a powerful experience to come from. The only option I had was to let Martha continue.

At 17 years old, I needed somebody to tell me things. The principal at my previous school had not engaged with me that way at all, but there was a counselor at the continuation school, and he was checking in on me. He asked why I was there, and I told him that I got kicked out of school, but I didn't really tell him why.

I probably didn't even know why, but he dug and then dug deeper, and then he realized that it was because I was working all this time and that my dad was sick. He got to the root of it and because he took the time, he thought he could do something to help me.

I looked tough, I had big eye makeup, and I looked like a gang member too. He saw beyond that and said if I could do a year's worth of catch-up work in four months, I could go back to the high school that kicked me out.

That was the first time I ever heard somebody give me hope, hope to get out of where I was, and a plan. He gave me a very specific plan. The only challenge was that somehow, I had to put my job on hold.

But I still needed money, so I talked to my manager, the company owner, and told her the situation. She said I could work on the weekends, even double up on the weekends, and we'd figure it out, but during the week I should focus on school. Now, she was one of my believers - my first believer in business.

The counselor at my continuation school was my other believer.

I was working, I was studying in the daytime at the continuation school, I was going to night school, and I was doing all kinds of extra things to try to get back to that high school. There was a little fire in me that wanted to prove to people that I wasn't a bad kid, that I wasn't a bad influence like everybody thought. I didn't want to be the kid who was not going to make it.

Within four months, I was back at that high school with my chin up and everything on track, and I graduated on time. It was quite a learning experience for me. I still knew nothing about college though. I didn't know anything about my future.

Now, when people ask me who I am, I tell them I am a combination of a lot of different things. I'm a combination of coming from a different country, of not knowing anything, of people believing in me, and of opportunity.

How powerful and inspiring hearing about that moment was. I will never forget how it made me feel. I then asked Martha why, in her opinion, there are notably few Latinos in higher positions, and what you do to increase the numbers?

In my opinion, technology is a very privileged career. You learn

HA NINO - ADOBE DIVERSITY CONFERENCE/KEY NOTE

"I was born in a shack with no electricity and no water."

And now look!

technology in colleges and universities, and you learn how to work in technology at school but what if we can't afford it?

Schools, however, cost a lot of money and yes, there is a small percentage of Latinos that can afford those schools. Those are not the Latinos I am talking about here. I can tell you that in the Silicon Valley area alone, almost 40% of the kids in school are Latinos and maybe two or three percent of us have the required money to go to the schools where recruiters are hiring from.

Also culturally, under-served Latinos don't truly know what the education system is. Our parents don't know it, so how can they teach us. We blindly enter this academic environment and hope that somebody will guide us. We might ask questions, but it's very hit or miss.

Those who have the privilege of entering industries like technology often have parents that are well educated, who know the educational systems and have money saved up for specific schooling purposes.

The Latinos and Latinas I'm speaking of do not have that, so it is hard to enter the environments where technology companies are looking to recruit. I said hard, not impossible.

However, I have seen a small shift. In the last few years there has been a big emphasis on diversity. Honestly, if I could have a banner, I would say: "If you're looking for diversity, look in diverse places". Simple! Let's do that. Because we are not in the places the recruiters are looking at.

We should be looking to recruit kids from different places. Look at community colleges. Look at kids that might offer something different.

Look at kids with a story and life experience. I tell you, in my case, when I must solve something or do something with a smaller budget, I don't panic. I get super resourceful, super passionate because the diverse background I come from called for it. We are used to being on a budget.

There are so many values of under-served talent that are not on LinkedIn profiles. So, when we are talking to this diverse talent, we also need to dig deeper to find out what value they are going to bring to the organization that is different. So why are there very few Latinos in the technologies? It's because we don't believe we can be there. I am there, so I am proof. The few of us that are there need to be louder.

Another reason is we're not in the places the companies are looking at and the recruiters that are looking for talent are looking for the same people in same places, therefore they get the same outcomes. It is time to change it up!

What are their beliefs and attitudes? Where do they spend their time, and so forth, these are such important factors. I remember a number of years ago talking about that diversity of thought, and what would happen if people came in and brought in that adversity and diversity of thought Martha mentioned. We'll get into that in a moment.

I asked Martha why is it so important to own your own story as a Latino, and to hide the best bits of life? I know that our true story is not usually on our LinkedIn profiles. We don't tend to share our secrets or achievements.

I think professionally, it is still taboo right now. People like me, who do put their stories out there for all to see, have been through it and we have overcome it, and we found value from it. The younger generation are still working on that.

I think seeing profile samples like Rocío's and other people that are using their story for betterment is a good progressive thing and I hope that Hispanic people can begin to own their story at a younger age, because it just gives them so many more years to make a difference.

I didn't start owning my story until a few years ago. It takes a lot of reflection, it takes a lot of deep thinking, it also takes a lot of other people to make you feel safe and be able to own your story. It takes others to help you heal those facts of shame we keep so silent. A big lesson for me is owning my facts. That's hard but it's so healing.

What are the facts of you personally as a human? I was undocumented, I was smuggled into this country as a child, I lived in poverty. Just say it. Those are facts. They are literally just facts that you can do nothing about. Fact, I was kicked out of high school. Fact, I overcame it. Fact, people helped me out. Fact, I couldn't have done it without them.

Once you look at your life in those terms it becomes a little easier to talk about. When you take the taboo from those negative things away, you start to feel a little better about who you are and who you may be tomorrow, and then, importantly, who you can help. When you put your true story out there, other people will recognize their own stories in yours. And if you can overcome hard times, then so can they. So, it's important to own your story, not only for yourself, but to tell it, for the benefit of others.

Bringing humanity into the workplace is probably one of the most important things anyone can do. I get it and hope this book enables readers and others to embrace this shift to empower our young.

Once in a while, I would say to those I was with, when I was in university that I was a teen mother in graduate school. People would be shocked as I was in my early 30s. My response? Wow, look at where I am, a serial entrepreneur, in school, working 70 hours a week, and you're telling me what I did was wrong when I was 14 years old? - That, the best that I could have done, considering the circumstances - was a mistake?

I was empowered by the response Martha gave.

Not only did you do that, but you also raised a good human, you should be proud. Instead of people looking at it as a negative, they should recognize that lady is amazing.

That is how owning your story and changing the narrative, and putting it out there, begins to change the perception of kids like those in that continuation school. They're not bad kids, they're just dealing with bad circumstances. They're misunderstood, because nobody is talking, nobody is digging deep into these situations.

This is why owning your story is powerful, you become okay with yourself, and that is hard to do. I have had my insecurities. I have been in tech jobs and felt like I didn't fit in. I talked to new people at a high level and the whole imposter syndrome kicks in, but once you start to own yourself as human - and there is truly zero you can do about that past stuff - you move forward. You get the strength to have others learn from your story and move forward, maybe even heal a little bit of their own life.

That is super-important.

At the end of the day, you can bring your whole self to work and once you do that, magic happens.

It is important people compartmentalize that because I think during the pandemic, we were possibly forced to bring our whole selves to work. I hate to say this, but maybe it was a little bit of a blessing for the work environment, because you might be in your bedroom with a crying child, while the Amazon guy is knocking at the door and the dog is barking. We can't switch us. That's life! You can't change your personality because you're on a Zoom? No! You can't do that. If you did, it's probably exhausting.

When you're in an interview don't switch either. It's hard to keep up the theatrics. Sooner or later your true personality will be found out – just be your whole self everywhere.

Speaking about that, I asked Martha which values she thought were underrepresented and underserved? Or, as some people call it today, 'marginalized talent', and what it can bring to an organization?

We all come with different backgrounds. I think that looking in the same places to hire might give you the same type of talent options. I think that value is found by bringing something different to the table, that special thing that maybe makes us stand out from the rest.

Perhaps it is something that we grew up with, maybe we had to help our parents work at a store, or we had to help our father in the mechanic shop, maybe we had a good work ethic from the time we were 10. I mention this because I feel like we need to own some of

*"The poorer Mexicans like me
don't have educated parents,
so there wasn't much talk
about school, it was all work."*

those differences that we grew up with and bring it to the corporate table as a benefit.

We are resourceful because we grew up with no resources. My advice to those who think they might not have as many check marks as others. Perhaps make your own check marks and; bring that to the interview table. I guarantee many will have the same check marks but if you speak about something different, you might actually catch some attention.

Back to the subject of lack of resources, I grew up stretching my money. That made me an excellent budget manager. I have managed multi-million-dollar budgets well and it's because I grew up with nothing. I believe that being different and having a unique background can benefit a corporation.

We also usually grow up very family oriented and bringing that whole family vibe into the workplace can translate to a much better work group environment, which means better retention. It is harder to leave a family than it is some stranger who's just on Zoom every now and then. I think loyalty is huge, and we can bring loyalty to the team.

I've been at one company for three years, one for two years, one for five years, and Adobe for more than 15 years. It's a long time, there's loyalty involved, because at most of those companies I felt like they were my family, I have friends there. It felt comfortable in that office and therefore I stayed longer.

Being in an office is new to many first-generation immigrants. Entering this environment and getting a job there means we were hired, and we are now CYCLE BREAKERS. You 'as a recruiter' just made a whole difference in our lives, the lives of our parents, our children's lives, and the lives of generations to come. This was a multi-generational hiring effect.

Now, perhaps we can send our parents on vacation, we can have insurance for our children, and the generations to come will be so much better off too. There is so much value that we can bring to a corporation, and we will be grateful and bring it for a long time, but there is also value that corporation can bring to many with just one hire. It's a win/win.

What a concept, to be able to say we can work together this way and look at it through Martha's lens and see there is so much behind the budgeting, the retention, and the individual gifts we can bring if we shout about them.

I want to mention a small company attorney firm that I have recently spoken to as an example. The CEOs attorneys make half a million. If he loses one attorney, he loses half a million. That half million, is more than a million dollars when all is said and done, because he must replace that attorney as he may lose clients as a result of the cases that they can no longer represent. Imagine that 'as a CEO'. It's not half a million for him, it's a couple of million. What we are bringing with the concept Martha mentioned, is loyalty. That is what companies are currently missing out on. Now businesses are trying to put retention programs in place, to attract the people that bring that energy and loyalty we have, into the organization.

I wanted to know Martha's further thoughts on retention.

Latinos have a lot of energy; we have a lot of heart. We are motivators, we are gatherers, let's nurture some of that. Make us feel comfortable at your organization so we can make others comfortable, too.

I know companies struggle with retention. Companies should consider under-served talent because it's not just a job for us. It's a new life. Now, just make us feel like you care, with words of affirmation. We can't assume. Remember, we are new to these environments. We need to hear it. We also need to feel it. Make us feel like family and we'll stay there longer.

That is a whole different experience and conversation coming into the workforce. I asked what advice Martha would give those entering the workforce right now?

First, congratulations for entering the workforce! It is a hard thing to do if you are first generation; it's a whole new world for you to learn. There will be many people in the organization that might have been there 10 or 20 years - learn from them.

One thing I learned when I came into tech is that I didn't know everything, in my case, I didn't know anything tech and that was OK. It's OK to ask somebody's advice for five minutes, or even for 15 minutes. If you love what a person is doing, take them for coffee and learn from them, ally with them, have them be part of your journey, then maximize that time.

Many of these folks, especially in tech, come from amazing educational backgrounds. I work with people from Stanford, Harvard, Yale, you name it, and I feel like I now have a little bit of Stanford, Harvard, and Yale rubbed off on me too. I hope they can learn a little about my background as well. Perhaps together it's better, I think so. My background brings a lot of life lessons with it. I'd love for others to learn them with me too.

You know the old saying. "You are who you hang around with."

That is the truth. Hang out with those you want to learn from and continue to learn from them. Maximize your time with everyone, use that environment to your benefit because, believe it or not, there are so many people out there that want to help you out and want to see you succeed.

I think sometimes as Latinos we are not comfortable asking for help or to say we don't know. We need to change and grow culturally, to learn to get comfortable with being uncomfortable.

Leading on from that, I asked what is the impact of people not asking for help when they feel like an imposter or an outsider?

Lack of growth and being uncomfortable. When you're uncomfortable, you probably want out and I think the impact is probably losing 'out' on an opportunity. Who wants to be or work in an uncomfortable place?

Therefore, the impact is probably less experience at a job and not getting those promotion titles from that growth opportunity because you remained silent and were uncomfortable asking for it. The impact could be less pay, less benefits or perhaps a lesser title. Remember, if we're not growing, that means that professionally we're probably not getting paid more.

My advice is to ask for what you want. If you don't, I guarantee there are others asking for what you were silent for – and they'll get it because they spoke up.

I think Hispanics are missing out if we let that imposter syndrome get to us. If you do, you're going to be stuck. I guarantee it. I feel that everybody has some sort of an impostor syndrome, Latino or not. I have white friends, Indian friends, black friends, and we all feel uncomfortable at times. So, knowing that is a game changer. We all have imposter syndrome in one way or another.

Some people think leaders are more interested, but are they more interested in the outcome? Are leaders out to get you when you're asking for support? Some think that if they get a coach or go to a workshop for personal growth, that it could be seen as fixing a problem, that there is something wrong with them. Is that really true? Martha's reply made a great point.

If you have a good leader, it should not matter. It should be a benefit. They should recognize that an employee wants to grow and is smart enough to ask for help and seek advice. If a leader is feeling uncomfortable with that, I think that is their problem, not yours. There is nothing wrong with asking for help. You should always push your employees to grow more. If somebody does come to you, and you are a leader, let them because they're coming to you for a reason. Plus, the better they look, the better you look too.

I wanted to confirm the idea the other way around, when the employee is thinking there is something wrong with them. What if their boss asked them to go out and do something to improve themselves, or to take a course?

There is nothing wrong with you; your leader simply wants you to know more. Your leader just wants you to grow and to benefit the organization more. There are organizations that don't have these extra perks – use them, they are a gift.

I think we need to be humble and thank them because they think that we can be better with a bit more support. Don't take it as a negative. I want to stress, if anybody's giving you a resource for a coach or any additional help - that's amazing. Take it. Anything you can learn from another professional is always a positive. Your leader only wants you to be stronger.

Martha represents part of the two per cent of people in tech here. My next question was to ask how she got into this highly competitive industry?

Accidentally! I was 19, recently out of high school and working at a manufacturing company. The company was losing money by manufacturing in the US, so they were going to be moving the company to Mexico. They asked me to go, but my father had just passed and I decided to stay back. I ended up working in a business that manufactured office cubicles for Silicon Valley companies. And would you believe I ended up at one of those Silicon Valley companies.

Funny story. My time in the cubicle industry had run out. I was out of a job; I went to a temp agency looking for anything that paid over 15 bucks an hour. This is back in the days before Google, we had phones with cords on them, and sometimes the lines would be kind of 'choppy'. Speaking with the recruiter, I thought she said, there's an opportunity at a 'sand' company. "Sand" ..like by the ocean. I knew nothing about "sand" but if it paid the 15 dollars, I was there! I'm going to be in the materials business, or so I thought.

I had obviously misheard it, because when I got to the job, it was a 'sound' company, like sound for computers. And because I had zero fear of 'sand', I said "yes". I think if she had said a tech company in 'sound' I might have been intimidated and said "no".

"I think sometimes as Latinos we are not comfortable asking for help or to say we don't know. We need to change and grow culturally, to learn to get comfortable with being uncomfortable."

That was a pivotal lesson - I didn't need all the tech knowledge! There are non-techie people in tech. I'm one of them. I have made a career of over 25 years in tech, not knowing tech. At the time I didn't have a degree either. What I did have, however, was base skills. I had office skills, I had budgeting skills and I was confident about those skills and focused on those, I pumped those up during the interview.

People like to get stuff off their plates, so when I got to that company, although it was completely foreign, I learned, I asked questions and I asked how I could help. I did a lot of that. I needed to prove I belonged there and that I could add value.

I entered the tech industry accidentally, but I stayed there on purpose because I liked it. I learned, I got mentors, and I got coaching, I went on sales calls, I observed people and I was curious. I think all this learning got people's interest in me too, because one of those managers at that sound company took me aside and literally sat me down and asked if I was enjoying my job. He asked if I would be interested in other paths in the company. I didn't know any other paths aside from the $15 dollar path I signed up for. I told him I didn't know but would be interested in his guidance. He grabbed a board marker and literally drew the available paths. Hope paths! I liked that other people saw whatever was shiny inside of me and got it out.

I've been in sound, I have been in hardware, I've been in mobile - I did mobile before mobile was mobile - and I've been in software and services. At all those jobs, being adaptable was super-important, because technology changes all the time. You must be comfortable with change. I mean, I went from a time in the tech where computers were tethered to a wall to fitting in your hand and taking them everywhere.

What I was selling 25 years ago is not relevant now. It's better.

Perhaps, if there was ever an industry that people should get into, where you don't have to know 100%, it's technology.

Three, four years into tech, I was noticing people getting promoted, but I was not. Perhaps it was that nagging imposter syndrome voice, I wasn't smart enough, I didn't have what they had. I thought it was because most of the people I worked with had degrees.

That idea led to me to taking a gap in my work for the first time in my life and attend the University of Phoenix. I had been dabbling when I could at my credits since high school, but I had not achieved the goal of a check mark in the degree box. For about 6 months, I did what I had done in high school and focused and got my schooling.

At 26 and 8 years after graduating high school I finally had my degree. In parallel I had 12 years' work experience. Lack of this check mark makes people stress, coming up with a story as to why one might not have it. I no longer needed to stress about this – one less thing. If you are able, get your degree. Although it's not impossible, it is just easier to get in.

I recently learned there are many tech companies that are eliminating the degree necessity for coders and other like jobs! A step in the right direction.

Also do not be afraid to network. Network like a human, not like a scripted robot and don't be afraid to use LinkedIn. Post, comment, follow companies you like, people you want to learn from. Get yourself out there!

That is the story of how I got into this very competitive industry of Tech. It is worth noting that when I was there, I worked it and I worked it hard. It has been an amazing journey and now, because of the way that I got in, and because of my background, I am super-passionate about having other people believe that they can enter it too. And I know they can, because if a girl from a shack can do it, so can they.

I love that. I knew Martha's dedication to making a difference and opening doors for people so that they can walk straight through and break that cycle. Let's co-create together! That's one of my favorite words, 'Co-create'.

Most people with diverse backgrounds don't talk about their past. What was the pivotal moment that changed that for Martha; was it the moment she decided to talk about herself?

I didn't find that voice until a few years ago. I had kept that voice silent except with family. The pivotal moment that changed it for me was kind of an interesting moment. At Adobe, the Photoshop company I work at, I give tours of our fantastic buildings at lunchtime and there was this one group of kids coming in from the Central Valley where they grow strawberries and artichokes. I showed them the basketball court, the cafeterias, our ping pong tables. When I looked at my tour group, I noticed a boy and his eyes were watery. I asked him what was wrong. He said, "this is all good but people like me don't end up at places like this".

Well, little did they know I wasn't just a tour guide. I was a marketer that had been there forever. I turned to him and said, "what? I am YOU". I proceeded to tell him my story. I told him the story about me coming from a shack, being in poverty, and how I was kicked out of school. I told him the truth.

*"If you're looking for diversity,
look in diverse places."*

That moment was a game changer for me, because it was the first time that I realized I had to tell this kid that he can be at this place too, because I was him; I am him. That event started the journey and with me feeling more comfortable with my story, that day I felt a little bit healed.

Three months later, Adobe had a diversity conference opportunity, where they were looking for people with diverse backgrounds and stories. If your story entry was selected, you might be able to speak on a stage. Might? Might was a 'chance'. I had already told the kid some of my story, now I tell it all. I had nothing to lose, but everything to gain. I always wanted to speak but this was not a kid. This was Adobe leaders. This could be risky.

I had so many insecurities. Then I thought about my kids and the advice I would give them if they had an opportunity. In that moment, I hit submit to the 'My Story' entry. A few months later I was a closing keynote at that conference in front of 1200 people, it was glorious. Gloria Estefan was there too, it was ridiculous. My mother also was there. With tears in her eyes through the entire talk she cried with pride as her little girl from a shack proved to everyone that she had made it. This moment changed my life. I haven't stopped talking since!

After hearing that incredible moment of enlightenment, how that can inspire others, I asked Martha how someone turns their adversity into treasure?

Well, first you must believe that what you have already been given is a treasure in and of itself. That the life you have is not all negative. Take the victim mentality away from it because it's too easy to think it's all because you were in poverty; it's because you had nothing, because your parents were not educated.

I think you turn it around when you start to say that you did have those issues but think you don't have them now. Remember the facts, but also that you're able to turn things around.

Then you start to feel like a superhero that can help people using your backstory. We are all humans, after all, and if you got through your circumstances, if people have helped you out, that's that superpower you need to do the same right there. That is the energy we need so that other people can feel better about it.

Once you realize that your adversity can help other humans to open doors, you'll feel better about your story and maybe heal a little bit. Once you start you won't want to stop, because who wants to stop the gift of helping other humans?

I know so many people are going to benefit from reading this and knowing there's another human being out in the world who has been vulnerable, and they've succeeded and continue to succeed. So, that's the beautiful thing, as we see more of us out there telling our stories others will start to feel more comfortable with telling theirs.

My One Golden Nugget on leadership is "If you're looking for diversity, look in diverse places."

My One Golden Nugget on tenacity is "To not give up, to look for help and to ask for assistance. Keep going."

My Golden Nugget on grit is "No matter where you come from, it doesn't matter. It is where you end up that matters. So don't give up."

"No matter where you come from, it doesn't matter. It is where you end up that matters. Don't give up."

Martha Niño

OGN INTERACTIVE
Martha Niño
Scan here
to visit my profile

José M. Hernández

HISPANIC JOURNEY

NASA Astronaut, Speaker and President/
CEO of Tierra Luna Cellars, Inc. Scientist/Engineer,
Entrepreneur, Farmer and Wine Maker

The stories shared in this book are remarkable, stellar, life affirming and inspirational, but perhaps only one can truly claim to be out of this world. José M. Hernández is an award-winning, patent-holding NASA astronaut who flew aboard the Space Shuttle 'Discovery' as flight engineer in 2009 on a 14-day mission to the International Space Station. He has worked at NASA Headquarters in Washington DC and also in the Office of Legislative and Intergovernmental Affairs helping develop space policy, NASA's annual budget and interacting with Congressional members to promote the President's vision on Space Exploration.

His books 'Reaching for the Star's and 'El Cosechador de Estrellas' are touchstones in personal and professional growth and in business he has a track record of pushing the envelope to create new markets and opportunities. No wonder a film is being made of his life!

If you are anything like me the thought of going to space makes my heart sing - I can't think of anything other than love that would top that experience, but I had to go mission control and say it: 5, 4, 3, 2, 1, José Hernández, what makes *your* heart sing?

I feel a lot of joy in being able to motivate and inspire others. I have had a number of experiences that have enabled me to get to where I am today and everything I've done in my personal and career life has molded me into who I am now.

I think it is important for people to recognize the value of what they are going through today, and how they can turn that into fuel for success. I love being able to walk somebody through this idea and have them realize the awesomeness of what each day brings, each today.

I feel that many people perhaps to minimalize the work that they do, because they happen to 'only' work in a sandwich shop, or at a grocery store and they feel like this should not be taken into account as it is something that they are not overly proud of. They say: 'Wait, at some point I'll have a real job or a real career.'

When I reflect on my journey, how I got to be where I am now, I can honestly say to anyone I meet, that every job I have had has contributed to everything I do each day in my professional role.

On a personal note, my heart sings for la familia, my family, especially when I hear good news, like my oldest son is getting his PhD soon. My daughter just received her Master's degree in data science, and that makes me very happy. I have a special needs daughter, Karina, who has taught the whole family what unconditional love is all about. We have learned so much from her and are all blessed by having her in the family. In every family there is one kid that is different from the rest. I don't mean it in a bad way but rather that my youngest, Antonio, nonchalantly approaches things from a different perspective. As a parent, when we do not understand this, we tend to worry. He's starting his sophomore year in mechanical engineering and it would not surprise me if he ends up doing something extraordinary with his life. When I look at all my kids and my wife, I did something right. With her love, my five kids are the product of that. I can smile every day. They all make my heart sing.

I have had so many people who have been influential in my life, I had to be inquisitive and ask who had been José's greatest role model and why?

I don't have one person who I would say is my greatest role model. I think there are different role models for the different parts of what

"*I feel a lot of joy in being able to* **motivate** *and* **inspire** *others.*"

makes me an individual, for example, work ethic. Here, I believe my father is my biggest role model overall and then my mother for making me a decent human being.

My greatest role model career-wise is Dr Franklin Chang-Díaz, the first Hispanic American NASA astronaut. My role model from the technical side, is a former boss, Clint Logan, with whom I worked in developing the first full-field digital mammography system for the early detection of breast cancer.

Honestly, I have a whole set of role models that I look up to and that I have tried to emulate to try to make myself into a better individual.

My niece is interested in space and José spoke with her to inspire her dreams because he is never too busy to help others. That is an extraordinary way of being. What a wonderful legacy to be able to impact the lives of many through the choices that he makes and the way that he shows up in the world. We talked about his view as a role model himself.

I have tried to do my best in terms of being a role model. I talk to kids that want to be astronauts, and many other careers and I share a five-ingredient recipe my father gave me. I like to share my story, giving conferences, and I constantly ask myself how I can reach a bigger audience, so I started writing.

After that, I thought that the ultimate audience I could reach would be by having a movie of my life story, and now I am lucky enough that Netflix and Amazon were interested in filming my story. I'm so excited that in the last few months of 2022 the movie filming begins for Amazon Prime. We have the actor Michael Peña playing me and the movie is going to be released in the latter part of 2023. I am very excited about going to that premiere.

I promised José to post the release everywhere when we have the date so that we can all see it.

Throughout these interviews we are learning that certain parts of our culture bring different results. I put this to him and asked which attributes of being Hispanic had been, and are, both a blessing and a curse as he achieves his dreams.

From a blessing perspective, I think it has been the can-do attitude, the tenacity, the not being afraid of hard work from the very beginning. The downside is the fact that you feel like you've been judged before you even begin, so you feel that you're not being given the opportunity, that there's always doubt things are going to get done when tasks are assigned to you. And then, suddenly, they get pleasantly surprised.

Make no mistake, people like Rocío and I did not start life on a level playing field, we had to take a big shovel to level it. And that requires work, not self-pity, to decide to level this playing field with this shovel come hell or high water.

Speaking of leveling that playing field I wondered what José thought Hispanics can achieve in the next decade?

I think we are at a point where the minority is becoming the majority and this is why you hear and see such conflict between different groups, because they don't want to give up the power, they don't want to give up the decision-making processes.

But no matter what this wave is going to come in, it's going to be overtaken, and we will be in a position of making decisions. Whether we are in the Hispanic community, African American community or

Asian community, we will be in a position to make political changes, policy changes that are going to be more even keeled to help everyone in the community, not just certain segments, not only certain socio-economic levels of individuals.

Carlos Quezada had joined us on the interview, and he asked José this: One of the things you and I share is that early on in our childhood we were uprooted many times, going back and forth between Mexico and the US. Do you feel like that experience was detrimental to your growth? Also, did you feel like it contributed to where you are today?

I think originally it may have been a detriment to the growth because you get interrupted in terms of your education process. Speaking Spanish at home and English at school and with many interruptions, you miss out in terms of learning certain aspects, for example, in the English language, then you have to play catch up. But I think, once you catch up, which didn't happen for me until I was well into college, then I think it's a blessing because I was an individual with a diverse background, a person who's easily able to accommodate different changes in the environment.

When the rules change or a project gets canceled, you look at other opportunities, and you ask how you can make this better. A perfect example is when I was at Lawrence Livermore Lab and I worked on a Strategic Defense Initiative project developing an X-ray laser. At that time the Soviet Union broke apart and the justification for such grandiose and expensive projects went away. We canceled that project and rightly so, but while my colleagues in that project went off and found other jobs within the lab and lasers in defense systems, my boss and I stayed behind and posed the question of how we could use this technology for another application and not waste all the development we had done.

That is when we got the idea of developing the first full-field digital mammography system for the earlier detection of breast cancer, a device that gives clear images and means that radiologists see images with much more information content so that they are able to look at possible precursors to cancer earlier. Everybody knows that the earlier cancer is detected, the greater chance the patient has for survival.

I am convinced this device has saved hundreds of thousands, if not millions of lives in the process.

What I am saying is that you take advantage of these types of changes, moving around a lot, making new friends and going to new projects or creating your projects because of the fact that this was in your background, this was in your DNA, and you don't get phased by it. You don't run to the security of an existing project, you're not afraid to start from zero and begin something new, so, that's exactly what we did.

That is a powerful idea, using the gifts of adversity for change and innovation. Now we were speaking of being a child and having a lot of different experiences, José has achieved one of the greatest things that every child dreams about, becoming an astronaut. Who has not dreamed of that?

It was time to discover his journey from the day he decided that he wanted to become an astronaut.

The dream was conceived when I was 10 years old, watching the very last Apollo mission live on TV. You can picture a 10-year-old boy holding on for dear life to a rabbit ear antenna black and white vacuum tube technology console TV, well, that was me watching astronaut Gene Cernan walk on the surface of the Moon and listening to the reporter Walter Cronkite narrate.

"Make no mistake, people like Rocío and I did not start life on a level playing field, we had to take a big shovel to level it. And that requires work, not self-pity, to decide to level this playing field with this shovel come hell or high water."

It was a December night in 1972 and I went outside and saw the Moon in its full glory then came back inside to listen to the astronaut. I was hooked. This is my calling. This is what I want to be. I want to be an astronaut.

I shared that newfound dream with my father and mother. She only had a third-grade education, but my dad was wise enough to listen to that dream and take it seriously and he did two important things. He empowered me in believing that the dream was possible, and he also gave me a five-ingredient recipe to succeed and said if you want to do this you must follow these steps.

First, define your goal or purpose in life. I said: 'I want to be an astronaut.'

Second, recognize how far you are from your goal. I said: 'Well, you know, being a migrant farm worker's son can't be any further away than this.'

Third, draw yourself a roadmap from where you are now, to where you want to go because you have to know the way to your destination by yourself.

'What is the fourth part?' I asked, and he said: 'You are doing it already by being in school. It's preparation; you must prepare yourself according to the challenge you choose. And you have picked the big one, so you will also need to go to college.'

And then, pointing outside, he said the fifth and final part is effort. He told me: 'You know that the effort you put out Saturday and Sunday, then seven days a week during the summer, picking fruits and vegetables? Well, you put that effort here into your school books.'

Then he finished off by telling me I must always give more than people expect. That is the recipe to succeed.

Of course, I had my own sixth ingredient - perseverance. I had the tenacity because NASA rejected me not just once or twice, it wasn't until the 12th time that I was finally invited to be part of the 19th class of astronauts. It was by following my father's recipe, and adding perseverance, that I finally got selected. It was a lot of hard work, blood, sweat and tears throughout the process of many disappointments, but along with disappointments, came some victories and I was finally able to achieve my dream.

Carlos had another question for José relating to a podcast he had heard stating that, and this is something that I think we all need to answer, in the community where we were raised the destroyer of our dreams sometimes lies within our inner circles, our family or friends, saying we're not going to achieve that - things like that are not for us. The question was how did that manifest itself' and how did José overcome that?

It didn't really happen much to me because of the words of my father and that my parents kept us in school. During the harvest, the only time we went to work was Saturdays and Sundays, then seven days a week during the summer. When school was in session, we were in school.

I remember my father's friends used to make fun of him; the naysayers would call him dumb, because he had grown his kids in school instead of working in the fields. Slowly but surely though he built his house. It took him longer, but he built it.

That taught me a lot when I used to tell people I want to be an

"NASA rejected me not just once or twice, it wasn't until the 12th time that I was finally invited to be part of the 19th class of astronauts."

astronaut. I quickly learned that when I said something about it, many would make fun of me. I took the route my dad demonstrated and at that time I decided I was just going to work hard because I'm going to do it and no one has to know except me.

Then I worked my butt off. Sometimes it's best to keep things to yourself, and just go forward.

Carlos had another point to put to José; that one of the things that also seems to happen is that the path to the top gets lonely as you start climbing and start having some level of success. We start to shed the old community and build a new community.

Is that something that you've measured as well as you've been progressing through your career, that you just naturally start building kind of new groups or new communities that are more supportive of what you're doing?

Absolutely, that is what we have to do, but the fact that you find yourself lonely as you move up should be a red flag to you, it should be a sign that you need to take time out and look behind you and ask yourself who you can help to come and join you. Not the egotistical attitude of saying you'll get to the very top first then help people, because the chances are if you do get up there you are not helping along the way. The tendency is to forget about those people.

That's very important to fix. I'm proud to say that I belong to a foundation called Space For Humanity and their idea is access to space for all. We got the blessing of being able to send the first person from our organization on a Blue Origin flight. I pushed for Katya Echazarreta and she flew up to space about a month and a half ago, to space.

I don't want to be the only Latino flying and the more of us that have come up here, the better it is. I pushed hard because we need to give opportunity to a Latina who hadn't flown in space. These are the things that we must all do. If you're up there lonely and not looking back and helping, you are part of the problem.

My son drives me, and I asked José what the role of his family is in his success?

I think the role of the family in my success is the fact that they are very supportive of the things I do and of sharing my time with others who are not family because they know it's for the greater good.

They also contribute in other ways. My daughter Vanessa does a lot of outreach with her TikToks and uses me as an example, in terms of helping folks reaching their dream. My wife, when I was off being an astronaut, was very impressive running the whole household. While I was busy training, she was almost a sergeant with five kids. She did a phenomenal job in making sure that the i's were dotted and the t's were crossed when it came to parenting.

That allowed me to focus on my training and not have to worry about what's happening at home and be distracted. I was always assured that things were running very well at home. That's a lot of support. That's something you don't get a lot from many homes. I've been blessed and thank my wife of 30 years and my five children because of that.

We don't talk about politics in this book for obvious reasons, but I had this question in my mind: How is the Hispanic drive enhanced or held down by the American system?

Well, again, I think right now there is an uneven playing field from day one. Most Hispanics, most African Americans, go to public schools and I found out quickly when I went to college that even though I was an A-grade student, not all public schools are created equal.

The thing that affects us the most is the fact that in poverty-stricken areas we need to improve resources for public schools, we need to have good instructors, and not babysitters. Those are the things I think hurt us most, that we're not paying enough attention to the education system, especially the early portion of the education system in our communities, the elementary schools. We need to make sure we beef up those areas and make it such that our kids will be able to compete once they go into college or high school.

On your journey, what was the worst day of your life? What happened and how did you recover from it?

Getting rejected by NASA and not becoming an astronaut - so the worst day of my life happened 11 times!

No one likes rejection and neither do I but at the same time, even though it was a bad day each time being told I was not going to be considered for further evaluation to become an astronaut I gave myself a chance to soak in it.

This is how I would pick myself up. I said: "Hey, what's the worst thing that can happen if I never get picked up by NASA as an astronaut?" Wanting to be an astronaut motivated me to go to college, motivated me to go to graduate school, motivated me to become a pilot, a scuba diver and to learn a third language - Russian. It motivated me to have a kick ass job at Lawrence Livermore National Laboratory.

I allowed myself to soak in the disappointment for a while, but I realized I had it pretty good. I told myself to be grateful for what God has given me, and the things I have.

By the next day I was bright eyed, bushy tailed, and once again dedicating myself to my career and moving forward waiting for the next selection cycle.

Hispanics are not as well-known as other cultures like Indians and Asians for their scientific contributions, what does José think we can do to increase the inclusion of Hispanics in the scientific world?

I think we have to do a lot more outreach and level the playing field, especially during the early ages - elementary school is when you have to do it, making sure that the opportunities are there for kids and also give them a sense of pride in our culture.

Historically, there's a lot of math involved in our culture. You look at those pyramids that have been built, you look at the fact that the Mayans invented the concept of zero, we've studied the stars, long before Galileo studied them, and we know a lot about the stars. Look at how the pyramids are placed and the winter solstice and the summer solstice brilliance where you're able to see the serpent on the pyramid when the shadow appears – all these amazing things that take a lot of engineering and math.

We need to make the Latino student proud of the fact that it's in our culture. We have this ability, that they too are able to do it, if they just apply themselves.

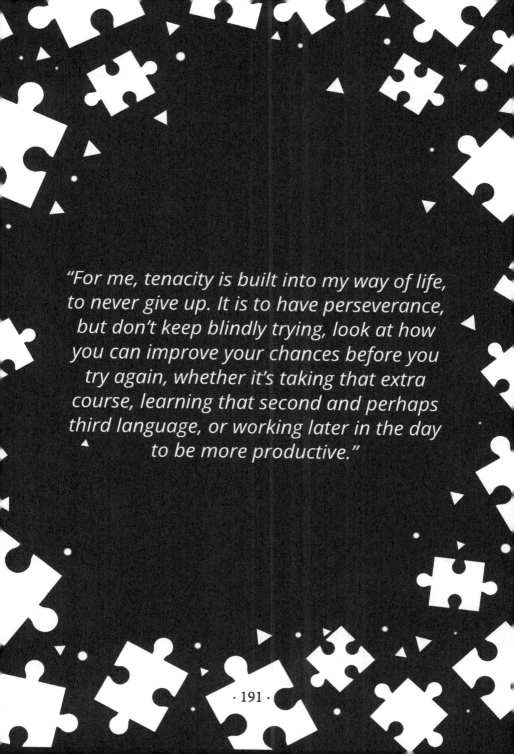

"For me, tenacity is built into my way of life, to never give up. It is to have perseverance, but don't keep blindly trying, look at how you can improve your chances before you try again, whether it's taking that extra course, learning that second and perhaps third language, or working later in the day to be more productive."

The subtitle of the book is: Leadership, Tenacity and Grit. What do each of those words mean to José?

Leadership to me is being a good example. As a role model, you lead by doing good yourself and having a strong work ethic. By definition, you become a leader, you don't seek to become a leader; leadership comes to you. I strongly believe that people tend to gravitate towards people that want to do good because they want to be like you.

For me, tenacity is built into my way of life, to never give up. It is to have perseverance, but don't keep blindly trying, look at how you can improve your chances before you try again, whether it's taking that extra course, learning that second and perhaps third language, or working later in the day to be more productive.

All these things require the grit to roll up your sleeves, to not be afraid to get dirty and work in the trenches. I feel the minute you think you are too good to make 10 copies of a paper that you need to make copies of, you've got problems because your administrator isn't always going to be there. You should be able to go and do the things you wouldn't ordinarily be accustomed to doing.

Lastly, I wanted to know if there was anything José felt was important to say that we had not covered.

I think the million-dollar question for me is, what's your next mission? What's your next goal?

I bring this up, because I challenge myself with the same questions. I feel I am at a point where I have reached a certain level of success because I put together a five-year plan. You get there, and you realize you don't have a second five-year plan. Now there is a movie and much more to come. I think my story is powerful. My story inspires, and this is why I went out on the speaking circuit. I wanted to increase my outreach, so I wrote three books, the first book 'Reaching for the Star's a self-penned biography and a middle reader book 'From Farmworker to Astronaut' where I take the reader through my 14-day space mission while reflecting on what it took to get to space and finally a children's bilingual illustrated book 'The Boy Who Touched the Stars.'

From there, the next logical step was to take it to the masses, so let's make a movie! Now we are doing that. From that perspective, from the astronaut story, and reaching the masses, I think I can say mission complete once the movie from Amazon Prime comes out.

From a family perspective, I continue to help all my kids through college with zero debt, and to make sure they studied what they are passionate about.

Now, from my personal point of view, I ask myself what is next for José? What is my next goal? And my next goal is very different. I have bought some land and planted a vineyard because I felt it was important to go back and work in agriculture, as that is where I started life.

That is my therapy when I'm caught up in the office with all the hubbub. It is wonderful. There's nothing more refreshing than getting on the tractor and plowing the rows in between my grapes, doing it myself. It's great. I love it.

But then, what else now that I have mastered that? my father showed me how to manage the vineyard, from planning all the way to harvesting, and I can do it by myself, so what's the next goal? Well,

I thought, why should I have to sell all my grapes to a winery? Why can't I make my own wine? So, I started making my own wine. And that is how Tierra Luna Cellars was born.

Now I have three varieties of wine and I'm selling it direct to consumers and just had a meeting with a supermarket chain in Southern California, North Gate, and we are to start selling that wine in their 42 supermarkets. My goal is to grow big enough that hopefully one day, someone like Constellation Brands, or Gallo Winery say they want to buy the brand but with the brand comes me and we can grow it to a bigger scale. So those are my plans - grandiose, but achievable.

We now go a little bit off script, as Carlos wanted to ask José if he believed in the law of attraction where, if there's something that you're going after and you put it out there, to God or the universe, the intention will actually help you to make it true.

Agreed! I know I'm going to be doing some good consulting with HPE. I keep pushing. It will happen. It is the power of believing. You tell yourself enough, you convince yourself enough, and then you start behaving and making moves towards that direction.

The key is that you don't look down the road and see that ahead is a big hill to climb, or that it is a long distance. Instead, look at the next 10 feet, and you will get there. That is the way I do it and eventually I reach the top of the hill.

I will sell 'my brand' one day to a Constellation brand or similar company, and we will scale it up a hundredfold in terms of how much wine we will be producing and placing on dinner tables.

Believe in the law of attraction and be very committed to what you want to accomplish in life.

I love it. José echoes what Jim Rohn used to say: Go as far as you can go, then go further. Take those 10 steps; go further, you'll figure it out along the way. And at the end of the day, the only one that needs to hold the roadmap is you. And when you hold and own that roadmap, life is amazing.

"Believe in the law of attraction and be very committed to what you want to accomplish in life."

José M. Hernández

OGN INTERACTIVE
José M. Hernández
Scan here
to visit my profile

Angélica Killion

HISPANIC JOURNEY

Operations & Process Improvement Professional

I started my interview with Angélica by asking what makes her heart sing.

I am happiest when helping others. It might be baking a special dessert, volunteering at school, teaching a disaster preparedness course or my favorite, helping people tap into their potential to create a better future for themselves.

Life story

I am a native-born, first-generation immigrant. My family lived in Tijuana, México. My mom legally crossed into the United States to give birth to my brother, sister, and I, so we would have greater opportunities in life.

My mom grew up in severe poverty; her home life was a constant struggle and placed obstacles ahead of her. She lacked the support of her father, a typical *machista* who cared more for his wants than his family's needs. She loved learning and was devastated when she had to drop out of school after 6th grade to start working and provide for her family. As a child, chronic ear infections and a lack of medical care led to her becoming deaf in her left ear.

When I was five years old, my mom became good friends with another mother in México who would leave her five-year-old daughter to watch her younger brother while she was at work. She would tie her toddler's leg to the leg of the table so he would not be able to crawl far. When my mom learned about this, she brought the children to our home to care for them. That five-year-old and I became lifelong friends.

When I was eight years old, my parents divorced and my mom, siblings and I moved to the United States. I started school in the middle of second grade, with no understanding of the English language. I cried when I could not communicate to my teacher that I needed to use the restroom. Fortunately, a wonderful English as a Second Language (ESL) teacher spent months with me in a closet-sized room, patiently teaching me the intricacies of the English language and better equipping me for my future.

Our relocation to the United States, for me, began a way of living within two countries. My home, school and future were in the United States, yet my primary language, culture, and roots—father and grandfather—were still in México. In México, I understood the people and how the world worked; yet I no longer belonged there. In the United States (*el otro lado*), I had yet to figure it all out. I was a Third Culture Kid (TCK), someone who grew up in multiple cultures and countries and struggles to belong.

As a child growing up on both sides of the border, the cultural differences between the two countries was very apparent to me. For example, showing up unexpectedly at someone's doorstep may be perceived differently. In México, I have always received a warm welcome when I have shown up unexpectedly at a friend's house, while in the United States, not calling before visiting risks a response equivalent to "WTF." Another notable cultural difference is the speed in which time passes changes when I cross the border. It seems to slow down in México, where spending time with people is far more important than sticking to a set schedule. Time appears to speed up in the United States, where often, getting things done has a higher priority.

Living a new life in the United States was not without struggles. In fourth grade, my teacher was so angry with me that she grabbed my arm very hard and left a mark. I ran from my classroom, crying all the way home. Thankfully we lived a short distance away. Between

*"Any day could be our last.
Be grateful for what you have
and stay focused on what's
important to you."*

sobs I told my mom what happened. Grabbing my hand, she marched me back to school, stormed through the school office, passed the secretary without a word and continued through the hallways, with office personnel struggling to catch us.

Once inside my classroom, my mom went up to my teacher and gave her a stern lesson in Spanish in front of the entire class and office personnel. She made it clear that her job did not involve physically abusing children and advised her there'd be severe consequences if she did this again. My mom then demanded I interpret her message "exactly" how she said it; I did, although I'm pretty sure my teacher understood the gist of it from my mom's tone, volume, and facial expressions. That teacher never put a hand on me again. This was one of many lessons I learned from my mom about standing up for myself.

My mom's limited hearing made it virtually impossible for her to learn English. On more than one occasion, when she felt disrespected, she called on me to interpret both the literal message and the precise sentiment. She loudly communicated to these individuals that they should strongly consider a different occupation since they *clearly* did not like the one they had. Interpreting her passionate outbursts built my confidence when speaking with others.

Even though our family depended on government assistance to survive, we often found ways to help others. In 1987, one of those ways was for me to help long-term residents gain legal permanent status by filling out lengthy forms to apply for the Immigration Reform and Control Act (IRCA) of 1986 (*La Amnistia*). These complex applications required applicants to provide extensive documentation including fingerprints, employment history, proof of continuous residency, letters from sponsors and more.

As a thirteen year old, I was kept busy for months filling out forms and describing the exact documentation Immigration required. It was common to come home from a long day at school to find someone waiting for me to assist them with their amnesty forms and my mom standing by with an afterschool snack. The expectation was for me to help because I could. I was happy to do so, even though the forms and process were extensive. I learned that I had the ability to make a lasting difference in someone's life.

When I was fifteen and a half, my mom accompanied me to apply for my first job. I was hired immediately, and for the rest of high school I juggled a job and my academics. Ten days after my 17th birthday, I married my first boyfriend. I did this against my mom's advice.

Along with my wedding vows, I vowed to continue my studies after high school no matter what and signed up for a two-year Electronics Engineering program. During this time, I alternated between living with my first husband and my mom, worked two jobs and went to school full-time. I didn't drive or have a vehicle and relied on public transportation, traveling four hours daily. I often left and returned in the dark. Those days were long.

For safety reasons, I had to be friendly with my neighborhood drug dealers. We had mutual respect and stayed out of each other's business. One day, after a long day at work, I was grateful to receive a ride home from a female colleague; little did I know it would be my last. Even before my colleague put her car in park, the drug dealer began walking across the street towards us. He casually approached with his right arm extended and opened his fist to show the drugs he was holding, while I desperately tried to get his attention to wave him off. My colleague innocently looked at him and at the contents of his hand, not fully grasping the offer. I frantically leaned over her, waving my hands hysterically, and said "No!" The dealer immediately recognized me, apologized and quickly walked away–yet the damage was done.

At 21, I gave birth to my son, received my degree in Electronics Engineering and moved in with my first husband. Moving in together did not go well and my son and I returned to live with my mom. My first husband and I divorced shortly thereafter.

While working as a customer service representative at a copy shop, I boldly told our Xerox technician "I can do that job." The next thing I knew, a Xerox manager stopped by my work to observe me in action; he hired me on the spot. I loved that job! The role involved finding creative solutions to problems; it combined customer service and troubleshooting of electromechanical components within my assigned territory in San Diego County. I spent my days servicing multifunction devices in a variety of interesting spaces ranging from preschools, to submarines, to strip clubs.

In an interesting turn of events, I not only found a job I loved, I met the love of my life. He was the technical specialist of the team I joined and we spent many hours together while I learned my new role. We started a life together after a couple years. We both enjoyed the flexibility and unpredictability of technical service and soon had an opportunity to become small business owners servicing office equipment for Xerox customers.

As a small business owner, I discovered my passion for leadership and management. My husband and I built a team of service technicians to take care of our customers. Unfortunately, three years later, Xerox stopped outsourcing the servicing of their equipment and we lost our business; we were devastated. We both returned to work for Xerox as service technicians until a work-related injury resulted in the loss of my job.

I felt defeated after losing our business, and then the job I loved. That's when I decided to go back to school. Unfortunately, being a first-generation college student, I didn't know my two-year degree in Electronics Engineering was non-transferable to a four-year university and had to start from the beginning. I completed my Associate's degree in General Studies, Bachelor's degree in Management and a Master of Business Administration back-to-back; I only took one semester off to give birth to our daughter.

I intentionally focused on our children and their interests for several years. During this time, I volunteered for many different organizations, including my daughter's school, the local police department, the Alumni Chapter of Mortar Board Honor Society, and two local Community Emergency Response Teams (CERT). I continue to volunteer with some of these organizations where I have met many amazing people.

In 2021, I took a temporary position at a shelter for unaccompanied minors from Latin America; the experience was extremely rewarding. When the shelter closed, they offered me a position within a much larger shelter two hours away. I agreed and discovered one of my most rewarding roles so far, one where I supported youth care workers and enabled them to make a difference in the life of vulnerable children. My experience in mass care further connected me to my passion for disaster preparedness and response work.

Ultimately, I am grateful for my mom and the opportunities she created for us despite her limitations: severe hearing loss, not

"Once I had children, I always looked for opportunities for them to be exposed to new and different things so that they could grow and develop their own interests."

speaking English, having limited resources and being unable to drive. Because of her, our family is breaking the cycle of poverty, domestic violence and lack of education. We are investing in our children and our collective future.

What challenges did you experience as a little girl while helping take care of your family's affairs?

My mom became the apartment manager for every complex we lived in to save money on rent. As the oldest, I did my part to help the family by being her interpreter. Interpreting the English language before I was fluent in it or was part of the culture was difficult; I encountered people who made fun of me for not knowing a specific word or phrase. I would almost cry when my mom asked me to call a certain apartment handyman, knowing he would laugh at my poor English. I vowed to become fluent in English and learned the benefit of being able to communicate in both languages.

These experiences helped me empathize with others who struggle to communicate and made me more perceptive to the intricacies of culture and language. I learned to observe all aspects of language including body language, facial expressions, intonations and other cultural indicators.

How can we create our own opportunities and be more resourceful?

We must continuously create our own opportunities. In the third grade, my fellow students discovered their appreciation for Mexican candies; since I visited México twice a week anyway, I decided to capitalize on this opportunity by starting a business selling Mexican candies out of my backpack at school. I sold candy during lunch and recess and got in trouble for doing so a few times. This small business generated some much-needed dollars for our family and gave me a sense of accomplishment.

The end of the month often called for using our resources in creative ways. It was hard to hear my brother and sister asking for a glass of milk when we did not have any. During those times when we ran out of food staples, I made the most of our connections with our neighbors by borrowing eggs and oil to make cupcakes then selling them door-to-door to make enough money to buy eggs, milk, oil, bread and another box of cake mix. After I sold the cupcakes, my family went grocery shopping and I returned the borrowed ingredients to our neighbors. Being able to earn enough money to buy a few groceries for my family felt very rewarding.

How did you transcend your less-than-ideal childhood environment?

As an eight-year-old, I immigrated to the country where I was born. We moved into the same apartment complex as some of our extended family; they were the only people we knew. It did not take long to notice the illicit activities that some of my family participated in, such as using and selling drugs, going in and out of prison, buying stolen goods out of the trunk of a car and stealing from their own family. I realized that was not what I wanted.

My mom always prioritized our wellbeing. She kept us as far as she could from my extended family's destructive behaviors. She raised us to be honest and hardworking and expected us to do well in school. In spite of the fact that my mom could not help us with our homework due to her limited education, she supported us by creating a quiet area for us to work and brought us snacks and drinks.

Being poor was part of my childhood. My mom stretched the dollar as far as she could; she purchased familiar, affordable groceries in México and got very creative with meals. I have fond memories of eating *caldo de papa* (potato soup) and *enchiladas de cebolla* (onion enchiladas) and now understand those meals were created out of necessity, taking advantage of inexpensive ingredients.

Not finding anybody in my family whom I could look up to, I literally looked across the street to my best friend's house. She had BOTH a mom and a dad and lived in a house with a backyard. Her grandma and grandpa were involved in her life and lived around the corner. Their family shopped at Price Club and brought home more groceries than I had ever seen in my life. I decided this was the type of environment I wanted to live in and resolved to do whatever I had to, to create it.

What holds us back?

Sometimes our own family holds us back. When I was 12 years old, an older family member told me how little she expected from me. She professed that I would never graduate from high school or learn to drive a car and that she expected me to get pregnant soon and not do much else in life. Those words hurt; I did not understand why she said those things and promised myself to prove her wrong.

At times, our friends and families think our goals are unattainable or don't understand our drive and criticize us for wanting something different, something better. They may say to us, "you think too much of yourself" or are *creída* for not being content.

My advice is to be intentional and bring others with you— celebrate each person's step forward. Words are powerful; use them to lift each other up.

What destructive behaviors have we historically normalized within our community?

Let me tell you about my Abuelo. He was an unscrupulous, uneducated, male chauvinist gambler and alcoholic with a bad temper who humiliated his family and never expressed love or compassion. He spent his paychecks as soon as he received them, coming home empty-handed to his family. His family lived in fear of his violent, drunken outbursts which happened often, especially at 2am when he'd wake them up and proclaim, "I am the one in charge here!" and challenge them to disagree. He beat his wife and terrorized his family.

Unfortunately, my mom continued the catastrophic cycle of domestic violence and alcoholism when she married my father. Like many women in her situation, my mom put up with my father's damaging behaviors and extramarital affairs until their divorce.

Growing up, I experienced the violent effects of too much drinking firsthand at family gatherings: an uncle slammed his head through a police car window; a cousin beat his wife when he got drunk and my brother and I had beer bottles thrown at our car as we left a family gathering. This conduct was accepted and normalized; what drunks did was simply an annoying and inconvenient part of who they were.

Sadly, I continued the same pattern of alcoholism and domestic violence in my first marriage. This is the type of behavior which has plagued our families for generations.

Culturally, excessive alcohol consumption at gatherings or celebrations is seen as a badge of honor, as though you can't fully enjoy the moment unless you're inebriated. Now I see the extent to which the experiences that my grandmother, mother and I had growing up, affected our choices in life. It's important to remember that our children are always watching and learning and are likely to repeat what they see. We must transcend these historically normalized destructive behaviors in order for us to empower our future generations.

What has been the most challenging situation you faced and how did you overcome it?

One of the most challenging situations I have faced in life was taking my infant son and leaving my violent, alcoholic husband. My first husband was my first serious relationship; we met while I was in high school and got married the summer before my senior year.

He was controlling and abusive from the beginning yet I stayed with him for several years. Why? For anyone who has not been in this situation, the answer is not straightforward. I knew my husband had a troubled childhood and I thought maybe I could help him have a better life and future. When my husband was sober, he was nice and apologized for his drunken behavior; I thought things would be different next time—that was not the case.

When my son was a few months old, we moved into our first apartment. After a couple months, he reverted to his drunken behavior and I asked him to move out. The nightmare did not end there. In his final violent outburst, he showed up drunk to visit our son and became physically violent; he held us hostage, threatened to kill us and pulled the phone cord from the wall when I tried to call 911. Police officers arrived and my husband was quick to assure them that everything was OK; with my son in my arms, I pushed my way through the door to escape to safety.

What happened next shocked me. He held two large kitchen knives pointed at his chest and threatened to kill himself while several police officers aimed their weapons at him, yelling at him to put the knives down and a police helicopter circled overhead. Thankfully, our one-year-old son and I were safely behind the officers. He finally gave himself up and was taken into custody; as they turned him in my direction to handcuff him, he threatened to kill my son and I as soon as he was released.

That was the point when I decided to leave this man for good. I knew what I had just gone through was not the type of life I wanted for our son. It was one thing to decide to stay with my husband for myself and quite another to subject our son to his erratic and dangerous behavior. I moved back in with my mom and got a restraining order. For several years afterwards, he stalked and harassed me at work, home and anywhere in between.

What core beliefs must change for us to make progress?

We must erradicate the belief that we have been bound to for centuries that women are inferior to men. The negative part of *machismo* is a root cause of the destructive behavior against women that manifests itself when men want power over women and resort to violence.

Not surprisingly, it begins with what we tell our children. Growing up my mom was told she "needed to listen to the man because he was in charge"; consequently, she never developed or experienced a sense of independence while living at home. As a child, the disparate expectations for males and females was explained to me with the ubiquitous phrase "Él es un hombre", or "He is a man". I questioned my mom often, especially in my teenage years and never received an explanation that made sense. For her, those words said it all.

What specific experiences shaped you to become the involved mother you are today?

Growing up in the *barrio*, I had few opportunities to engage in extracurricular activities. In the summertime, the only thing we had to look forward to was the portable swimming pool on our school's blacktop. While I have fond memories of having fun in that pool, our community lacked sports, clubs and any after-school activities. The lack of opportunities to stimulate my brain and my body as a child played a major role in how I chose to raise my children.

Once I had children, I actively searched for opportunities to expose them to new and different activities so that they could develop their own interests. Whether it was an after school club or a summer camp, they had many options to choose from. As a result, our children discovered their unique interests, developed confidence, gained leadership skills and created long-term friendships. Although I did not have these options growing up, I am grateful for the opportunity to experience these activities alongside them.

What are some of the challenges that you have faced as a woman in the workplace?

Working in the male-dominated field of office equipment repair, I often received interesting looks when I informed customers I was there to service their equipment. The most memorable was on a military base. After introducing myself and letting the customer know why I was there, he responded, "The repair guy is coming out to fix it." I reintroduced myself and clarified why I was there and he had the same response. I was frustrated. I stated assertively, "I am your service technician and I am here to fix your copier!" and showed him my toolkit. With a look of disbelief on my face, I asked him, "Do you want me to fix your copier or not?" He apologized and walked me to the machine.

As the Service Manager and first-level technical support for copier technicians in the field, I spoke with customers often, especially when their machine was experiencing a recurring problem. When customers called to complain that their technicians were unable to fix their equipment and requested to speak with the Service Manager, they were surprised when I answered the phone. When visiting upset customers on-site, they were shocked to realize that not only was I the manager, I could also fix their equipment.

How has death shaped your life, and what have you learned from these experiences?

When I was five years old, I had my first experience with death.

A five-year-old neighbor and his grandfather were killed when a retaining wall fell down on top of their home while they slept.

At 17, I planned my first funeral for my 14-year-old brother-in-law who was murdered by a gang member. It was the most difficult of the dozen funerals I have planned in the United States and México.

I have watched a loved one die and discovered two bodies. These experiences have given me a much greater appreciation for life. Any day could be our last. Be grateful for what you have and stay focused on what's important to you.

Let me leave you with a bit of advice. Communicate your wishes to your family in advance to avoid misunderstandings and family drama. My family knows my wishes: donate my body to science and have a celebration serving delicious food and a cake worth waiting for.

Golden Nuggets

- We are more resilient than we think.
- Keep the curiosity of a child.
- Empathize with others—we are all on our own journey.
- Life is too short to care about what others think.

OGN INTERACTIVE
Angélica Killion
Scan here
to visit my profile

Jose D. Beteta

HISPANIC
JOURNEY

Co-founder & CEO, Raíces Brewing Co.

It is always a good day when I speak to my good friend, Jose Beteta. A Costa Rican by birth, he was the first person in his family to attend and graduate College.

Jose is the Co-founder and CEO of Raices Brewing Co, a LatinX-owned and operated brewery next to the Denver Broncos Stadium. He served on the Human Relations Commission for the City of Boulder where he applied his commitment to social justice.

Jose continues to serve in a wide range of leadership roles and was appointed by Governor Hickenlooper to serve as Co-Chair of the Minority Business Advisory Council.

He has achieved amazing things, some of which you will read about later, but first I asked Jose to tell us about where he came from and how he got to be here in the USA.

I was born in 1980 in San Jose, Costa Rica, the second oldest of five brothers and two sisters, one of whom sadly passed away last year. We come from very humble beginnings and at the tender age of 12, my family made the journey to the US in search of a better life for us.

My dad was able to get into the US with a visa, but the rest of us were denied entry because of our financial status so we took another route and in 1993, while crossing the border in Mexico, we were all detained.

Under the 'Catch & Release' program we were released with an order to attend court a month later in San Diego but decided not to go to court because we were convinced we would get deported. Instead, we headed to Maryland, where I grew up.

Most of my family eventually obtained US citizenship in 2001, although I had to wait until 2018 and spent a lot of time feeling uncomfortable. It wasn't easy, but despite that, I was the first one in my family to go to college. When I graduated from Howard University, I graduated with a degree in Business Administration and Information Systems.

I started working in IT jobs while my wife was doing an internship in Boulder, Colorado. I visited her and loved the area. I knew that I wanted to move there because the pace of life felt different, the people seemed more genuine, and I felt relaxed.

In 2012, we made the move to Colorado, and I was introduced to a Latino Chamber of Commerce. There was just one person running it and they had lost interest, and I was asked if I was interested in being involved. The website was old and out of date and it had only a handful of members, and I saw it as an opportunity to apply the skills I had learned in IT to bring the organization up to date. I wanted to make it vibrant and alive, and one of the first things I implemented was rebranding it as The Latino Chamber.

I created meetings and programs to attract new members and made it a relaxed place to make genuine connections that focused on our Latino heritage. It worked, and we grew from that early handful of members to more than 150 in a short space of time.

I had noted that there was, and is, a genuine economic power behind our Latino community - around $2.1 trillion in annual GDP - that was not being taken into consideration at the time and was something I felt needed much more attention.

The Latino Chamber afforded the opportunity for Latino businesses

"I have learned to move through life like water. To remain fluid and flexible."

to network with big corporations and other non-Latino businesses. For the large corporations who engaged with us, it gave them an opportunity to work with a diverse group of Latino businesses and earn a 'pat on the back' for their Diversity and Inclusion credentials.

It was a win-win for everyone, and we went from an annual budget of $8,000 to over $120,000 which allowed us to have even more impact. We created a leadership program for women and activated other programs for younger people. I was very proud of what we achieved.

On May 4th, 2016, the idea of creating a brewery came to me!

I wanted to create a Latino brewery to attract more young professionals from our community. Denver, Colorado, was the perfect place for us to start the Raices Brewing Co. and it became a mecca for craft beer.

I cannot take all the credit though. My wife 'Tamil' was instrumental in its development, creating cultural programs that focused on music and art. We brought in an expert, Martin Vargas, a Puerto Rican who had been working in the industry for a decade, and the three of us created a very successful business marriage. We won eight national awards for four of our beers, and we were listed as one of the top 20 breweries in the country by 'USA Today'.

In a nutshell, the brewery has become a multicultural community event center where we represent and display our art and culture, not only from the programs that we create, but also by inviting the community to contribute, and use the space that we facilitate and help curate.

"I never forget where I came from and continue to be active in advocating for immigrant rights. I am a big supporter of the underdog because I was one."

"In a nutshell, the brewery has become a multicultural community event center where we represent and display our art and culture, not only from the programs that we create, but also by inviting the community to contribute, and use the space that we facilitate and help curate."

When we first opened, we had seven employees, now we are close to 30. We continue to grow and become more popular thanks to constant improvement, new ideas and 'outside the box' thinking.

As an immigrant, what was the greatest lesson you've learned since coming to the United States?

It kept me humble, and made me always appreciate my roots, which is why my partners and I decided to call the brewery Raíces, which means 'roots'. To me, it represents my cultural heritage, my background, and my history.

I never forget where I came from and continue to be active in advocating for immigrant rights. I am a big supporter of the underdog because I was one.

What differentiates you from other Hispanics?

I guess attitude towards life is what would separate me from other Hispanics and other human beings in general. I have had a very long and tough journey. Because of that, I have since learned to move through life like water. To remain fluid and flexible. When I come across barriers I pivot, I look to find other ways to accomplish whatever I have in my mind.

I find it is important to be very flexible and, of course, very community-oriented, but I am also aware that I don't have all the answers, and that I do not need to rely only on myself. I can ask for help and assistance.

I feel that 90% of the things I know I have learned because of my attitude and how I've pushed myself to find answers, but it is also down to continuous learning. I wouldn't say I'm a bookworm, but I do like to fill myself with a lot of information and educate myself on different topics.

I have always focused on elevating my thinking above race and country. I think about humanity and existence at a higher level constantly. At the end of the day, we are all just humans. The color of your skin, where you were born, what you look like, how you sound, how you look, none of those things mean anything to me. What does matter to me, however, is your humanity, your compassion, the way that you move through life, and the way you interact with others and nature.

What is your driving force in the midst of chaos?

I have been 'down' so many times on my journey. What I've learned is that it's never the end of your world.

My 'One Golden Nugget' of wisdom, when faced with chaos, is: 'Push through and see what happens'.

I am not afraid of hitting rock bottom and having to start again. Now, with the driving force of having a family, it makes my instinct for survival even stronger.

Earlier, I mentioned that one of my sisters had passed away - that was during COVID, and she was only 26. After flying back from the funeral in Colorado, both my wife and I caught COVID and ended up in hospital. Thank goodness that my son, who also came to the funeral, didn't catch it, and while we were both in hospital, he spent a month staying with my father-in-law who is 84 and lives with us.

"The most important asset you have is your brain. Use it wisely and educate yourself as much as possible. It is the biggest investment that you can make in your life."

"I am not afraid of hitting rock bottom and having to start again. Now, with the driving force of having a family, it makes my instinct for survival even stronger."

My wife and I were both intubated in hospital beds for a month. Following that, we had another month recovering at home, both in the basement, hooked up to oxygen tanks and away from my son and my father-in-law. We would talk and wave at each other through the stairwell and it was really hard not to be able to interact with them or have the chance to give our son a hug.

Looking back, we really were on the brink of death. During that most awful of times, my thinking was consumed with how we were going to leave things should the worst happen. At the same time, I was also on my laptop trying to keep my business affairs in order and take care of my team.

Now that we have moved through to the other side of COVID, I believe we have all come out with a different perspective on life.

Who most inspired you to be who you are?

It was my parents. They both worked really hard, and they also have an amazing story.

My father gave up college to be able to raise us, and my mother comes from a background where she never knew who her real father was and her mother was pretty much absent, so she had to raise herself. When we came to the USA, they were both working three jobs each, to make sure we had a place to live and food to eat while my siblings and I went out to educate ourselves to create a better life.

My mother-in-law, who sadly passed away seven years ago, was also a big inspiration to me. She was a big community activist who came from very humble beginnings and then eventually earned a PhD in Community Relations.

She fought for the rights of Puerto Ricans - access to water, land, and for other social issues. My mother-in-law was as humble as they come and was never somebody who would be waving her title in your face. She was very well spoken, but she had a lot of grit, a lot of force behind her.

And lastly, and perhaps more important, my wife... She has always been the biggest source of inspiration to me. She comes from a background of strong cultural identity and has educated herself as highly as possible. She has been the driving force behind the cultural projects and community at the brewery and she's an inspiration to me daily.

Jose, what specific contributions do you want to be known for?

I want to be known for how I raise my son. I try to raise him in a way in which he can be free to be anyone in life he wants to be. Just as long as he respects other people, and doesn't impose opinions on others, like religious beliefs, because I think that we can all live much better in a society where we can have differences without hurting each other.

I would also like to be known as someone who cares a lot about community and stands up for the underdog, and who, hopefully, inspires other people. And for reminding them that there is always a way - maybe it's not straight ahead, but there's always a way!

And lastly, I want to be known as a good human being.

How are you paving the way and changing the course of humanity for other Hispanics?

I think that it is by showing the way I've done things. You don't need much to be able to accomplish the things I've accomplished.

If someone is at a standstill, feeling like they don't know where to go from here, I would like to remind them it's simply a matter of self-education, putting yourself out there, and taking risks. You must put in the time to invest in those things. You don't necessarily have to have money to be able to succeed in life.

The most important asset you have is your brain. Use it wisely and educate yourself as much as possible. It is the biggest investment that you can make in your life.

How have you benefited from the efforts of those who have come before you?

I stand on the shoulders of giants. My parents paved the way for me to have the opportunities, I have had help. I have enjoyed all the things I have accomplished. They opened doors, and all I had to do was walk through them.

When I became the first 'undocumented commissioner' in the country (a landmark moment!), it wasn't my doing alone. There are people, who have, for decades, been working for those rights, for those changes, and for the ability to reach that equity in our communities.

What advice would you give to other parents for supporting their children?

I would say support your kids by giving them a roof to shelter under and food, and then, let them be themselves.

So many times as parents we can create filters that hold back our children's potential and stop them being who they want to be. I believe they should have strong personal ideas of who they are, where they came from, and what their potential is. Energy is limitless.

My advice would be, don't try to shape them into something they aren't meant to be, let them decide what they like and dislike. Give them core values and a strong foundation on how to take care of themselves as they become adults and instruct them how to be a good human being to other people.

What opportunities do we have, as Hispanics, to bring our 'whole selves' to the workplace?

I think the opportunity is not just for us, it is also for other people, different ethnic groups, to enjoy our flavor. We should be more comfortable with who we are as we start to learn the power behind everything that we do - look at our financial contribution, and our numbers in the workplace. I believe it is Latinos who are the highest job creators.

Thanks, Jose. Finally, what makes your heart sing?

As soon as my son was born, my mindset about the world shifted, it became very much about what I want to give back to this world. The legacy my wife and I are going to leave so that my son will be proud of us. That has become the main driver in both our lives.

OGN INTERACTIVE
Jose D. Beteta
Scan here
to visit my profile

Jose D. Beteta

Alejandra "Ale" Spray

HISPANIC JOURNEY

Community Empowerment Manager

I met Ale when I had the privilege to share the stage with her at the Hispanic Contractors of Colorado Trade Association. I immediately recognized that she was a woman on fire and on a mission.

She works in construction, as Community Empowerment Manager for the Mortenson Denver operating group. Mortenson is a top-20 commercial builder, developer and engineering company in the US, operating in the commercial, institutional and energy sectors.

Ale's job is to develop and maintain client relationships with a special focus on community participation plans such as making the most of opportunities for small, women-owned and minority-owned enterprises.

Ever since we met, I have followed Ale's career and seen the amazing work she's doing in construction and engineering. We've had coffee, we've connected, and I've found she is a truly remarkable individual. A Mexican immigrant, she is acutely aware of the hurdles that women and people of color face and works tirelessly to improve representation on Mortenson projects.

As I said, she's a woman on fire, a woman on a mission, and as the number of women in construction continues to grow she's a voice for women in the industry as well as for our wider community. She has a huge heart and works tirelessly to improve diversity; I was so pleased she agreed to be interviewed for this book.

I began by asking Ale to share the things that make her heart sing.

As an immigrant finding myself in a new country it was really a question of how I assimilated my culture into this new culture. It makes my heart sing to think of the progress I've made coming to the United States and building a successful career as a woman in the construction business, opening the door and showing others that there are no limitations. Only those you put upon yourself.

The other reason my heart sings is my two kids. I have two teenagers - a 17-year-old daughter and son who's 14. Nicole and Alex and my biggest inspiration and motivation.

How did you find your way into this business?

I was born and raised in Guadalajara in Jalisco, Mexico. My parents divorced when I was 12, so while my father was part of my life, I was raised mostly by my mother. As a working professional mom, she was my inspiration. I looked up to her and she showed me that all things are possible, to find different options whenever I got a "no" for an answer.

With that mindset, I went to university and secured a degree in civil engineering, the only woman among 23 men, and was ready to take the world by storm!

In 1999 I moved to Colorado, where I found out that the degree and professional license I'd spent five years studying so hard for was not recognized in the United States. That was a slap in the face and the dawn of a new reality - I was in a new country and realized that in order to join the workforce I had to start again from the bottom.

Even though I knew the language, the cultural shock was hard to adapt to. I spent six months waiting for my work permit, so I would watch kids' TV shows to improve my English - I remember watching *Sesame Street* every day just to learn how to pronounce the words.

"In 1999 I moved to Colorado where I found out that the degree and professional license I'd spent five years studying so hard for was not recognized in the United States."

I didn't want to leave my apartment because I was afraid I would get lost. I didn't have any network, professional connections, references, or friends, and was unsure how to start applying for jobs. That was a pivotal moment in my journey because I remember deciding there was no benefit gained from criticizing the system that didn't recognize my degree - as my mother would always say: "You fall down, you learn, you get up, dust yourself off, and you keep going."

But without the degree being recognized I couldn't go back to construction as easily as I thought I could, so I found a job as a translator with a manufacturing company that made plastic components. I worked there for two years, but when the company was acquired and closed doors, I realized it was the Universe showing me it was time for me to get back into construction.

Now that I was fortunate enough to have references, I applied for a position at AMI Mechanical where the owner, Manuel Gonzales, told me that he was willing to take a chance on me if I was prepared to work hard and put my heart and soul into the job.

I started as their estimating coordinator, working with customers, looking for new business opportunities, but also developing my own skills both personally and professionally. Over time I grew into the position and that's how I became involved with the Hispanic Contractors of Colorado Trade Association. I started out as a volunteer on one of their committees and 10 years later secured a place on the Board of Directors, then in 2017 became President of the board for two terms.

My career was taking shape and I felt like I was succeeding!

I spent 17 years with AMI and in my last position I was taking care of their marketing strategies, social media, and proposals as the Marketing Director, while also in charge of business development duties. I was reminded one day that I had succeeded in all this despite English being a second language, and it made me feel extremely proud.

It was difficult to leave a company that had helped me develop and grow as a person and professional, but when one of my clients, Mortenson, asked me to join their team to oversee their community outreach initiatives and help develop relationships with their trade partners, I saw it as an opportunity I couldn't turn down. When you make that jump into something new, you never know for sure if it's going to work out, but I knew I had to keep growing and keep challenging myself.

Sometimes the regret of saying 'no' can be heavy in your heart, so I started at Mortenson in 2019. Six months later the pandemic hit.

My role was to focus on supporting minority-women-owned running companies in the construction business. It involved a lot of direct contact, personal meetings and in-person relationship building, but as COVID took hold we had to pivot everything and connect with people via a screen. I found that really challenging, but I made it work for us. I think that's what us Latinos do best; we rise to the challenge.

What's the most important thing you learned as a Hispanic that enabled you to succeed in America?

I think being bilingual. Sometimes as Hispanics we feel perhaps ashamed of our language and heritage, but being bilingual has been my superpower!

*As my mother would always say:
"You fall down, you learn, you
get up, dust yourself off, and
you keep going."*

I would say to people, don't be afraid to use it because it's the beauty that connects with your people. When I first came to the United States, I didn't want to talk, but now, it's my pride. Embrace it.

Tell me an example of how you have excelled in business because you are Hispanic?

When I was running the marketing for AMI Mechanical, our competitors were going to networking events and talking with people who could potentially become our clients. No-one from our organization was attending so I decided I would.

The first event was daunting because I was self-conscious about my accent. I remember standing in a corner and realizing that nobody was going to come and talk to me, so I had to push myself out of my comfort zone.

When you do that, growth happens. I read a quote recently: "Failure is not the enemy of success, being in your comfort zone is." And that's so true. I allowed the feelings of being afraid to push me, not to overwhelm me. I asked questions, I made sure to remember the names of people's children and wrote them on the business card they had given me, and quite naturally I found I grew into the role of business development.

A wonderful memory I have is receiving an award in 2018 from the local marketing professional society as business developer of the year. I was up against five other nominees, who were all amazing people with great reputations, and I thought there was no way I could win, but I did. I remember crying with joy!

However, leadership comes with sacrifice and even though I knew the hard work would pay off I sometimes I missed tucking my kids in bed and missed going out with friends.

I owe my resilience and grit to my mother; I am aware of the responsibility and honor of representing Latinas in an industry that is aiming for more diversity.

If you had to pick one moment from your life that best illustrates to others the struggles and grit that make you who you are today, what would it be and why?

Again, it's from AIM Mechanical. At that particular time, I was working as a receptionist, and they were downsizing. I took a call from someone who wanted to speak to the CEO, and I said I was unable to help. The person on the other end of the line got mad at me. He was so frustrated he called me a stupid Mexican.

I just froze. That was the first time someone had been offensive to me without me being able to see them, but even though in that moment I was shocked that this person was trying to hurt me, I took a step back, absorbed it, and decided I would use the experience to empower myself. I wasn't going to let it get to me.

What is it that makes you a global leader in your field?

I think working in an industry where it isn't commonplace for a woman. In Mexico, when I decided to be an engineer, there were very few women pursuing that career. On my part, it was really stubbornness to prove a point to my father that I could do it.

How do you see the American Dream now shifting to becoming the Latino Hispanic Dream?

· 239 ·

"Sometimes, as Hispanics we feel perhaps ashamed of our language and heritage, but being bilingual has been my superpower!"

"Failure is not the enemy of success, being in your comfort zone is."

The dream is whatever you want to make it. It's the opportunity that you look for.

As a minority we need to start having a voice so that we are listened to, harder and louder. In our culture we are taught that you just keep your head down and don't make trouble, but enough with that - we have to make trouble!

We need to have a voice so that we can advocate for each other. When politicians are talking at Capitol, State or Federal level, you need to know how they're going to affect you. We need to gain the power to say we disagree and be able to ally our community and make the politicians listen.

We need to create trouble, but good trouble.

That's powerful and it leads perfectly into my next question - does our humility limit us?

I think being humble is the right mind set to adopt. In our culture we are taught by our grandmothers to be humble and never forget our roots.

I never forget all the blessings that I've been given and as my mother would say, with these blessings comes great responsibility. We can and should feel proud to share our accomplishments to show others what is possible in life, but we must be honest and human.

I believe Hispanics have more challenges and obstacles, but at the same time, we have the drive, the heart and the passion. Never confuse confidence with arrogance - we can still be confident and share that confidence with the world. I believe we owe that to our community.

You are an expert on diversity and the challenges faced particularly by women of color. What are the major challenges you see repeatedly and how have you helped correct them? What would be your key pieces of advice to women you have not worked with directly in those situations?

I don't consider myself an expert; rather as a constant learner of the continuous and unique challenges women of color face on a daily basis.

Some of the major challenges I see are a lack of representation at upper-level management. Sometimes the decision of having a family comes with the price of delaying professional growth, and if you decide to focus on your career you can get chastised for not caring enough for your family so there is always the guilt of having to pick one or the other.

Secondly, there are limited opportunities to be in those higher roles, so we end up fighting against each other for that seat at the table and it is perceived as women being mean to each other.

Lastly, there's the equal pay gap. Women of color have to work longer to earn what a white male earns, so we will always be behind the pack in this career race.

My advice is to support women who are struggling to find the way to combine having a family and a career. There is no balance so let's stop using the 'work/life balance' cliche.

Evaluate if your company is open to disclosing salaries so that you learn what others in a similar role are making. Mentoring women who are entering your industry so that they feel there is someone advocating for them goes a long way to helping them find their voice and express their ideas in a professional manner.

*"My advice to young people is to enjoy
all the good, the not-so good and even
those ugly lessons we all experience
in life, and appreciate the people
that cross your path because they all
provide a life lesson."*

"Be **confident,**
but stay **humble."**

Tell us a little about the community plans with small ethnic businesses that you were working on before the pandemic. What were the goals and key elements? Perhaps you would share some of the successes from that time.

Our company has an established supplier diversity program which is a part of its culture. It isn't just about constructing buildings; it's about transforming communities and making a long-term impact. Our approach has been to connect with local organizations, attend community events, meet entrepreneurs and business owners, and learn about their companies. All our 13 offices have the same goal, to empower our communities through economic inclusion. At the same time, we also work with local schools to inspire and connect with students interested in construction.

Now that your journey has taken you to such a senior role, what key elements or steps would you repeat or even change now and how would you advise a young member of our community who is starting out today, given the advancements that have happened in recent years?

While there is always something you look back on and wonder how things might have worked out if you had done something differently, I believe I am where I am because of the life experiences I have gone through. Regret doesn't add any value - you live, you learn, and you keep moving forward.

My advice to young people is to enjoy all the good, the not-so good and even those ugly lessons we all experience in life; to appreciate the people that cross your path because they all provide a life lesson. Take care of yourself because you can't help others if you are not in a good place, and that saying "No" sometimes is not necessarily a bad thing.

Take the risk - that is where the growth happens! And no longer 'fake it until you make it', you need to be YOU, authentic YOU. There is always something to offer regardless of your education, tenure, or age.

Is there any topic that I have not asked you about that you feel is important to share in this book?

There was a moment in my life where I went through an identity crisis. It was after becoming a USA citizen. Visiting my family in Mexico I didn't feel like I belonged there anymore, but as a new USA citizen I hadn't found my Latino community, so I kept asking myself: How can I be a leader or even a role model for my kids if I don't know where I belong?"

I learned that I didn't need one label to define myself. I am Mexican, I am American, I am a mother, I am a daughter, I am a professional, I am an engineer, I am a community member, and I am proud to be all of these.

Remember, if you are facing an identity crisis too, find your true calling and be the best you can be!

"Keep grinding and keep knocking on doors because one of them will open."

Alejandra "Ale" Spray

"Take the risk - that is where the growth happens!"

OGN INTERACTIVE
Alejandra "Ale" Spray
Scan here
to visit my profile

Frank Barragan

HISPANIC JOURNEY

Founder - Barragan Media

I met Frank, the Founder of LA-based digital marketing company, Barragan Media, through a mutual friend in Burbank, California, on one of my extraordinary retreats and networking opportunities - I always do business and pleasure at the same time.

He is an amazing entrepreneur, and we share the same mantra - he is Mr. Unstoppable, and I am Miss Unstoppable. We've had many extraordinary conversations about business life, family, people and transformation.

I started our interview by asking Frank his recollection of how we met.

I think one of the first things that struck me about you is that we use the same mantra of being unstoppable. I hadn't met anybody else that used that before. It is a very special term. I even got a tattoo of it because it means a lot to me. Meeting somebody that also embodies that mindset was really cool and you have great wit and an amazing personality, so we got along right away.

I wanted to know what makes Frank's heart sing.

I think certain places in my life and past experiences, are the things that have made me really feel alive. I put on an event called Noche de Ciencias (*A Night of Sciences*), where we brought in a group of people from the community, I think it was 150 families or so. We taught the kids about STEM - Science, Technology, Engineering and Math - by doing some hands-on experiments, and we talked to the parents about the importance of higher education for their kids.

These were people of lower income and under-served communities. I remember standing there in this big auditorium and when the people started coming in it was so touching; seeing the kids engaged and the parents in the other room learning about the importance of higher education was magical. I feel like there is something about inspiring people, teaching people how to live a better life, what they can accomplish and how to set a better path without limitations, that really makes me feel alive.

I asked Frank to tell me about his story - what has his personal journey been?

I feel like I've lived two lives - the life before I attended Landmark, a personal transformational program, in 2012 and the life after. One of the biggest reasons why I went into that program was because I was frustrated with my life, I wasn't getting ahead at work, I felt like I was stuck, and that there was no advancement.

The other big thing was my weight. I've been overweight for a large part of my life and I just felt like I could never slim down. It would go up and down all the time, like a roller coaster. I thought it was always going be like that, but when I enrolled in the Landmark program among the first questions they asked was: 'Who are you being that is allowing this to happen? Who do you need to become that would be able to conquer this weight issue?'

At first, I didn't understand what they meant, but they simply let me sit with it for a few minutes until finally I came up with the term 'Unstoppable'. If I was unstoppable then I would not let anything stop me from getting to that goal, even if it took 100 cycles of going up and down, to find the formula that works for me.

That moment shifted a lot of things in my life, and it started with the weight. I lost 60 or 70 pounds and left my job because I had always wanted to start my own business. The weekend after I did that program, I submitted my letter of resignation without 2-week notice,

I burned that bridge on purpose so I wouldn't be tempted to go back.

I started my business, Barragan Media, and I've been doing that for 10 years now. It has given me a different outlook on life, one where anything is possible, and I get to create anything I really want. I just have to visualize it, put in the work, and nothing can stop me.

A big part of my journey in life was going through that experience. Before that, I felt like I was going through life half asleep, going through the motions and to be honest, it felt like I wasn't really living.

I also have to thank a really good friend of mine, Cynthia Grande, for enrolling me in Landmark.

I've been there too. I've done that. Transformation is a key and it's not something that's typical in the Hispanic community. It takes courage to have those conversations. It takes courage to move forward. It takes courage to decide that we're going to be part of whatever it is that we're doing to transform our lives and life becomes easier.

One of the beautiful things about Landmark is that you walk in on a Friday as one person, and you walk out on a Sunday a very different person, because you get to face your fears.

Yes, you get to see your blind spots. You get exposed to that and you get a new skill set. It is very eye opening.

Would you say that without doing those three days that weekend you wouldn't be where you are now?

Definitely. I don't know where I would be now, or what I'd be doing. It had a huge impact. Three days to Unstoppable!

"I started my business, Barragan Media, and I've been doing that for 10 years now. It has given me a different outlook on life, one where anything is possible, and I get to create anything I really want. I just have to visualise it, put in the work, and nothing can stop me."

I asked Frank, as a Hispanic what is the most difficult thing you have had to overcome? And what specifically did you do that differentiated you from other people in the community?

One thing that is big in any ethnic group is its culture - that really drives a lot of who we are and how we grow up. Overcoming the limiting beliefs that come with any culture is a major challenge.

In the Hispanic community, there's this big thing about humility, which is good to have. However, the idea of being overly humble is really pushed, you're told not to show off, not to brag about what you do, what you know, your accomplishments and successes. You are taught to not talk about that stuff because other people that maybe haven't accomplished anything may feel bad.

That means sometimes it's hard to share things you know people could be inspired by, but if the details aren't being shared, you're not telling people exactly how or what process you went through to get to where you are. One of the biggest challenges for me, growing up in a Mexican family and culture, is this thing about being able to fully tell my story and share it with others.

It's frowned upon to talk about successes, and we have to get past that. It doesn't matter what my family thinks, or what the extended family, friends and the culture think, we must share our success.

When I was involved in The Society of Hispanic Professional Engineers, there were these Latinos that were successful, that went to college, and had very successful careers, but it was a really small subset. People from our culture are doing this, but nobody knew about it. I think that is a downfall of our culture because you would have kids in the under-served neighborhoods that would never hear about the successful Hispanic engineers, and they should, because it's very inspiring to see somebody that looks like you going to college, being a successful engineer.

Frank and I agreed on this point, so I asked what needs to happen to change that?

You never know who's watching or who might get inspired. I was building websites from a very young age, and I remember my ex getting inspired by that, and then eventually teaching her kids to do that. They all went on to do technical stuff.

That really hit me because I didn't know that I was inspiring anybody at that time. I was young and dumb, and I didn't really know any better, but because she didn't know anybody that was doing what I was doing, it struck a chord. This was back in the 1990s when programming was still a mystery.

There's a lot of times in my life where it's happened that I'm doing something different, big or successful, and somebody that I had no idea was watching, gets inspired - seeing me doing it showed them it was possible. There's a lot of power in putting yourself out there and doing what you're doing well because you never know who's going to get inspired.

Beautiful. My next question to Frank was, as a Hispanic, what was the most difficult thing he's had to overcome, and what specifically did he do to differentiate himself from other people?

The most difficult thing to overcome is mindset - getting past limiting beliefs. I think it's instilled in our culture that some things are not possible. You want to be an astronaut? We are told that's not really possible. I remember I wanted to go into little league when I was really young and my dad told me I wasn't good enough for that.

*"It's frowned upon to talk about successes, and we have to get past that. It doesn't matter what my family thinks, or what the extended family, friends and the culture think, we **have to** share our success."*

I was blown away; it just didn't feel good.

How did I get past it? A big part of it for sure was taking the Landmark program, but another part was the sense that I've always been different because I've always been looking for ways to become better or to become more self-aware. I felt like an outcast, I never felt part of the group, so I've always done my own thing - marched to the beat of a different drum, as they say.

I think that helped to distance myself from a lot of these limiting beliefs that are part of the culture.

I wanted to know what Frank thought Hispanics could be contributing to every facet of life that we're not currently doing.

Interesting. I think every culture, every ethnicity, provides something of value to the world in different aspects and a lot of times it's very similar - so you have scientists that are African American, scientists that are Hispanic, and scientists that are from Latin America and so on. We have these commonalities, and it doesn't matter where we're from, what culture we're raised in, or what city we're tied to, there are successful people in all these different cultures.

I don't think there's anything particular to the Hispanic community that we contribute, but I keep going back to this idea of successful Hispanics being more vocal about their path to their achievements and how they have overcome obstacles. It's very similar to what we're doing here - I think we're just not visible enough and a lot of the kids growing up don't think that they can do some of the things that we've done or could be because they don't see the role models. If they don't see a model of somebody that looks like them, they don't think it's possible to be a scientist, astronaut or engineer.

Latinos are the fastest growing group of entrepreneurs in the US - a 44% growth rate in the last 10 years, according to Forbes, against just four per cent for non-Latino owned firms.

I asked Frank for his thoughts on what drives Hispanics to become entrepreneurial.

That's a great question. Entrepreneurship is sparked by the need for innovation - where there is a need there's going to be an entrepreneur who comes up with a solution. It's about finding a need.

I think one of the things about Hispanics, specifically Mexicans, is that we tend to be very entrepreneurial - people just hustle because they need to put food on the table. Now, because the economy isn't as strong as it was, let's say in the US, you have to get creative with how you hustle to bring home the bacon.

When you see the people that come up from Mexico to the US, they tend to be hustlers - they'll set up small taco shops on the corner, or they sell blankets under the freeway, they'll do whatever they need to do. That's the biggest entrepreneurial demographic right now. They just tend to be very, very hustle-oriented.

What makes Hispanics unstoppable in the midst of chaos?

Hispanic cultures, but I see this specifically in Mexican culture, have a lot of ties to family and being very close knit. In Mexico, you tend to have multiple generations of families living together, whereas in the US many families have segregated themselves and older parents maybe live in a nursing home.

In our culture, you know that your grandparents live with you until

"There's a lot of power in putting yourself out there and doing what you're doing well, because you never know who's going to get inspired."

they pass away. In Mexico, my grandmas lived with my uncles and we would go and live with them for a while. We have big families living in the same area and in the same community.

Family matters a great deal to Mexicans, and to Hispanics in general, so I think that's the motivator that they use to drive them. In terms of chaos and uncertainty, I think they always keep the family in mind and focus on how to support and provide for the family.

There are pros and cons to that, because sometimes when you're focused very tightly on the family, you get stuck in a herd mentality and it can be hard to break away from that.

As a Hispanic, what significant contributions have you made that maybe other people have overlooked?

Honestly, I don't think I've contributed anything specifically, but I think there are things that I've helped with, like putting together that Noche de Clencias event, where we brought in maybe 600 or 700 families over 3 years in the San Fernando Valley, an area that is under-served and under-represented. Being able to impart some of that missing wisdom that wasn't being given to the kids and to the parents, that's probably one of the biggest contributions I think I've made to the world in general.

What do you think people don't know about Hispanics, that if they knew would change the way that they engage with us?

That we are just like everybody else, we are all very similar in what we strive for, like being able to support our families, being able to contribute, to give back to the world, to leave the world better than how we found it, and in the process becoming better versions of ourselves.

I think everybody wants that. I think a lot of us still don't know how to do that. We don't know how to get there, or even know that's possible, but I think at the core, whether you're Hispanic or from another ethnic background, we all want to become better versions of ourselves. We want to contribute to the world in a positive way.

Frank's voice does not sound Hispanic to me, and he doesn't look particularly Hispanic either. I wondered if he thought there had been times when that changed the opinions of other people in his favor?

I totally understand the question because I feel that a lot of time how you think people see you is how you're going to react and how you're going to present yourself. I don't particularly play the race card, or the Mexican card, or the Hispanic card as that doesn't come into my view a lot when it comes to my personal life or my business life.

Sometimes I feel like an outcast, because I grew up in a predominantly Latino neighborhood where I saw some of the stereotypes of Latino culture, or Mexican culture; things like the Chicano movement. That movement was big here in LA, but I never subscribed to it and I never felt part of it. I never really saw the benefit of alienating myself from everybody else. I always saw people in general because when you start thinking that people see you in a different way you're going to act differently, and you're going to be reactive instead of being proactive.

Based on that, I think people may treat you differently because you're being different and treating other people differently. I don't see myself as Mexican, I just see myself as a citizen of the world that happens to have been born in Mexico and come to the US. I think that has had an impact on how people see me.

Do you think that those who look and sound more Hispanic are having a different experience to you, even though they're at the same level of success? Or does that not count when you get to a certain level?

It doesn't matter as much when you get to a certain level, because I think what it takes to get to that level of success is resilience. So, whether you think that people see you a certain way or not, if you're very resilient, if you're unstoppable, if you don't let things get in the way, you're going to make it happen, whatever it is you want.

It gives me more peace of mind to think of myself as a citizen of the world instead of being Mexican. I think at some point, it doesn't make a difference to success, but, for example, in building relationships I think that's where it would make a difference. I have seen Hispanics that have the mindset of just sticking to their Hispanic relationships, and they don't build outside of that. They don't have other connections. I have all kinds of friends, from all ethnicities and because of that I make connections very easily.

What do you think stops most Hispanics from achieving the level of success they're capable of?

I think it's all mindset. Some people just believe that success is not within reach for them. I think they've been taught that even if they get educated and want to graduate, the focus should be on simply getting a job and providing for the family. I think that holds back a lot of Hispanics from gaining the levels of success they could achieve.

I know that not everybody that goes to college is successful, but it does give you an edge - statistically, going to college and getting a degree gives you a better chance. I think the reasons for that have to do with context - those individuals who went on to college tend to

"The most difficult thing to overcome is mindset - getting past limiting beliefs."

come from families where there was an expectation that they were going to go to college. That's the common thread I found by asking successful people - their parents expected them to go to college, there was no question about it.

It was very similar in my family. I think the ones that don't go to college, like their families before them, the expectation isn't there - you just go out and work so you can provide. It is the context, wrapped around education that makes a big difference.

What situation in your life have you overcome that has contributed to every facet of your career?

One hundred percent it has to be the weight. That has been one of the most challenging things I have worked on, and it has spilled over into many other areas of life. I see the similarities between how I was able to overcome that obstacle and how I've applied the same things to business.

A big part of it has been learning how to be consistent, learning how to have a formula that works and executing it day in, day out, week in, week out and not stopping. Ever! That's the sense of becoming unstoppable - you just keep going until you get there without stopping.

You might have a few periods where you fall down, but you get back up. There's this really cool Japanese saying – 'Fall seven, get up eight.' You just keep getting up, it doesn't matter how many times you fall, you keep getting up and you keep going and you keep going.

Learning that I was able to overcome being overweight because, at one point, I thought it was not achievable. That really gave me the confidence and the knowledge to say I can apply this to all kinds of areas in my life.

Which one technology product has changed your life?

100% It was my first PC, because that's what I started working on. I got a PC at 15 when, fortunately enough, one 'fell off a truck!' That's how I started to pick up learning to get on AOL, getting online, getting on the Internet, starting to do web design and building websites. That changed my life!

Which book would you recommend to others?

The book I would recommend is one of my favorites, not just about making money, but in general, and about mindset. It's 'Think and Grow Rich' by Napoleon Hill. It's one of those books that I keep reading over and over and every time I read it, I get something new about what it takes to really become successful in getting what you want out of life.

At the end of your life, what will you be known for contributing?

The biggest thing for me is being able to inspire people to overcome their limitations, or their limiting beliefs, being able to help them see that they can be the best version of themselves, or they can become a better version of themselves.

Not that I'm keeping track, but I'm not sure how many people I can impact. There are people that I know I have inspired over the course of the past 10 years or more. I think that's the biggest contribution that I can give back to this world before I die.

My One Golden Nugget in grit is to "Never give up! Very simple, never give up, don't give up until you get to your goal."

"Focus on the message that you're trying to impart to the people that are following you. It's not about you, it's about them and about what you can inspire them to do."

"My One Golden Nugget in tenacity is to find a word that inspires you. For me it's 'Unstoppable'. I feel like if I'm unstoppable I can do anything. So, find something that you know, a motto or word that inspires you."

OGN INTERACTIVE
Frank Barragan
Scan here
to visit my profile

Adrianna Abarca

HISPANIC JOURNEY

Founder & Board Chair of the
Latino Cultural Arts Center

Adrianna is the Founder and Board Chair of the Latino Cultural Arts Center of Colorado located in Denver. She has long dreamed of creating numerous institutions where the local and state-wide Latino communities are confident that their history and artistic expressions are accurately represented.

Her community interests, volunteer time, and resources have been dedicated to creating places for artists, families, community, and scholars to gather.

Forty years ago, her family started The Abarca Family Collection to support the work of artists of Mexican decent. Included are paintings, photography, prints, sculpture, textiles, and folk art. These works of art and a large selection of books will be housed in the future Mexican Heritage Museum, which will be run by the LCAC.

Her parents came from humble beginnings. Her father, Luis, was an immigrant from central Mexico, and her mother, Martha, was raised in an orphanage in North Denver. Adrianna attended North High School and would not have planned to attend college had it not been for the insistence of Vice Principal, Dr. Martha Urioste. Thanks to her mother's support and the guidance of her mentor Dr. Cordelia Candelaria, she acquired a BA degree in Latin American Studies from CU Boulder. After college she worked for 5 years in the arts in San Francisco, including The Mexican Museum.

She returned to Denver twenty-five years ago to participate in the family-owned business, Ready Foods, which is celebrating its 50th Anniversary. Now that her daughter, Arisela, is in college, Adrianna dedicates most of her time to the Latino Cultural Arts Center.

To build her knowledge of cultural representation, Adrianna traveled extensively to meet artists and crafters throughout the United States and Mexico. She has been a volunteer, collaborator, and financial supporter of Denver's Museo de las Americas, Mexican Cultural Center, Su Teatro and the Chicano Humanities and Arts Council. Adrianna advises on culturally relevant programming and Latino outreach with the History Colorado Center, the Denver Art Museum, and the Museum of Nature and Science. She was a Founder and for 13 years served on the Board of Directors of the Latino Community Foundation of Colorado.

Adrianna has curated works from the Abarca Family Collection for numerous exhibitions for the Arvada Center for the Arts, the Museo de las Americas, the Emmanuel Art Gallery at Auraria, and most recently, for History Colorado in Denver and Pueblo. Education is at the core of what she does. She is passionate about the preservation of cultural identity and a comprehensive and accurate representation of history.

She hopes to leave a legacy of learning and cultural pride for generations of Latinos to come and strives to teach young people about the value of passion, hard work and dedication.

I met Adrianna in our community, she is an amazing person with a big heart, and I have loved and admired her ever since. She is creating a beautiful cultural center that helps people really reconnect, and she introduced me to Clínica Tepeyac which helps people who may not have the funds to get medical care.

I started with my favorite question, what makes your heart sing?

What makes my heart sing are acts of beauty, the expression of beauty through nature, and the expression of beauty through artistic creation.

This co-author has a great knowledge of our culture which we will discover in more depth later, but first I wanted to get the story and the journey that has led to her current success.

I was born in 1964 and grew up in Northwest Denver. My father was an immigrant from Central Mexico, my mother was Irish American and raised in an orphanage in North Denver. They met when they were young. It was love at first sight, and they started a family.

We were raised with a great appreciation for our Mexican heritage and are fortunate that we traveled to Mexico on a regular basis. I was raised with kids whose families were of Mexican descent and had been in Colorado for several generations. By the 1970s, most of them had lost their cultural identity and were deprived of the historic knowledge of the contributions that their families made to the development of what is today the Southwest United States.

Only a few of my peers were not able to speak Spanish, and we struggled to create a new cultural identity for ourselves. We didn't relate to our parents' experiences, nor could we relate to what was being imposed on us by a society that wanted to acculturate us. We felt we were in "no man's land", stuck somewhere in-between. It was a subconscious struggle that we were not equipped to articulate. When I went on to higher education, I was able to pin-down what led to some of that confusion and angst that we experienced growing up. I went to Brown Elementary, Lake Jr. High and North High School.

The NHS vice principal, Dr. Martha Urioste, strongly encouraged me to go to college. Other than her, there was very little support from within the system, and the counselors offered no guidance. Fortunately, my older brother went to college, so I knew that it could be done. Even then, I had to figure it out on my own.

My parents didn't have the expectation I would go to college, but they were supportive. My first year, at the University of Denver, I experienced tremendous culture shock. It didn't feel like the community and city I grew up in. For the first time, I was surrounded by young people who grew up in economic privilege with a higher level of education.

I wanted to go to a small university, and I didn't want to venture outside of Colorado, but DU was too insular. After finishing my first year I transferred up to Boulder. I expected CU to be more diverse, however, it wasn't much better. Eventually I found my community; I ran into a fellow Chicana that I went to junior high with, and we clung on to each other for dear life to get through the experience. We joined the UMAS (United Mexican American Students) and MeCHA (Movimiento Estudiantil Chicano de Aztlán) and found others who had come from similar backgrounds and experienced similar struggles.

The biggest blessing was taking a Chicano Literature class with Dr. Cordelia Candelaria. She mentored me and brought me in as an intern in the Chicano Studies Department. The fact that CU had a Latin American Studies degree helped me stay engaged and want to pursue my degree.

I did two semesters of study abroad in Spain. It was my first time away from home. I was able to use Spanish, and it was invaluable to see things from a different perspective. I realized that traditions that I had always assumed were Mexican had Spanish origins. During and after my trip to Spain my identity struggle continued. I didn't feel a true connection to the Spaniards because I came from a distinctive cultural upbringing. Being able to study Latin American Studies helped me to identify with a bigger experience and appreciate our amazing diversity as Latin Americans.

I moved to San Francisco for five years but returned to CU Boulder to get my degree. It was very important to me to feel that sense of accomplishment and to show that I had the discipline to complete that chapter of my life.

A lovely story with some very honest comments. As stated, the inability of many people of Hispanic background to speak Spanish may be a benefit in that they've interacted unconsciously with others in a different way than if they had spoken Spanish.

I wondered if she thought that was a benefit or a loss?

It's a tremendous loss to lose a link to one's culture as valuable as language. Nobody should be limited to just speaking one language. Other worlds open up to you with every language you learn, and that's very beautiful.

Did Adrianna think that there is an element of a loss of culture, which is disadvantageous?

Not speaking, reading, and writing in Spanish well is highly disadvantageous. It puts big limitations on your ability to communicate with all of Latin America (with the exception of Brazil) because you don't share a common language; a big foundation of heritage. In the US we are told "that English is the only language we need to use."

"We were raised with a great appreciation for our Mexican heritage."

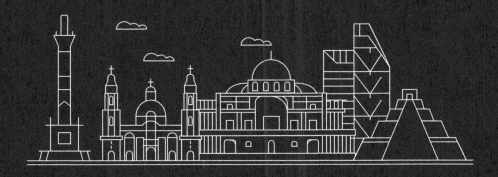

"It's a tremendous loss to lose a link to one's culture as valuable as language. Nobody should be limited to just speaking one language. Other worlds open up to you with every language you learn, and that's very beautiful."

Okay, so I asked, just as a caveat to that, was she suggesting that we are withheld by our own cultural community because we don't speak Spanish? Are we seen as an outsider because of that?

Oftentimes, yes. A lot of my peers are not capable of communicating well in Spanish, and it's very frustrating and embarrassing for them. They feel ashamed for not being able to speak Spanish because the people who are Spanish speakers don't understand why, if they have Spanish surnames, or if their parents spoke Spanish, they don't. Are they incapable or somehow not intelligent enough? What's wrong with them?

I understand that. Does Adrianna have an understanding or a grasp of the Spanish language now?

I had to work very hard to "recuperate" Spanish. There were a lot of factors keeping me from learning Spanish: although my father was completely fluent, my mother didn't have the linguistic capability to use Spanish. In addition to our parents not speaking Spanish at home, most of my peers didn't speak it and it was not taught until junior high and not very well. Additionally, it was not encouraged by society, and we felt a need to create our own cultural identity. I shunned Spanish until I got older and realized what I had been deprived of or had lost. It was very difficult to travel to Mexico and not communicate freely with my family.

I can imagine that was very difficult for her to do. Shunned in school? Is that because you had American teachers? Or was it that they were suggesting that because we are in the United States, it wasn't necessary?

In school we took Spanish classes, sometimes with native speakers, but they just didn't have the ability to convince us that it would benefit us to learn this language. It was a very frustrating experience. At the time, we didn't have many Spanish language radio and TV stations or a social acceptance of using Spanish in public. Many parents of kids I grew up with were physically hit and told they were stupid for speaking Spanish as children. We didn't believe Spanish was something good.

I had a million things I wanted to say about that. I think I know because I grew up in southern Texas, and that was the case. Spanish was not something that we were allowed to speak, even in the schools. Not only was society saying you can't speak Spanish in the schools, but that was also the experience. They used paddles. Children were hit. They were called 'spicks'. They were hit with a paddle because they spoke Spanish back in the day, and that's when I grew up in the 80s.

That happened to the previous generation to mine here in Colorado, but I'm amazed that it lasted that long in Texas.

I want to say that it was probably the early 90's and around the time that I was starting university that I remember hearing a story. It was a different time in this country. Every state was different. At the time, in Texas, there were lawsuits, one was specifically brought to my attention. There were some ladies who were hired because of their ability to be able to speak Spanish, then, and because they were speaking Spanish at work privately with each other too, they were fired.

I had a moment with my grandmother when I was 14 years old. My Spanish was very basic up until that point. She said that I should be embarrassed to be a Mexican and not speak Spanish. In that moment,

I thought that never in the world again will my grandmother be embarrassed of me for not knowing how to speak Spanish. However, I thought that Spanish was just one language. There are many Hispanic subcultures, and I was learning my Spanish, basically, on the street. Sometimes I was using different dialects, I would just piece things together. Later, I started to make the distinction, over some years in fact, of each of the different Hispanic language subcultures.

Adrianna had also mentioned encouragement, and that her brother was encouraged to go to college because he was male. I understood from other conversations we had had, that the Hispanic community often, while it seems quite strongly matriarchal in places, (a lot of the influence certainly seems to be grandmothers and mothers) does not push for the education of our young girls and seems more focused on a traditional female role in the family.

I asked her how she would suggest that we encourage Hispanic girls to go to college, or is it no longer a problem?

It's still a problem. You have to create that expectation early on, so that there's an assumption that you're going to continue either in higher education or through vocational school or some other form of training. You must encourage a sense of curiosity that is nurtured throughout the child's lifetime. You must nurture an insatiable appetite for learning, so that if an individual does not have access to a good education through the system, that they have a means to get around it, either by accessing books or the Internet, or gaining knowledge directly as an apprentice.

I think what she had been saying here is exceptionally important. Adrianna had obviously experienced this in the modern world. That there is, perhaps still, not the level of education directed at, or the expectation of it, for Hispanic girls.

I continued with my previous point and asked her this directly, "Do you feel that culturally, women in the Hispanic community are still seeing and feeling that they should be at home? Or is that changing?"

No, I would say absolutely. If they do go on to higher education, for the most part, they're expected to live at home to stay under the wing of the family and not live in a dorm or live in another city. It's very hard for young women who want to leave home or study somewhere else. There's a lot of fear imposed on our young women about going too far from the family unit. There is a fear of her being sexually active or sexually exploited, and historically, young women were expected to marry at an early age. The norms are starting to change, but females are encouraged to stay in the nest for as long as possible and not fly away too soon.

Does Adrianna think that there is a fear of dilution of the Hispanic bloodline and culture by marrying outside? Or is that gone as well?

I don't think that's necessarily a huge factor anymore. I would say because of media access that there's not as much pressure to keep a culture "whole" or "pure", so to speak.

I hoped she could expand briefly on what she had learned about the beauty of Latin diversity during her time in Spain.

I want to be very careful with using the word 'Latin' diversity because it's not Latin. It's really Latino, as in Latino Americano, as in Latin American diversity. If you just use Latin without the American, it's tied to Europe. If you bring in the American, then it's tied to the Americas. In Spain the professors didn't address the tremendous diversity of The Americas. It's helpful to use the three racial makeups; Mongoloid, Caucasoid and Negroid. The Mongoloids are of Asian/ Native bloodlines. The Caucasians in the Americas are/were from various parts of Europe or the Middle East primarily. The Negroid blood came from the Moors in Spain, and then the Africans that were brought to the Americas as slaves.

I needed more on this; it was a very different piece on diversity.

For people who don't have much background in this area, the mixing that happened in the Americas is historically huge. Then there is the religious diversity, primarily with the influx of people of Jewish heritage. For the longest time, there was a denial of that Jewish, African and Asian heritage. Those conversations are starting to be had. A great number of people in the Americas have a combination of all three races, therefore having different branches of humanity represented in their bloodline. Throughout the centuries there has been a lot of mixing!

And, what did she think was the advantage of that?

It's a huge advantage. If you go to the countries where people are diverse, like Colombia or Venezuela, they acknowledge that most of the population is of mixed race. Regardless, sadly, there's always going to be discrimination based on skin color. Diversified communities have a sense of "We're all in this boat together". We all come from conquered people and have some history and ancestry in common.

You find more commonality when you are a mixed-race person. You likely have a lot of internal identity struggles, but at the same time, it gives you different sources to pull from for inspiration or a sense of pride.

Here is a piece that we haven't covered before. I think the gifts that appear when we have been exposed to language and culture, because we can think differently and because our minds are expanded in ways that they normally are not, are really fascinating. I recently had my DNA tested. Coming from Finnish background as well as Jews that came from the Middle East and Iberia, I was always wondering why many diverse people would approach me and assume I was "one of them".

Even Greek people come up to me and say, "Are you sure you're not Greek?" I had no clue until I got my DNA that there are so many different parts to me. I love the fact Adrianna mentioned that sometimes our familia, because of fear, do not allow our kids to go to university. They may go too far away. There is the fear of losing them. There was a man from Nebraska who came to visit my uncle to recruit him for football. They told my grandmother they were going to give them a full ride scholarship, everything. She insisted that he not leave home.

Immediately after high school my uncle got married and worked in a tire shop for the last 33 years of his life. It robbed him of an opportunity to grow and to expand and to be who he really wanted to be. She was afraid, but she didn't know.

Even with my younger cousins, I have one that's 20 years old, and last time I went to go visit her she said, "I want to become a traveling nurse". And that's amazing. "I'm here to support you. What do you need?" her father stated, continuing "I don't want her to leave home. If she's going to go to college, she can just go here".

I wish we all knew how much we are depriving our next generation of the ability to explore, like going to Spain and being able to learn.

I felt sure that international experience must have shifted the way Adrianna, and others, see the world forever.

Generations ago there was an economic necessity to keep the family close. If someone's going off into college, then they're not contributing to the household income, which is very real for a lot of families. I noticed in the Chicano community, oftentimes there was a fear that a person would get further along than you because they're educated, and they know things that you don't know. Maybe you'll be seen as dumb, and they're going to be seen as smart. You can feel insecure about the fact that you really don't have an education, that you can barely read and write.

It creates an insecurity of, maybe they'll think they're better than me. That individual is going to know about or have access to something they don't. An older person may fear that younger family members are going to be exposed to the "wicked ways of the world".

Some of the fear probably came from a strong Catholic upbringing. "You have to keep your daughter pure until she's married". If she's out running around in the world, you can't send a chaperone to follow her everywhere. It sounds funny now, but it wasn't that long ago that, that was the prevalent thought process.

Changing to religion, I asked if religion still plays a very large part in the Hispanic community and did she still apply those things to her own life?

I sent my daughter to a dual language Catholic school so she would be as comfortable learning in Spanish and English from a young age. Her school didn't expect her to be baptized or take the First Communion. It gave her a cultural understanding of the cultural importance of Catholicism in Latin America. I wanted her to understand how many of her peers were raised, indoctrinated into the Catholic religion.

Had that been an advantage for her daughter?

Not a huge advantage at least overtly. Down the line when she hears about Catholic beliefs and celebrations, they won't be a mystery to her. It's an educational tool. It's a bonus, in a way, to have another opinion or another view. I left it to her to decide what she did or didn't believe in the religion she was being taught. She was left to come to her own conclusions.

I've seen this recently, even among our highly educated Latino American women that, even their young children, at times, may be embarrassed of our culture.

What were Adrianna's thoughts about that?

There is great pressure to be like everyone else in this country. To dress like everyone else, to watch sports, to make English your strongest language, to acculturate. There are certain things that are changing now in the world. For example, sexual identity is being challenged on a very large scale in this country. But there are still a lot of things we are pressured to conform to; Certain norms that are considered part of 'being American'.

'The children whose mothers come from Latin America are struggling with their own cultural identity.' How did she feel this could be addressed?

A really good approach that they can take, which we didn't have the

"You must nurture an insatiable appetite for learning, so that if an individual does not have access to a good education through the system, that they have a means to get around it, either by accessing books or the Internet, or gaining knowledge directly as an apprentice."

opportunity for, is to introduce their kids to their heritage(s) through children's books. There are so many beautiful bilingual, bicultural, kid's books, not just books that are translated into Spanish. I think if a child sees someone that looks like them in a book, and reads of experiences that are similar to theirs, it can create a certain amount of ease. If you're not exposed and can't see that mirror reflection, you're going to always feel like an outsider. It could be hugely helpful to take your kid into the communities and experience some of the food, the festivities, the joy. Expose your children to the music, which is oftentimes very joyous. If you or other adults are proud and knowledgeable, that will transfer onto your children.

Such a beautiful answer. I thought about a million places where I could take these children to look at our culture and enjoy the knowledge that comes with that. **Adrianna continued...**

If the parent(s) or family members, teachers or peers are proud, that pride rubs off on the kids. But if they're ashamed, all those negative emotions can be projected onto young people very easily.

Being of Mexican heritage, we're very fortunate for our proximity to Mexico, it's much harder for other Latinos from further away. Living in the Southwest US, it is common for families to take a bus or drive to Mexico. If you're from Southern Mexico, Central America, South America and the Caribbean, it's much harder to reconnect to the homeland through travel. It's harder to hold on to the connection with family and traditions. It's very important to acknowledge the good fortune we have due to our proximity. Immigrants whose families are halfway or all the way around the world have it tough.

Remember that it won't be just Hispanics who read this book and the term 'homeland' is mentioned.

I asked her if, in her opinion, Mexico is seen as the homeland of Hispanics in general.

Mexico is seen as the "homeland" specifically to those who have recently migrated from Mexico only. It's not seen as the homeland for many people from what is today the Southwest US. Although most of the land was part of Mexico until the Treaty of Guadalupe Hidalgo in 1848, their family didn't come from what is modern Mexico. Their family origins had a distinct history and culture.

Each Latino ethnic group has its own homeland, however, there is a very real Latino connection to the Virgin of Guadalupe. The Catholics claim that she was sighted in Mexico, and her myth and image were/are used to great advantage, however, she is known as "The Patroness of the Americas". Even more important than her Catholic identity, she represents "female energy". With the Native Mexicans, she was associated with Mother Earth and is a mother figure. When many of us refer to Mexico as the homeland, that's the 'womb' we came from. We see ourselves as having been birthed from that land, with a very specific connection to our Native spirituality.

As Adrianna had such a depth of our culture both past and present, the One Golden Nugget team suggested we extended the conversation within this chapter, that we should go into a little bit of history. Adrianna obliged...

Yes, the whole Southwest was purchased by the US for a very small sum after a 2 year war that ended with the Treaty of Guadalupe Hidalgo in 1848.

Sounds silly, but I got a tingle about that going into the book.

I think it is essential that there be a historic component because many people don't have that historic background. And a lot of this could get lost without that historic context.

I'm not an actual historian, but I'm going to throw in a couple of things that you can chew on. I think that it's important to have a conversation around 'where Latin America is.' I once heard that Latin America is wherever Latinos or *Latinoamericanos* are. I was amazed how many Latin Americans are living in Barcelona, Spain. It will be amazing to see if their children have any sense of what or where their parents came from. Will they transfer their cultural traditions and stories of their countries to their children? Will these European born children self-identify as Latinos?

Will they organize themselves as a collective, and will they celebrate historic events such as the independence of their country? Are they going to keep the dances and the music alive? Or are they going to encourage their kids to assimilate into "Spanish culture"? What will that become, and what will be their connection to Latin America?

Geographically these immigrants and their families are very far away from Latin America. It's fascinating to me, that even though the Mexican population in the United States historically has been in the Southwest, today we have *Mexicanos* all around the country. From my perspective, the US is part of Latin America.

Then there's the question of how one Latino relates to another. What makes us unique, and what do we have in common? Should we encourage unity among Latinos, or should we maintain and encourage diversity? I think a Latino can be distinctive and find commonality at the same time.

Many years ago, I saw a film from the US called "Latino". It was about Chicanos in the US military fighting a war in the 1980s between the Sandinistas of Nicaragua, (that the US pit against their fellow Central Americans) and the Contras from El Salvador and Honduras. The Chicanos soldiers were very conflicted and wondered why they were killing people that looked just like them. As Latinos we oftentimes see our commonalities and share a mutual respect with one another.

Given that Adrianna agreed to speak about history, I asked if she would give us further insights about the journey, the things and events that she would like people to remember before they are lost.

I'm amazed by the recent 'reverse migration' happening between the US and Latin America. Amongst ourselves we sometimes joke about a *"Reconquista"* (a Reverse Conquest) because so many Latinos are coming into the US. We're taking back the lands that, long ago, were taken from us. Historically, our people traveled from the North to the South. Now, because of economic necessity, political pressures and violence, our people are migrating from the South to the North. If I were an academician, is something that I would be writing about, because I think this reverse migration is fascinating.

I want to mention here, that we have to be very cautious about using the terminology *"reconquista"*, because conquest is an act of violence and genocide. That is why we say it 'tongue-in-cheek'. A Reverse Conquest would infer that Latinos are coming north with the intent to conquer. We are, quite simply, seeking the opportunity to better our lives, and those of our families.

According to one of our other interviews in the book, by 2050, we will be the biggest demographic in the US. I wondered what her thoughts would be on the balance of power shift.

We are not a military force. We are a passive force. We're not bringing in disease. We don't have a religious itinerary. It is not even close to a conquest, but rather a forced human migration pattern. Most immigrants would much rather remain in their countries if they could. Out of necessity, many Latinos migrate North. The conquest of the Americas was a very bitter pill to swallow. Our 'Native blood' is very indignant about the suffering and brutality inflicted by the Spaniards. Our 'African and Asian blood' has suffered equally as slaves, exploited labor and victims of discrimination.

I really appreciate that. I felt the conversation was also necessary. Adrianna had clarified it in my mind. I think it's important, the necessary migration from north to south. The fact that there are benefits for both the US and indeed, the Hispanic community.

Adrianna had brought up the word *Latinidad*. The first time I ever heard that was at an event that we both hosted in 2021. I wanted an explanation of that word for our readers.

I don't have an exact description. It is more of a feeling of unity among Latinos. It's finding the shared cultural commonalities, for example, in the food we eat. It acknowledges our diversity and sense of pride. It's the feeling of being part of something bigger than oneself.

What are the pros of going with Latino versus Hispanic? Is there a shift? What were Adrianna's thoughts?

I've been very conscientious of the terminology since college as a

Latin American Studies major. After college, I lived in San Francisco at the time when the Latino community, which was very diverse in the Mission District, confronted the word 'Hispanic'.

We weren't comfortable with this terminology. First of all, it's an English word. In Spanish it is *'Hispano'*. That word is one layer of linguistic conquest. It was bad enough that we were conquered by the Spaniards. Now, we are also being linguistically conquered by the 'Americans' (as people from the US like to call themselves) calling us something else in English. For people of mixed heritage, the term 'Hispanic' over-emphasizes Spanish blood. The vast majority of Latinos are mixed race and most haven't had a direct connection to Spain for centuries.

It is important to explain, and to be very clear, that there is a notable difference between being Spanish-surnamed and Hispanic. A lot of Native Americans have Spanish last names that were imposed on them. There are many layers of imposition tied to the terminology Hispanic.

Some people may ask, "Why are you saying Latino?" Let the readers be clear on this: Latino is not the same as Latin (i.e., Spanish, Portuguese, or Italian). It identifies a place of origin, that place being Latin America.

Growing up in Colorado, as part of the Southwest, we were taught to identify ourselves as "Spanish" (in English). Ironically, we didn't speak Spanish. The logic was that if you were Spanish, you were European like 'them', and that you would be less discriminated against. You were pushed to deny your Native, or possibly Asian and/or African blood. There were a lot of other Caucasians in the Americas. What if your last name wasn't Spanish? Did having a French or German last name make you any less Chicano or Mexican or Latino? Unfortunately, another imposed division is between Native Americans in the US versus those living further South. Natives in the US speak English as their second language and the natives in Latin America speak Spanish (with the exception of Brazil) as their second language.

Words and language are often used to divide and conquer, or to impose something. In my opinion, "Hispanic" is a terminology that came with an agenda. Hispanic is a 'safe word' and a term that allows politicians and people of European descent to feel safe. They often do not take into consideration that, maybe, it is not a comfortable term for us.

Given her strong feelings on the use of terminology and language, what would her opinion be if the title of the book had been '*Latinidad*, A Story of Leadership, Tenacity and Grit'?

It would feel more comfortable to me. The Hispanic Journey as a subtitle would have been more pleasing to me. In this country *Latinidad* is becoming an embraced identity because it shows unity.

What is Adrianna's definition of the word *Latinidad*?

Latinidad is an evolving heritage that proudly overlaps Indigenous, African, Asian and European identities and traditions.

She had said *Latinidad* is a modern word. What would be an older word for the same thing in her mind?

Hispanic or Hispanic-ness? Only a small component of our population is comfortable with Latinx, and for whatever reason, academia has pushed Latinx. Very few people self-identify as Latinx unless they are from a younger generation who don't think it's correct to conform to gender norms. I, personally, would stay away from using that terminology, but it should be acknowledged.

The 'Latinx' term is often used now. Is Latinx, as a description, a problem because you are from an older generation, I asked?

The older generation may say that it's not good Spanish or English: it's not Latinx America, it is Latin America. If you want to call yourself 'Latinx', because that is how you see yourself, that is great, and I am happy to call you Latinx. It is the same with the socio-political terminology 'Chicana/o/x' being an identity you give or call yourself, versus, one imposed on you.

Fascinating, and as always, Adrianna's knowledge and views of these things were worth a deep dive. I asked her to talk more about the history behind her last comment.

The *Chicano* identity came out of the Chicano Civil Rights Movement in the Southwest US, which started in the late 1960s. There are different theories on the origin of the word, but it came from within the Mexican American community, and it is a political identity. It was a reaction to people calling themselves 'Spanish'. *Chicano* is in the masculine form. As girls, or women, we use/used *Chicana*, the feminine.

Back in the day, we didn't use the "x" at the end. Very few young people today identify as Chicano, unless they grew up with people who self-identified as such or took Chicano Studies classes and prefer to use that term for themselves.

Denver, Colorado in the USA, was a stronghold for those demanding social change. There was a call to educate ourselves about the history and cultures of our people. We were as a community then deprived of that knowledge because it was taken away from us, mainly by being ignored, by the school systems throughout the Southwest and beyond.

When Adrianna mentioned 'taken away from the education system', did she really mean she did not learn history because she was educated in America and history was taken out of the education system.

As a child, we did not learn about Latin American countries or the histories and contributions of Latinos or any people of color in the US. There are surely aspects of history that have been excluded in education throughout Latin America as well, where there's also a lot of discrimination aimed at people who are of a dark complexion.

It is very important for us to have the most accurate representation. I would say almost every media piece about me is now written or corrected by me. It is important that our message is correctly seen and heard.

To conclude, because the book is subtitled with the line *'Leadership, Tenacity and Grit'*, I asked Adrianna's advice for Latinas in particular, to learn from her, that which she believes will better contribute to their future?

Often, what you're trying to accomplish may scare you, or seem unattainable. Have a conversation with yourself every day and reaffirm your abilities and dedication. Tell yourself that you're going to figure it out. There are going to be days when you're the only person who understands what it is that you are trying to accomplish.

It's a lonely road, so you have to be very self-assured. Silence your doubt with, *"I'm going to figure this out. I'm going to do this"*. You must be your own best advocate and admirer. As females we have to make opportunities to show our abilities and create our own models of success.

If you're not curious or don't desire to learn more about what it is that you're taking on, you need to find something else to dedicate your energy towards. Keep looking until you find something that you experience and dream about every day, find your passion.

That is exactly what it's about! I followed up by asking the most difficult thing she had faced and overcome? How did she do it?

The most difficult obstacles have come from important men in my life not being supportive. It's very painful to always feel like you'd have to prove yourself to them. You only have to prove yourself to yourself, but you feel like you need their approval. Culturally we were raised to believe that we need men's approval, which is so damaging. I have had to be rebellious to overcome the blockades, even if they're just emotional, and challenge the limitations put in front of me time and time again.

Sometimes successful Latinas come across 'way too strong' according to some of my male friends. Sometimes I have come off a seminar stage and men come up to me, and none of the women come up, because we are too intimidating, too confident, but the remaining men are not engaging up to me because I'm a Latina that 'knows too much!'

I had a few last questions:

What does 'leadership' mean to you?

Leadership is setting high standards and high expectations. Lead by example and with generosity.

I pushed for a specific example of that in her life.

As the Founder and Board Chair of the Latino Cultural Arts Center of Colorado, I have had to put myself in a leadership role. I've had to be able to mentor and guide my younger staff. I've had to acknowledge where I lack skills and when I don't have the knowledge I need. If I make less than stellar decisions, I have to admit my vulnerabilities. I encourage the very best from my staff and give them recommendations and suggestions so that they can grow. I might plant ideas that they can take ownership of and make them their own.

What does 'tenacity' mean, and what is a specific example of tenacity?

Even though you don't know everything, hopefully, you have the desire and the intelligence to somehow figure it out. Surround yourself with talented people who share your convictions and goals. If you don't have what you need in the beginning, but you have a vision, you must believe that you can accomplish that dream.

I like that. That was a great answer. It says everything.

"Leadership is setting high standards and high expectations. Lead by example and with generosity."

What does 'grit' mean to you and why is it important?

Grit is being persistent, and the willingness to do the unpleasant work when you have to. If you're not willing to do the grimy work, you shouldn't expect someone else to do it for you. I learned a lot from being in a family business which is celebrating its 50th anniversary this year.

"Do not be afraid to get unpleasant."

"There are going to be days when you're the only person who understands what it is that you are trying to accomplish."

OGN INTERACTIVE
Adrianna Abarca
Scan here
to visit my profile

Roy Love

HISPANIC JOURNEY

President ANSO - Association of Naval Services Officers,
Speaker, CAPTAIN USN (Ret), RBLP-T, Rider Coach

I was blessed to connect with Roy through Ed Vargas, who is also a co-author of this book. Roy is an extraordinary individual who was working to support veterans with their mental health.

During the writing of this book one of our supporters and friends Eduardo Ibacache Rodriguez sadly took his own life - an event that had a profound effect on all of us. For me, it became important to use this book to help shine a light on, and create awareness of, a topic that perhaps we don't talk about enough in our community - our mental health.

After retiring as Captain following 30 years of active service in the US Navy, Roy Love is now President of the Association of Naval Services Officers. These days he blogs as 'The Road Eagle' recounting his travels and celebrating all that's good in life from the saddle of his motorcycle. His thirst for life knows no bounds and in his business life he is a highly skilled and successful leadership coach, mentor and speaker. As he says: "I believe love, dignity and respect for one another is the key to a meaningful and fulfilling life."

What am I good at? Everything I put my mind to. People matter more than money, possessions, or status."

Here, Roy makes his case...

In 2022, our nation is dealing with a pandemic, global warming, natural disasters, significant racial tensions, political disunity, and a looming recession driven by high inflation and economic uncertainty. These issues are affecting us all. Many experts are saying that we are experiencing a mental health crisis of unprecedented proportions. But does living with stress, going through bad experiences in our lives, and dealing with demanding times, financial difficulties, job loss, and failed relationships mean we have serious mental health problems?

Human beings are resilient. We can move beyond these experiences and begin to feel whole again. Established by Mental Health America in 1949, May is Mental Health Awareness month in the United States (MHA ND). Mental Health America (MHA) proclaims itself the nation's leading non-profit dedicated to addressing the needs of people with mental illness and promoting good mental health for all people. Its goal is "to increase awareness of the importance of mental health and wellness in Americans' lives and to celebrate recovery from mental illness" (MHA ND).

MHA warns that we are living with increased stress, mandated and self-imposed isolation, and unprecedented levels of fear and uncertainty, and it is exacting a heavy toll on our lives and health.

To differentiate between severe mental health issues and not being temporarily mentally healthy due to hardship and stress, Dr Lucy Foulkes, an academic psychologist who specializes in mental health and social development, says that: "We do need to encourage people with milder or more transient difficulties to talk: first because any form of distress is horrible to experience alone, second because what seems mild may be the beginning of a more serious problem. But we need to figure out a way to talk about these negative emotions without sending the message that there's something dysfunctional about you for feeling that way." (Foulkes, 2021).

I agree. Dealing with my past personal pain and distress while also supporting others now helps me understand what she is saying.

I know many of us are reluctant to seek help from others. As a child, I believed I had to be strong, not show emotion, and be the man

"Human beings are resilient."

of the house. As well-intentioned as my parents may have been, there are times in our lives when we need the help of others. I want to teach my children how to be resilient without losing their humanity while bottling up feelings to the point of being unable to cope. As parents, we owe it to our children to understand mental health issues and how to address them.

In a study about mental health in America, MHA reports three significant findings concerning our youth:

1. "Over 60% of youth with major depression do not receive any mental health treatment. Nationally, fewer than one in three youths with severe depression receive consistent mental health care."

2. "A growing percentage of youths in the US live with major depression. 15.08% of youth experienced a major depressive episode in the past year."

3. "Over 2.5 million youths in the US have severe depression, and multiracial youths are at greatest risk. 10.6% of youths in the US have severe major depression (depression that severely affects functioning). The rate of severe depression was highest among youths who identified as more than one race, at 14.5% (more than one in every seven multiracial youth)."

These figures are alarming, especially for Hispanic and Latino families, who I believe have a large share of the multiracial youth described here. It is incumbent on all of us, parents, uncles, aunts, grandparents, brothers and sisters, and teachers, to understand how this affects children around us. We need to do something about it. Our children are our future, and if we don't care for them now, these problems will affect them in adulthood.

Many of us went through trauma when we were young because we did not have the help and support needed. Understanding the problem now can help us find solutions.

Tied directly to mental health issues, we must also consider the implications and impact of suicide on our society. "Suicidal ideation continues to increase among adults in the US. 4.58% of adults report having serious thoughts of suicide, an increase of 664,000 people from last year's dataset. The national rate of suicidal ideation among adults has increased every year since 2011-2012. This was a larger increase than seen in last year's report and is a concerning trend to see going into the COVID-19 pandemic." (MHA ND).

September is suicide awareness and prevention month. As I write this, it is the beginning of the month, and this year I have pledged to support the MOVEMBER Foundation's fund-raising efforts to improve men's mental health and suicide prevention and lead the fight against prostate and testicular cancer. I have supported this global movement to help men live happier, healthier, longer lives since I became aware of it five years ago.

Before that, as a Naval Officer, I supported the men and women entrusted under my care by the US Navy. I don't do this solely as a labor of love but because I see it as an obligation. I served in the US Navy for more than 29 years after spending four years at the State University of New York, Maritime College, a Merchant Marine Academy.

Through three tours in command, as Captain of a ship, a Training Squadron, and the most populous Naval base on the West Coast, I witnessed many instances of sailors going through tough mental health challenges.

As a Commanding Officer, I was responsible for addressing and responding directly to suicide attempts and suicide ideations among my troops. While I never lost one of the sailors under my charge to suicide, I did work with many fellow Captains who did.

The impact on the crew and the families cannot be fully expressed in words. Our men and women in service struggle with the pressure of serving their country, difficult times in combat zones, and the stressors' of deployments, family life, and sometimes, financial insecurity.

While in the Navy, I did everything possible to serve the men and women under my charge. Danielle DeSimone of the USO wrote an article in which she says that the rate of suicide among active-duty members has been at an all-time high since 9/11 and has increased over the past five years. It may be the highest rate of suicides since World War II. We must do something to make this right.

The MOVEMBER (ND) Foundation says, "Globally, the rate of suicide is alarmingly high, particularly in men. Too many men are 'toughing it out', keeping their feelings to themselves and struggling in silence." MOVEMBER aims to reduce the rate of male suicide by 25% by 2030, and I want to help them get there.

We must do everything we can to stop men from dying too young. We must collaborate with them to support our service members, first responders, and veterans. My journey has led me to this moment in my life, where I will do everything that I can to change this. It is important to me to do this, and help men overcome the traumas they have been through, so they can live healthier and more fulfilling lives.

There were times in my career when I questioned whether a sailor

"*As a child, I believed I had to be strong, not show emotion, and be the man of the house.*"

might be making up something to get out of work, but I quickly learned that it is better to offer help than to judge without understanding. Empathy and love must be at the forefront of all our interactions with the people we work with and serve. Whenever I had trouble with what I heard from or about a sailor clamoring for help and support, I thought back on my own lived experiences.

Let me tell you my story; perhaps you'll understand why I care so much for people. BJ Nebblet said: "We are the sum total of our experiences. Those experiences – be they positive or negative – make us the person we are at any given point in our lives. And, like a flowing river, those same experiences, and those yet to come, continue to influence and reshape the person we are and the person we become. None of us are the same as we were yesterday, nor will be tomorrow." (Goodreads ND). What follows is the story of what led me to become who I am.

"Cállate. Los hombres no lloran." "Shut up. Men don't cry." I heard this so many times growing up from my mother, my brothers and sister, the kids in school, their parents, in movies, and so many other times. It was common in the Dominican Republic for mothers and fathers to beat their children in public while screaming at them and calling them names, all the while telling the boys, "Los hombres no lloran," or "shut up, or I'll give you a real reason to cry."

I don't know if men don't cry; I know I did. When I was a kid, I always cried after a beating — tears, rivers of tears flowing from fear. One by one, tears of suffering and frustration fill the cup of despair, which eventually overflows. Despair is the destroyer of hope, the extinguisher of life. But we can overcome it.

Tears aren't just for grief or joy. Tears are part of the physical manifestations of the pain inflicted by an abusive parent, a bully, or older siblings. Tears make you feel cold, and your body shudders incessantly when it is crippled by fear. It is a horrible, miserable feeling of shame. I hated myself for being a crybaby.

I learned to run to avoid beatings. I knew that bringing home good grades gave me an advantage. Mom liked to be told her kids were brilliant. She got mad when my older brother didn't do well in school. I learned to be a good, obedient, and faithful boy, to avoid beatings. I learned to bury my feelings and shut my mouth to avoid beatings. I learned not to care, and I learned not to feel. It didn't always work.

Sometimes, Mom beat us because she was angry with my dad. He was hardly home, always out with one of his girlfriends, but he was a good dad. He never beat us. Yeah, I used to wish my dad was at home more. Mom might have been nicer to us then. It sucks to live with parents and not be loved by them. It's worst when they tell you they love you but that you make them angry, and that's why they hit you.

Anger. Anger is power. Anger can creep into your heart and hang out there. It never leaves; you push it back and keep it there until you need it. Mine just kept growing.

After moving from the Dominican Republic to Puerto Rico, I had many more fights in school. My dad was Puerto Rican but, as an outsider, the full Puerto Ricans called me many names. Their favorite one for Dominican kids was "plátano," meaning plantain, because that's our stereotypical meal, I guess.

There were other insults, but I fought for my dignity every time. Mom taught me to fight and not to cry. Still, I cried after every fight - this time from anger and frustration. "Los hombres no lloran," Mom would say when I got home from school, bruised, with red eyes. I would bite my lip, feeling more defeated now than after the fight.

Release. I finally turned 13; this was the year I would no longer cry after a beating. I started Junior High School when we moved to New York City. It was a tough school. There was a fight in my school almost every day. I had one every few months. The smartest kid in the class, popular with the girls, and always quick with jokes, I needed to fit in, be loved by my mom, and not feel weak.

I was fighting with a school bully who had been scarred on his right cheek from a knife fight. That made him tough. I remember exchanging blows, getting hit in the face, feeling the sting, and backing up. I recall something coming over me that would not let me cry. Something bubbled up from somewhere deep inside me, and all I could feel was anger and hatred at this boy who decided he would pick a fight with me because I was friends with a girl he liked.

I backed away, stood as still as I could, and just stared at him for what seemed to be an eternity. He just stood there, fists in the air, looking back at me. Neither of us said anything more. I turned around and walked away. I never cried again after a fight. Oddly enough, after this encounter, this bully became my fiercest protector in Junior HS, and I never had another fight until I got to High School. That's a story for another time.

I tell this story so you can understand my personal, undiagnosed struggle with mental health. I have never been evaluated for or diagnosed with mental illness, depression, anxiety, or other mental health problems. For many years, I lived the best I could without seeking help or support. I wish I had done it earlier.

*"I became the first
Dominican American
to Command a US
Navy warship."*

I am 53 years old, and I have cried many times. I cried when I was 11, and my oldest cousin sexually assaulted me. I cried when Aids took my oldest brother. I cried with anger and despair when I found out my now ex-wife betrayed our commitment by having an affair with someone close to us. My mom said it was my fault. So did my ex.

Sometimes, the ones who should love us the most are the ones who least support us. I wanted to kill myself. I thought about suicide for months. I think about those who would have cried if I had committed suicide, and I'm grateful for those who were there for me in those days. I started drinking heavily. I became angry again.

But I had friends and allies who cared about me. They pointed me in the right direction. And thanks to the accessibility of Navy Health and Wellness programs, I started seeing a counselor. Her advice kept me from going over the brink.

I slowly brought myself back together, recovered, moved on, and later met the right person for me. We have been married for almost 19 years now. She lets me cry when I need to and cries with me when it's appropriate. Crying is healing.

I cried several days after I learned my father had passed away. I fought those tears a lot. I cried the day I lost my newborn baby to premature birth. There is no worse or better reason to cry than the loss of a loved one.

But then, one day, I cried with anger and frustration after an investigator accused me of taking things personally and acting out of rage against a man who violated several laws. That's a long story, and one I will tell eventually, but for now, let it suffice to say that it is the day I knew my childhood trauma was still with me.

The anger of my youth has never left, and while I may live with it, it isn't who I am. I am centered, and I am happy. But I know the anger is still there. I just don't let it out. It also does not limit what I can do and how I perform.

Despite everything I told you, I have led a very blessed life. I was blessed with good teachers and great friends. My strong desire to stay out of trouble led me to isolate myself and learn. I focused on studying and escaped my reality in books, TV shows, and being outdoors.

In Junior HS, I had an incredibly supportive teacher. His name was Mr Medina, and he always told me, "Todo se Puede," in essence, everything is possible if you work hard. Because of Mr Medina, I was Salutatorian at my graduation, attended the best public high school in NYC, and eventually received a scholarship to attend SUNY Maritime.

I left home at 18 and joined the Navy. During 29-and-a-half years, I rose through the ranks with an impeccable reputation for excellence, driving and delivering results, and taking care of people. I became the first Dominican American to Command a US Navy warship, the first to lead an Afloat Training Group, and the first Latino to command the largest Naval base on the West Coast, Naval Base San Diego.

In all of these, I believe I am also the first Afro-Latino to achieve this. While in command of a ship, we received multiple Command Excellence awards, winning the Battle Effectiveness Award (Battle E), Retention Excellence Awards, and many accolades. While in command of Naval Base San Diego, we earned the Commander-In-Chief's Installation Excellence Award, which the base had not achieved in over ten years, and the Retention Excellence Award, as well as many others. I had a great career, despite the heavy load carried from my past. None of it would have happened had I taken my life. Suicide is never the answer.

The lived experiences, although I share them with you in this book, are not something I have ever shared with anyone other than my wife. No one in my previous jobs knows everything I have been through. That's why we should not judge others. My rock may be a mountain to you and a pebble to another. We must respect everyone and treat each other with dignity always.

My experiences did not limit my potential. But how and why was I able to overcome these things? In retrospect, I can say with complete confidence that I was only able to do what I did with the help of many great teachers, a multitude of friends who were there for me, as well as the support and allyship of many former Commanding Officers and bosses who saw potential in me, and invested time in forging me into the person I am.

I can also say that despite everything I have said about my mother and father, they taught me a lot. They cared for me as best they knew how. I suppose they did what they thought was proper, given the trauma they had to grow up with and the things they suffered, making them who they were. I owe them a great deal, and I now understand their pain, as I have heard their childhood stories and know mine pales in comparison. Like them, I achieved many things and overcame all the traumas I experienced.

I don't wish that anyone goes through what I lived because we can triumph and be successful without suffering. Still, I know that human beings are strong, resilient, and capable of overcoming anything. The things we are going through today are tests of our will and power, and we can get through them together.

"We must **respect everyone** *and treat each other with dignity always."*

Roy Love

My mental health matters, as does yours. Understanding my past taught me that I cannot do things alone. To maintain good mental health, I involve myself in several hobbies. I read, I write, and I ride my motorcycle while managing two businesses, serving as President of a non-profit dedicated to the recruiting, retention, promotion, and professional development of Hispanic/Latino Navy, Marine Corps, and Coastguard active duty and retired personnel. I also serve on several boards for other non-profits dedicated to improving people's lives.

I still love to read, and because of that, I have enrolled in school again. I am working towards completing a Ph.D in Human Capital Development at the University of Southern Mississippi. Attending a school a thousand miles from my house, allows me to ride my motorcycle across several states for a few days doing something I like to call M3, Mounted Mountain Meditation! It means riding my bike through the mountains while thinking about life!

Mental Health America says: "When you're mentally healthy, you can enjoy your life and the people in it, feel good about yourself, keep up good relationships, and deal with stress. It's normal for your mental health to shift over time – we all face difficult life situations. Creating positive habits is a great way to support your mental health when you're doing well and helps you build skills to use if you face symptoms of a mental health condition." (MHA, n.d.).

I no longer retreat into my mind, close myself off from others, and suffer in silence. We need each other. One of our greatest strengths as human beings is our ability to connect with others. Our superpower is our capacity for unconditional love and our strong sense of community. I may not have always sought help from professionals, counselors, and friends. But I do now.

My greatest help has been my excellent relationship with my wife and my love for my children. They are my reason for living. Helping others is what drives me, and what I have decided is my purpose.

I like to believe that life is the journey. In this journey, there are multiple possible paths, but the beginning is the same for all of us, and so is the end. In the beginning, others may limit our choices, but as we grow and head off on our own, the choices belong to us. How we travel and deal with the challenges along the paths we take determines how we feel in the end. We need each other to travel well and to complete this journey we call life in the best possible way.

References

Goodreads. (n.d.). BJ Nebblet quotes. Bj Neblett Quotes (7 quotes) (goodreads.com)
Foulkes, Lucy. (2021, March 29). What we're getting wrong in the conversation about mental health. The Guardian. https://www.theguardian.com/commentisfree/2021/mar/29/conversation-mental-health-psychiatric-language-seriously-ill?CMP
MHA. (n.d.). About us. Mental Health Month | Mental Health America (mhanational.org)
MHA. (n.d.). Mental health month. Mental Health Month | Mental Health America (mhanational.org)
MOVEMBER. (n.d.). About us. Movember - About Us - The Movember Foundation

OGN INTERACTIVE
Roy Love
Scan here
to visit my profile

Julianne Lechuga

HISPANIC JOURNEY

Health & Wellness Coach

Bioenergetic Medicine Specialist. The Wellness Shop 365

I love Julianne; she's quite a woman and has quite a story to tell. She's bright, curious, incredibly knowledgeable and the proud mother of four beautiful children. She's come up the hard way and in her early life had to endure a great deal of trauma. She's not alone in that, but she's very clear about how it has made her the woman she is today.

She's passionate about helping others and providing access to the things that will help all of us make our best possible lives through her website Thewellnessshop365.com. With diagnostic testing and custom coaching and consulting, Julianne is taking a holistic approach to address nutritional deficiencies and improve everyday wellness.

Julianne, what makes your heart sing?

Rocío, my family makes my heart sing with joy, it is the most beautiful thing to me. They motivate me every day to show up and be the best person I can be.

That's wonderful, family is so important to us all, but perhaps that's particularly true for you. Please tell me about your journey, Julianne.

I am a native of Colorado, and my family is of mixed ethnicity. On my dad's side, they are Mestizo, a mixture of Mexican and Indian; and my mother was of European descent.

My earliest memory is being five years old and living with my mom. She met my stepdad, and they ended up having a daughter. My stepdad worked two jobs to try to make ends meet. He was a true Hispanic and worked hard to provide for his family.

Unfortunately, my mom started taking prescription medications, and drinking alcohol heavily. She got so wrapped up in the drugs and alcohol that she was unable to take care of my sister and me. At the young age of six, I had to have had some motherly instinct because I couldn't sit back and watch my sister not be nurtured, loved and taken care of.

I started skipping school to be home with my little sister and took care of her while my mom was high and drunk. This of course wasn't sustainable and eventually my mother lost custody. This led to my little sister, and I, being separated, and it would be a while before we'd come back together.

Sadly, my sister and stepdad went their own way, and I didn't have contact with them. I went to live with my biological dad and my great grandmother. This was when I got the real taste of Mexican life. My grandma would cook all the time and we would have family gatherings and celebrations constantly. She taught me about hard work. I view this as the true spirit of what Hispanic life is. The best memories I have are of us making tortillas and sopapillas together. These were my most favorite times.

Living with my grandmother was when I really felt that big family experience and connection. I also found my connection with God there.

When my biological dad got his own place, I went with him and we moved to a predominantly Hispanic neighborhood. It started off well, I was still in elementary school and most of the kids were accepting of me even though I was a little lighter-skinned. I didn't necessarily fit in, but I was accepted by my friends.

"We would sleep in hotels or motels and when we couldn't afford to, we'd sleep under bridges or sometimes in people's backyards."

My years from nine to eleven were a total whirlwind. My dad started doing drugs and got caught up in cocaine. My mom came back into my life, at which point I went to live with her, but only temporarily. She had just come out of a halfway house and was living with a boyfriend, but she relapsed and started getting back into drinking and drugs and did the only thing she knew to make money, which was prostitution.

We would sleep in hotels or motels and when we couldn't afford to, we'd sleep under bridges or sometimes in people's backyards. It was tough and there were moments I just think it was by the grace of God that I made it through. Eventually I was placed back into the care of my dad, but by then he was doing heroin and his drug problems had escalated to a point where he couldn't function anymore.

Basically, he couldn't take care of me. I wasn't getting any food. I had dirty clothes. Our neighbors, who had taken care of me before, stepped in and I ended up living with other people in my community. I will be forever grateful to that Hispanic community for stepping in and basically taking me in as family.

But it was hard. Really hard.

When I went to school, I would get picked on and bullied about the clothes I wore, the fact that I was a white Hispanic, and I didn't fit in. It caused a lot of fights, so I was always changing schools.

My time with my dad ended abruptly when my cousin started molesting me, and then, my dad molested my cousin one night when he was extremely high.

Thankfully, shortly after that my great grandma and my grandmother pulled me away from that life. It had gotten to the point people were telling them that if somebody didn't help me, I was going to end up in a very bad place, possibly even dead.

My grandmother and grandfather took me into their home and for a couple of years I did well. I enjoyed school and was gaining friends and building myself back up, but I think I left who I was at the door. Everyone at the school I was attending were predominantly white and I just wanted to fit in so I kind of forgot who I was.

Eventually I ended up meeting some Hispanic friends that came into the school and I started hanging out with them. It was like a switch of a dime. Sadly, my old friends turned on me and claimed I was stealing from them. I got into more fights and ended up changing schools yet again.

Around this time my mom died in a car accident and my stepdad would come back into my life, bringing me and my sister back together again. I started building a really strong bond with my stepdad, stepmom, my sister, my grandma and grandpa. I worked really hard in school and was getting A's and making honor roll. I loved school and adored the community I was in - Hispanic and mixed, people from all different walks of life. I rediscovered my roots and had friends that honored who I was.

That was my life until my grandmother and grandfather divorced, at which time I switched schools again, going to John F Kennedy in Denver.

While attending Kennedy, I made it my mission to be the best student, and the best person I could be. I worked my hardest to be better than how I'd been raised and ended up being the first person in my family to graduate and the first to go to college. It was my goal

*"Things don't always work out the
way you want them to, and they don't
always fall into place the way you hope
they will. We all have this vision of how
we want things to be, and it doesn't
always work out that way, so you have
to be resilient, and be able to bounce
back when those complications and
roadblocks hit you."*

not to follow the path of my parents, I wanted to be like the strong Hispanic women in my life and wear it with pride.

That's a really powerful journey that Julianne shared with me - to be able to overcome those circumstances. She made a choice, a decision, and because of it, changed the course of her life.

I asked her, as a proud Hispanic woman, what did it take to be in your shoes today?

It took hard work and some blood, sweat and tears. People sometimes throw that phrase around and don't fully grasp what it means, but for me it was true. Some days were such a challenge that all I could do was cry.

Things don't always work out the way you want them to, and they don't always fall into place the way you hope they will. We all have this vision of how we want things to be, and it doesn't always work out that way, so you have to be resilient, and be able to bounce back when those complications and roadblocks hit you.

Those roadblocks can be people, or they can be situations. It doesn't matter, you are going to encounter them. The people who thrive get back up from those moments. They are the ones who will prosper.

Who has been your role model, and why?

My biggest role model was my great-grandmother. She had a heart of gold and was a hard worker. That woman brought family to life, she injected love into the air, and made me want to be the woman I am today, and the mother I am today. She brought light to me.

How has your family impacted your success?

When my first daughter was born, I made it my mission to go back to school and start doing something that would make her proud of me. We now have four daughters, and I have made it my goal that every day I wake up I show them what it takes to be the best person you can be, to show up no matter what circumstances stand in your way and be a strong Hispanic woman.

I just love them so much. They bring me so much joy and I want to show them what it takes to succeed in life, be their mentor and their guide. There are days when it doesn't always work out, but there are many more good days, and you flourish if you just stick it out and stay positive.

When and why did you choose to make the leap and become an entrepreneur, and what have been the advantages and disadvantages of doing so?

My husband and I started our business in 2020 when the pandemic hit. We wanted to help heal people from the inside out, spiritually, mentally, as well as physically.

Working for someone else, standing behind the scenes and offering good advice wasn't enough. We needed to step out from the shadows and put ourselves forward in order to help as many people as possible. It's not just about doing high profile coaching, it's about coming back full circle and helping those people who have been a part of our lives, the Hispanic community. Some of them may not be able to afford what we do but eventually we will reach those communities. Our goal is to help as many people as we can, so by the time they get to that point in their life where they're prospering, they're healthy and can enjoy all life has to offer.

"It took a lot of courage, tenacity and grit just to get things moving in the direction we wanted. Being an entrepreneur can be very difficult, especially in the beginning. You've got to show up every day, especially if you need to prove yourself."

The advantage of being an entrepreneur is that you really get to set your own stage, be your own boss, and that means as a company we can get out there and help as many people as we want. Starting a business, you have to learn how to structure yourself, you have to set a schedule because you are both the reason you can succeed and the reason you can fail.

And if you don't get out of bed in the morning and show up every day, failure will become inevitable. That's when people get scared, and they fall back into that job life because it's security, there's structure, and you have that paycheck coming in every month, but to really achieve success in life you need to run your own time management and be your own motivator.

Is there anything else you'd like to add, another reason perhaps that led you down the path of becoming a health coach?

A few years ago, I was struggling with Fibromyalgia and had a miscarriage. I was feeling ill inside, like my body was angry, and I didn't understand what was going on. That took me on a new journey, as I wanted to understand my body and not just take medications, which would only be a band-aid.

I was scared of prescription drugs because that was what derailed my mother, so I refused to take anything that was prescribed. I started doing my own research into alternative medicines and my husband and I met a holistic doctor who opened our eyes to amazing things.

It also opened a path for me to make a business out of helping people to not have to turn to prescription drugs because they are so addictive and some of them can be so bad for you. It really became a passion to help others that were dealing with similar issues find alternative ways to a healthier life themselves, so they can be the best versions of themselves everyday of their life and for their families.

Where specifically in your life, have you demonstrated leadership, tenacity and grit, and how has that served you on your journey?

When we first started our entrepreneurial journey, we couldn't get it off the ground. To make matters worse, we had filed for bankruptcy in 2019 and trying to get loans or help to get the business up and running was next to impossible. We weren't where we wanted to be in life and ended up really having to put our feet and claws into the ground and pull ourselves up.

At that time, we were getting endless rejections, but we both knew we were meant to be where we were, so we just kept fighting, putting in the work and eventually, people started accepting our ideas.

But it was hard. It took a lot of courage, tenacity and grit just to get things moving in the direction we wanted. Being an entrepreneur can be very difficult, especially in the beginning. You've got to show up every day, especially if you need to prove yourself.

How do you think Hispanics want to be inspired so they can achieve what they desire?

The best inspirational advice I can give to fellow Hispanics is to let them know we should be there for each other as a community, to lift each other up.

We are hard workers, but we don't need to be hard workers for the rest of our lives. We don't need to be in that job that takes us away from our families all the time because we're putting in so many hours to provide for them.

We need to be inspired to do things that will actually give our families generational wealth, we need to inspire them to do things that will help them prosper so that their families can thrive from what has been created, not just focus on a short-term job, where you're just over broke, showing up every day, and barely making ends meet.

What would you tell your 10-year-old self in order for you to prepare for your future?

I would tell myself that not every day is going to be easy, but your mindset and hard work will carry you. I would tell myself that amazing things will happen in my life that are going to give me courage, inspiration, and motivation.

So, keep going because nothing can stop you. You can do anything.

I think people get stuck in this mindset that life is going to be like this forever. But nothing is forever and if you work hard enough and put forth the effort, you will come out on top. You might have moments of failure but if you get back up and brush yourself off and do it again, you will eventually succeed and conquer!

What do you think are the greatest strengths of the Hispanic community?

When we come together, love each other and lift each other up, we can be a very strong community. Let's remember we are powerful in numbers; you can't do anything by yourself.

It is through the help and support of others that we get the privilege to be able to move forward. There is a lot of humility in our culture. Is it a benefit or does it hinder us?

Humility is one thing, but it is another to be arrogant, stubborn and bullheaded to the point where you don't accept help from others' and think you can do everything yourself.

Everyone in our community should be proud of who they are, where they come from, and know their worth. We should wear it like a badge of honor because we all deserve a seat at the table. We have to own who we are because then others will see it and be guided by that. Even from afar, you will be their mentor and can help them succeed in the same way because it's a ripple effect.

If you succeed and are showing you are proud of who you are, other people want to follow you. Be true to yourself and be unapologetically authentic. If you're silly, be silly. If you're smart, be smart. Never be worried about what other people think. I feel that sometimes we let others bring us down, perhaps it's because we are too humble.

I agree. Every Hispanic should step into their own power! Talking of power, you have a great story to share from when you were 16.

It's about knowing your worth. I was in a car with my uncle and biological dad. I don't remember what we were talking about, but we were bickering back and forth. I was doing really well in school and so I was proud of who I was and where I was going.

My uncle looked back at me and said: "You think you're better than everybody else."

And I looked at him with a dead straight face and said: "I don't think I'm better than everyone else. But I think I'm better than everyone in this car!"

At that point I had grown away from the environment I had been brought up in and I was able to talk for myself. It was really empowering for me to tell him that because I wanted him to know that I was not who he thought I was. I wanted him to know that I was going to be successful, and I wanted him to know that I would prove it to them all; and whoever was with me on that journey, I would be accepting of. But whoever tried to bring me down or get in my way, I had no qualms about asking them to step aside. It was really impactful.

Lastly, I wanted to talk about some of the people on Julianne's journey who had been great mentors for her.

Sometimes we don't express who we're proud to call mentors, or we don't share that with others because it's like a deep secret, but I think it is important to thank the people in my life who have really inspired me.

There's my stepdad and stepmom, Derek and Marlo Vigil; my great grandmother, Madeline Lopez; my grandmother, Susan Blanchard; Yolanda Ortiz; Debbie Lechuga; and Lorretta Muñiz. Then I have some entrepreneur mentors: Ed Mylett, Benjamin Hardy, Grant Cardone, Robert Kiyosaki, Matt Sapaula, Jessica Brothers, and of course, you - Rocío Pérez.

And last but certainly one of the most important, my husband Shawn Lechuga.

"Be **true to yourself** *and be unapologetically authentic."*

I would not be here today without these people, and I am proud to say that they have helped me become who I am and have guided me to where I am. I applaud and thank them for the grit, tenacity, love and everything that they have given to help me succeed.

Julianne's Golden Nuggets

"Leadership is to lead by example in ways that boost others' efforts in achieving a common goal."

"Have unrelenting determination and passion for your dreams and goals and make them big enough to make you hungry to work a little bit harder."

"Face any new challenge with courage and don't be afraid of failure. Some of our greatest ideas and knowledge come from failing."

One word I'd like to be remembered for is: Resilience.

OGN INTERACTIVE
Julianne Lechuga
Scan here
to visit my profile

Shawn Lechuga

HISPANIC JOURNEY

Health & Wellness Coach, Consultant
Dietary Supplement Specialist & Fitness Expert
The Wellness Shop 365

I met Shawn and his wife and business partner Julianne, many years ago. They were just an extraordinary couple. What they were doing for health and wellness awareness coaching and bringing their magic among extraordinary people, was truly inspiring and we connected about business again to share those insights here.

The first question was. What makes your heart sing, Shawn?

No doubt that's my girls. I have three daughters of my own and a stepdaughter. When I first met Julianne in 2008, she had a two-year-old that I came to know and love. At the time all my friends said, "you know she has a child?" I said "Yes!"

At that time in my life, I was looking for something, something different, something new. I was at a dark point in my life. I prayed to God for that gift, for a family. So those girls are my life.

Shawn's Journey

Everyone has a story. I'm just a regular guy from Littleton, Colorado. I have been through a lot. I have always been a very humble leader. I always give accolades and credit to others. My family heritage is half Italian, half Hispanic, and Mexican American. Our core family values are very strong. I grew up in a very loving middle-class home. I was raised predominantly by my mother and my grandmother. My dad and I had a very close relationship that revolved around bonding with sports and fishing. My fondest memories with my dad are our fishing trips.

I grew up playing sports, a lot of sports. I had a great childhood. I have no complaints about my life as a child. But, from a very young age, I always had a wild side, and I was very free spirited. I did not like listening to people when they tried to tell me what to do, or what I couldn't do. I wanted to express myself the way I wanted to.

Because I got into quite a bit of trouble in school and as I got older, I followed a strange path.

I started drinking at a very young age. And man, I loved it, being the life of the party. At that time, I thought, wow, this is really cool! That was until the years went by. I eventually became a high school dropout and left my junior year at 17 years old.

On reflection, that is really weird to me, because after growing up in a solid home, with two loving parents and loving grandparents, it's interesting how I became a high school dropout. I don't fully know why that happened. I think it has to do with how I disagreed with what I was being taught in school, and what I was going through at the time, but I had to find my own way.

Unfortunately, as I got older, the drinking continued, and the party continued. I had definitely lost my way. I love this quote, from a Bob Seger song, "I was surrounded by strangers, I thought were my friends". I thought these people were my life, I would do anything for those guys. And all they were, drinking buddies. Everything fell on me, including the bar tabs. Not a good start!

It was July 4th, 2009, when everything changed, right after I met Julianne, nothing really serious. We just started talking to get to know each other. I remember sitting with another friend of mine, I was sick of the life that I was leading. I was so tired of it. I just wanted a family and a wife to love. I wanted children, I wanted to do something with my life. That night I prayed hard, and sure enough, as the days went by, Julianne and I became closer. That next year, six months later, on

"Knowing, and understanding that, having the support of each other as a team, is the biggest thing that keeps us moving forward smoothly."

New Year's Eve, we were engaged to be married. Since then, Julianne and I started on a whole new journey and a whole new path.

That was a journey of transformation, making those different decisions and saying, 'Hey, this is where I'm going'. That is what differentiates people. It's not what happens to us, it's what happens for us, and what we then do with what happens for us.

As Shawn had grown up with more than one cultural background, I asked him for his opinion on what differentiates Hispanics from other cultures.

Well, seeing life from two cultures, with a family that is half Italian, half Hispanic, I can say the values of both cultures are very similar. Everyone is very close, we can argue and fight like brothers, but everyone is there for each other in the end. We have a family reunion picnic every single year, around the Fourth of July weekend. Some of us go the whole year without speaking but, man, when we come together, at that picnic, we really connect again. For me, culture on both sides is all about family. It's all about support. We may be all on our own individual life journeys, but I could pick up my phone right now and call any one of them and get advice or help.

As an entrepreneur, there are always decision moments. I wondered what his pivotal moment was. That 'I can do this' inspiration.

It was really kind of cool now I look back. At a very young age. I was just 11, me and my best friend at the time, who lived right next door to me, opened a lawn care and landscaping business for the summer and then a snow removal service in the winter. We also had clients paying for house sitting and pet sitting when they were away on vacation. It appears, from a very young age, I had the entrepreneurial mindset. I knew that I wanted to work for myself, I wanted to help people, and to provide services to others.

There were also many moments that changed my path in life. I would say the biggest one, as I got older, was that I got stuck into that nine to five job mentality, paycheck to paycheck, month to month. The word job is well known as standing for 'just over broke'. You make just enough money to pay your bills, and get your groceries, and maybe a little bit to go to the movies. For a lot of years, I was stuck in that mindset simply to support my family. I thought, then, it was a long-term plan.

As the years go by, without guidance, in a 9 to 5 you tend to lose a sense of who you are.

Probably, the pivotal moment for me, and my family's future, was the beginning of COVID.

It was March of 2020. We were all sent home from work in the middle of that month. Around two weeks later, I remember being with Julianne, we were sitting at the dining room table, and I said, "this is our moment, this is our time to change and to do whatever we want. We are here, stuck at home, we can either sit here and watch all this negative news they're feeding us, or we can read books and watch educational videos, learn and do. Let's do this while we have the gift of this moment - this is our moment in time to be whatever we want".

We now had the gift of TIME! So, boom!, we shut off all the TVs. We started listening to audiobooks, we started reading. I mean, just consuming all this knowledge of business entrepreneurship as fast as we could. We already had vast experience in fitness, exercise and nutrition, and helping others through holistic health care. I'm a teacher as well, I taught weight training for many years to big groups of people. This was our moment. We grasped it, we lived it, and we did it.

Now, here we are, a couple of years later, and we've gone down a few different paths and avenues since then, things have evolved and been learned. We have hit minor roadblocks, but each time we hit a roadblock, we went harder, we go harder.

There have been many times where we could have given up, and maybe said, this just isn't for us. An average person would perhaps have that short-term mindset, the instant gratification, whereas, as an entrepreneur, you have to know that it's a long-term journey. This is not overnight success. This is something that can take years in the making, and, even when you think you've made it, there's still more to do.

Knowing, and understanding that, having the support of each other as a team, is the biggest thing that keeps us moving forward smoothly. That is one of the things we have really seen, and learned, on this journey, that so many people are in this entrepreneurial mindset, but their spouse isn't on board. That, unfortunately, in my opinion, is where the collision happens. It simply doesn't work. When you have that support of each other, you have two like-minded forces, you have two brains, four ears, and four eyes to observe. Everything gets easier, gets better, and you support each other. So, I would say that pivotal moment was right at the beginning of COVID when we made that decision.

I think that moment was magic for a lot of us that looked at the opportunity and took it into our own hands. Also, that teamwork in a family business makes issues and challenges that are honestly shared, easier to deal with to move forward. Likewise, working with others you are close to, asking hard questions, even deep personal ones, being open with those you really trust, moves us forward.

Family can often divide and conquer a great plan. I have seen that happen and felt it personally when dreams and aspirations are not shared or recognized by parents or siblings. You DO make your own path, and part of that is learning to trust others, to know you can ask mentors to help you.

Next, as we know growing a business places a lot of stress on people, and as Shawn is a business owner in the holistic health industry, I wanted to know how he gets through those difficult moments?

We have different ways. Journaling, meditation, vision and prayer are the three best ways for me. I can't speak for everybody. The other thing we do, when the apprehensiveness of day-to-day business shows up, and the question of how we're going to make it through all of these different challenges is on our minds, or a day when we hit a roadblock, is to remind ourselves.

'Don't be afraid to step away!' In those moments we take a minute to go outside and play with our kids, or sometimes we take trips to the zoo, the park or even a road trip. Those are the times to regenerate. If you sit there, saying, "I'm staying here until this task is done", sometimes you're going to miss the great ideas, you're going to miss solutions, you're just going to come up with more problems, or you'll find yourself distracted. There is so much stuff online that you can distract yourself with.

"When the apprehensiveness of day to day business shows up, and the question of how we're going to make it through all of these different challenges is on our minds, or a day when we hit a roadblock, is to remind ourselves - *Don't be afraid to step away!*"

Don't be afraid to step away from the business. You will still have the big issues on your mind, obviously, but step away, get out in the sun and enjoy your life, because that's why we are here. Yes, we work hard and are all trying to create financial freedom for our family to enjoy life. However, if you're not spending time with those people that you love, enjoying the gifts of joy, what's the point of it all?

What is our greatest downfall as the Hispanic community?

Probably hard-headedness, arrogance and lack of communication. Everyone that I know is a go-getter and they are all very hard-headed, strong-willed people who, sometimes, are afraid to ask for help. They think, erroneously, that they have to do things all alone, without assistance, as if there is a benefit by doing everything themselves. I'm here to tell everyone reading this now, that mentorship, coaching, and networking are the best things that you can do. It will make life easier, better and more fun. In fact, you and I, Rocío, are a perfect example of that.

What do you wish that you could have known earlier as an entrepreneur that our culture doesn't speak up about freely?

Julianne and I are teaching our kids things they don't generally teach in schools. We take our girls on business trips, to conferences, and events, to expose them to the world of leadership, success, freedom, and entrepreneurship.

At school, I feel that they want to keep our offspring in an isolated, singular bubble, to keep each separate. In most schools in the US, the most important subjects, Finance, personal finance, money, business, economy, and most importantly – communication and interpersonal communication, are not taught to our children. We teach our girls how to communicate and speak to people. Our 11-year-old is proud to stand up in front of a crowd or in front of her softball, or basketball team and lead, speak, empower and inspire! Taking our daughters to our events, teaches them things they would NEVER learn in school! My personal mentor, Carlos Salguero always says – "Contacts make contracts" simply said and 100% true. At school, you can't work together with your classmates to figure out answers, they seem generally against this teamwork thing. They say cover your paper, you can't cheat, you can't do this, you can't do that. This puts the idea in our kids minds that they should do everything alone and by themselves. A great life does not function this way.

We are teaching our daughters to be a creator first, not a consumer. Doing this, you can open-up young minds to consume the things that they enjoy and design a future that they want. When you have that creative mindset, especially to gift it to a child, it opens up their world to all sorts of wonderful possibilities, one where we are not trying to shut them down into this one little area of thought, or limited scope, but one where we are trying to open their minds to different ideas. These children are going to be the next generation of leaders. Those with vision, and the collective wisdom to get this world running again. I think it is essential to develop creative attitudes in the young. Showing them the world of entrepreneurship is so important.

I have also done my best to promote the same attitudes in my offspring. Much of what I have shared with family, friends and in business has come from the wisdom in the books and words of others.

I have often found books a great way to expand my knowledge and thinking, I asked Shawn if he had a book that he thought I should take a look at. It turned out to be a classic.

*"We are teaching our daughters to **be a creator** first, not a consumer."*

I have a long list of books and mentors. One of the first books that I have read, and subsequently listened to many times as an audio book, is Napoleon Hill's 'Think And Grow Rich'. He developed what he called his own 'Mastermind' Alliance Board. Often these were people he had never met, people who would inspire him to create ideas. In my journal, I wrote, that's what I'm doing. I noted the most important and influential people in my life. I created my own Mastermind Alliance Board, and I wrote down their names and exactly what they were going to do to help me with using the teachings in their books.

My list, includes Napoleon Hill, Chris Voss, Bob Proctor, Dr Meg Meeker, Matt Sapaula, Robert Kiyosaki, Carol Dweck, Tony Horton, Grant Cardone, Lewis Howes, Benjamin Hardy, Ed Mylett, Carlos Salguero, Rocío Perez, Kent Barton (my cousin), Tyler Peterson (our good friend), our good friend, Loretta Muníz, Evelyn Barton (My dear Grandmother) who taught me so much, Debbie Lechuga (my mom), Allen Lechuga (my dad), and my wife, Julianne Lechuga. There are many more that have been such powerful and prominent leaders in my life.

These are all people that are influential to me. These, and many other business mentors, have taught me so much over the last two and a half years. I always check back to this list in my daily journal. I look back to see what I wrote each time they helped me. Creating that mastermind group was 'key' to me.

The next question to Shawn was... 'What would you say is key to being a leader in the Hispanic community?'

I have to go back to my networking, coaching and mentorship. You cannot be afraid to ask for help and remain humble. I grew up a very humble guy. I was playing sports. I was always one of the guys that were picked first to play baseball, basketball and football. I was a quarterback on the football team. I was a point guard on the basketball team. I played centerfield on the baseball team.

Also, a fun fact and achievements to date - I have a bowled 7 perfect 300 games and 4,800 series. I love competition on any level. I got used to knowing the people that I played with, and they were looking to me for leadership, and looking to me for answers. I remained humble, but I also took ownership of the team. Whenever we succeeded, it was because of all of us. It wasn't just because of me.

I was never afraid to ask for help, never afraid to say, why am I doing this alone? Everything or every idea doesn't have to be original. We are all, always, learning from each other. Nothing much, from any of us, is truly original. It evolves organically, through shared experiences and by listening. Take that knowledge, learn from each other, and then pass it on.

Shawn used the term, 'humbleness' in his answer, and we see it throughout many of the interviews. This humility, the humbleness, traditionally seems to be very much part of our culture.

Did he think that it is serving the Hispanic community well in promoting business? I'm not suggesting that being humble is not right when you're with your own team, but perhaps in terms of going out there into the world? Is there perhaps a little bit too much of it?

I think so. Absolutely. You need to be more of a strong arm at times. Another book that I love was written by Grant Cardone, it's called 'Sell, Or Be Sold' which states that if you're not out there selling you are going to be sold. That is what we, as a business, are doing. We have to sell ourselves every day. Day in, and day out, you must push your message, you cannot be afraid to communicate with people.

I noticed that with my family I would try to dig deep, especially on my dad's side, there's a lot of deeper roots over there. I wish I could go back in time and figure out where everyone is from and what everyone has done. To truly know and learn our family achievements.

Everyone is so quiet about it. They don't want to share names. They won't go into that detail. Recently my grandfather passed away. He had nine siblings, and there is so much knowledge and history there. They are all in their 80s now and they are slowly dying off.

Once they are gone, all that family history is lost. And everyone is too humble to say the good things they did and achieved.

I say, don't be afraid to share your story. I believe that it is a sin not to share your story and pass on that knowledge because, what we can share to one person, or many, that bit of wisdom from a moment in time, that will surely pass, might change their lives.

That was, certainly the thing that I had found as a founder member of OGN, that golden nuggets change lives. It can be one tiny nudge, one single idea, that shifts a thought pattern, and the future has a different path. Words are powerful, and ideas can change everything!

As Shawn had started a business with his wife in the COVID pandemic, one started with a few simple words in a moment of enlightenment, I asked him, 'In the beginning, you took time to

make a potential total shutdown of life into a worthwhile moment rather than just watching TV. As we are looking at leadership, tenacity and grit, what goals are you planning, and where are you going next?

We are on track to be one of the best-known holistic health and wellness coaching firms out there! Best known, beats best. To achieve that we are now working with the brand 10x, with Grant Cardone and more specifically Pete Vargas with 'Advance your Reach'. We are also working with him directly with the 10x agency, to build funnels to get us on large stages in front of our target audience. We want to be speakers on the big stage, to tell our story and have people come into our office, share their story and have us win together. That's the biggest thing here, to tell our clients that 'we win together'. This is not me telling you what you must do, or what you cannot do. We simply win together. That is our desire, along with featuring on as many big stages as we can, to talk and share our words, vision of health and wellness, and generally get out there in the world and make a difference.

As a company formed in COVID, how wide is your reach?

Right now, we are, largely but not exclusively, Denver centric. We first focused on the Denver Metro area. Now we have connected with the 10x community, we are rapidly expanding. We now have a following in Florida, North Miami and Aventura, Florida, Phoenix, Arizona, Milwaukee, Wisconsin, Las Vegas, Nevada.

The future is planned - with a big trip to Los Angeles, California in November 2022 for a very special workshop that will generate a whole new aspect to The Wellness Shop 365. Our business, the Lechuga name, The Wellness Shop 365, Live Well, Live Wise, Live

Shawn Lechuga

Don't be afraid **TO SHARE** *your story."*

Shawn Lechuga

· 351 ·

365 is now very well known around the Denver area. With focus and new connections, it is becoming known around the United States. As we continue to inspire people to Live Well, Live Wise, Live 365!

Excellent. Another great business from our community pushing forward, pushing hard to be seen. A good journey and one I am delighted to highlight on these pages. I, like many of those reading this, look forward to seeing the name 'Lechuga' on 10x.

Shawn, if you had a magic wand!! What would our communities be proud of?

When anyone gives me that magic wand question, when you're presented with too many options, it is hard to pick. You can have anything you want!

What would it be for our community?

It would be a community of full communication and collaboration. A community where everyone lifts each other up. It would be a community with constructive struggles. Obviously, everyone goes through that. If nobody had a struggle, something to solve, I don't think we would be here.

I think it would be a community where everyone is able to share their words, their knowledge and their opinion, without a violent backlash, where everyone is open to share an opinion, and where we all respect each other.

We cannot force each other to say, "Hey you, you need to do this, or you need to believe that, or you need to vote for this person". That is a personal preference. We are all individuals at our core. And, when you say you can have a magic wand... We all have a magic wand right here; in our heart.

I got this from somebody else. This is not my quote, this is from another gentleman that I follow. This is a quote from Coach JV. He says,

"What we believe in our hearts, we think in our mind, will eventually become our words and become our reality."

This is our 'magic wand' right here! It's in all of us.

I agree! Great answer.

Shawn, do you think that society should change? Is there still a culture problem between the Hispanics and the rest of American society, or is that now fading away, or has social media exacerbated it?

As a child I grew up in the middle class, more 'white side' of town, the white suburbia of Denver. The majority of my family grew up in the Hispanic or Latino areas outside Denver. We would visit them frequently and I remember as a kid it was a totally different culture, a different world, and I would sometimes be afraid to even look at others. I particularly remember lots of different gang graffiti.

Now, it seems like that gap has really narrowed. There is better communication. The word of love has spread more predominantly around the communities there. I remember being a child, over at my grandmother's during the summer, and every night on the radio or TV, there would be some sort of gang shooting or another drive-by shooting. As a kid that put in my mind, 'I'm afraid to go to Denver'.

Now, I don't hear about that gang violence every day anymore. It's very rare. It still happens occasionally, but I think that gap has really narrowed. I think that we are now communicating, talking better, and loving each other as a community a lot more. It doesn't seem to me now, that the Hispanics and the Mexicans only hang out with their ethnic group, or that the African Americans, or the Blacks only hang out with their groups either. It is a very mixed culture now. We have great friends from all different races. From when I was a young child to now, I'll be 40 this year, there is a big, and positive, difference.

I have seen big positive changes to how the cultural differences are melting. Also, how working and communing with other ethnic groups expands horizons and opens up great possibilities.

Moving forward, as a Hispanic entrepreneur, what is it that you wish people with our background would be asking more?

That is a huge question! There is a lot on my mind on that one.

Asking more??

I wish people would ask more questions! Instead of being that person who wants to talk all the time, be a better listener.

When we think of ourselves as lifelong learners, I think we have a different mindset about things. We don't know everything. We never will. We simply don't have enough years on this planet to know it all. Even if we had 1,000 years, we wouldn't know everything. So, I would say be a good active listener, instead of waiting for your turn to talk, listen. Listen to what's being taught to you. And then, ask more questions and listen again! and then ask more.

My personal mentors said, "If you have questions for me, or for anybody else, and we don't get back to you right away, keep calling, keep texting, keep reaching out."

When I was younger, I would have said, "Oh, I don't want to bother them. They're busy". I now know that you can't be afraid to ask a few questions, simply keep pushing. Of course, everyone is busy. But, if you want that answer, you had better go get it. Otherwise, you're not going to find it. You must have grit! And get a bit nasty. If you want something. *YOU GO NOW! YOU GO AGAIN! YOU GO GET IT!*

In June 2022, when we were in Nashville, Tennessee, I made a new friend, Roger Rojas. He produces podcasts, photo shoots and different media assets for entrepreneurs and athletes and others to get their word out.

I shared with him that Julianne and I wanted to start a podcast about health and wellness, and he suggested we start with a whiteboard session when we got home.

Roger is a very busy and successful man, and in the following two weeks there were many emails and texts and probably five contacts. Not only did I get the assistance and documents I needed, but he also personally offered to help with our future podcast ideas.

What I learned from that exchange was that persistence developed our relationship from an acquaintance to friendship because of respect. Now he knows I'm not afraid to ask and persist.

I wondered if, and how, Shawn thought we are maybe shooting ourselves in the foot as the Hispanic community by not thinking that we can be these massive wealth creators?

It is by not having the long-term vision; I go back to earlier in our conversation about how we were indoctrinated into the job system. You go to school, get good grades, go to college, get a student loan if you need to, and then you get a good job that barely pays the bills to support your family.

When you are stuck in that mindset, and then you try to go into an entrepreneurial side of things, it's very difficult to pursue and break through those hurdles, those roadblocks.

A lot of people meet one roadblock, and then they're done. They are already too afraid. They feel they need to go back to a job; they need that paycheck. They need this or that, no time to invest, or, it's the wrong time!

We shoot ourselves in the foot because we don't give ourselves time to grow, time to help each other. This life is a long-term journey. This is not an overnight success story.

If you're on a mission, keep your head down, stay focused on your vision and complete it. Know that the completion of the mission doesn't end with 'us' now. Our ultimate goal is way beyond ourselves. We want to pass these businesses' down to our children, and then, they are going to run with it into an even greater future. The mission continues long after we are gone. That is our goal. That, we as parents, create this legacy, this empire for our kids and our family.

It's not just for us, and I think that is another thing where 'we, as a community', do to shoot ourselves in the foot. We are too self-centered. We are always thinking about us and me, and what do I get out of all this. We're not thinking long-term. Surely in a modern world, you're not doing this selfishly simply for yourself. Our young people are counting on us for this opportunity of a real future. That

"If you're on a mission, keep your head down, stay focused on your vision and complete it."

Shawn Lechuga

*"When it comes to my family
I spell the word Love – T IM E."*

Shawn Lechuga

"The world is a constant evolution of change. You can either roll with it, take action and create, or be left behind."

Shawn Lechuga

"When I dance my daily dance, I do it like my family's lives depend on it. When I show up every day, we all prosper, and we can receive anything we desire."

Shawn Lechuga

feeling and focus on future things, can open up for them tenfold.

I think so many times that we don't think about the future. We don't think about what's going on. We're all happily able to spend $50,000 on coming to the party, yet we haven't invested in the family business.

What does that look like from a community perspective for us to be able to build from with that vision in mind?

Julianne and I were talking about this the other day, about investing in yourself. I don't want to call it luck. It wasn't luck, we had some investments that we made pre COVID. And then, during COVID, when the markets crashed, we didn't have a lot of money for us. We said, we're going to try make something happen, so we took action! It grew to a significant amount, unfortunately, not an amount of money to retire or make us financially free, but enough that we could invest in our business and invest in ourselves. Over the past two years we have gained close to the amount we have invested in ourselves for training, conferences, trips, books, knowledge and anything we could do to get better to go out there and win.

You *can* meet people on Zoom anywhere for free, but we wanted to fly to these places. We flew to Florida, Tennessee, Wisconsin, Nevada. And more. In all these places, we wanted to meet these people in person, because you don't really see who they are, or really judge their character, until you shake their hand, and have a beer, or a cup of coffee with them. We spent a lot of money doing this! We almost went broke again, investing in ourselves. I just told Julianne, "People don't have any trouble spending $400 or $500 on a bar tab, or thousands on the quinceañera, and what is that doing for you in the end?" What positive besides a fun time that you know you're paying for a lot of money to have a hangover the next day, feel like garbage, and your bank account suffers!

We decided to put this money out there to invest in ourselves, trusting that it's going to come back tenfold. When it does, then we can share our knowledge with everyone. We're not going to keep it; we're going to share it with everyone else. Our plan is to create a scholarship fund for students in low-income families so they can learn about proper nutrition, health and wellness. We also are going to set up a scholarship fund at our daughters' Catholic school where we can pay it forward and give others a chance at a great education!

Is there anything that you would like to add that you haven't told us that's important for Hispanic leadership, tenacity and grit?

What really changed my life, is simply to follow my own heart, and believe in myself. It all starts there. And, without doubt, my little black book, like I said earlier, journaling daily changed my life for sure. I read out bits of it to myself every day. On the very first page, I wrote, who I am, what I am, and what I am thankful for. The very first one is that I am healthy. I repeat that to myself every day. Because if we don't have our health, nothing else even matters.

Shawn's last reply also reminded me of all the successful people whom I have met, and read about, who do the same.

The attitude of gratitude mantra gets us through the less wonderful days and reminds us to smile and remember our blessings.

OGN INTERACTIVE
Shawn Lechuga
Scan here
to visit my profile

Pedro David Espinoza

HISPANIC JOURNEY

Tech Investor, Ted Speaker and Founder
& CEO – Pan Peru USA

According to the Voice of America, Pedro is the Robin Hood of Technology. As a teenager he released pop singles through Amazon, Spotify and Apple Music, founded a tech start-up while still at Stanford, and in 2014, at the age of 19, he started the SmileyGo platform to empower corporations to invest smarter. SmileyGo indexed the data of 1.3 million non-profits in addition to having users in 30 countries. Four years later he became CEO of Pan Peru USA, a venture that empowers 100 rural women to become entrepreneurs and plants 15,000 pine trees for reforestation.

A serial Internet entrepreneur, published author, lecturer, TED speaker and angel investor with a special interest in technologies founded by under-represented groups, Pedro is among the best of us.

I first met him in December 2019 when he was giving a keynote speech for the Tech Summit organized by LULAC in Denver, Colorado. Immediately, I knew he was someone I wanted to connect and build a relationship with. I was the only person who managed to get an autographed copy of his book that day as he was heading off to catch a flight.

I'm glad we stayed in touch and was even more pleased when he agreed to be interviewed for this book. I started by asking Pedro to share with me what makes his heart sing.

That's a great question, Rocío. I'm extremely passionate when it comes to empowering people and inspiring others through entrepreneurship and technology.

I was born and raised in Peru and came to the United States for higher education. I went to Stanford University School of Engineering and Berkeley Haas for a two-year business school program, and I saw that through technology we can change and inspire people when we create and launch products.

To give you one example, I am the CEO of Pan Peru USA, which is a venture that empowers indigenous women to become entrepreneurs in Pampas Grande. The experience of seeing these women evolve and change their mindset is fascinating. For example, from taking knitting as a hobby to it becoming a revenue-generating business model and launching their own start-up is incredible.

We began with one person and today we have 60 Latinas that are business owners and leaders. And that really fuels my heart to keep blessing, nourishing and helping these under-served human beings.

Please tell me about your journey.

Growing up in Peru, which is a very traditional, Latin Incan country, my hyperactivity and eagerness to participate, to ask a lot of questions, be persistent, be loud, and be smiley, was seen as a negative trait. As an elementary school student, a fourth grader, I fondly remember being given a behavioral clipboard and in every class my teachers had to monitor, evaluate, and grade my behavior and my emotional intelligence to ascertain if I was behaving well.

In 2005, my parents had to go through the USCIS immigration process and so we moved to Nashville, Tennessee for six months, for one semester. There, my hyper-activeness, eagerness, perseverance, persistence and tenacity that had been seen as a negative trait in Peru, completely switched.

I remember the first week of class and my classmates were asking me where I was from. With a smile I replied I was from Peru, South

"I'm extremely passionate when it comes to **empowering** people and **inspiring** others through entrepreneurship and technology."

America. I stood up, walked to the center of the class and pulled down the Rand McNally map and because no one knew where Peru was, I explained it was next to Brazil down on the Pacific Coast.

My classmates were inspired. People started clapping, but most importantly, my teacher, Miss Leigh Parrish really encouraged me in front of everybody. She told me that the fact I loved to speak in public, ask questions, play guitar and piano in front of my fellow classmates, and always participate, was leadership. She told me I could become a CEO, founder and innovator.

This experience completely changed my mindset. I realized these traits that came so naturally to me were a positive. So, when I moved back to Peru as a 10-year-old, I was extremely confident and at high school I ran for student government and was elected to the cabinet as President of both the Music Honor Society and the Business Honor Society.

In 2011, Japan had a major earthquake so I organized and hosted events to raise funds. That's when I started volunteering. I remember going to my mother's family hometown of Pampas Grande in Huaraz, which is nearly 13,000 feet above sea level in the Andes Mountains and used all my leadership skills to really make an impact for the women and children.

There's one story I always like to share that I should tell here.

When I was a freshman at college at Berkeley in California, I skipped a class, my Multivariable Calculus class. The class was at 8am and I woke up at 9.30am, super late, so I went to the Golden Bear Café where I noticed an 80-year-old businessman wearing a suit.

Now, I always remember my mom's Nugget of wisdom – 'Júntate con los mejores', which means 'surround yourself with the best'. With that in mind I asked myself if I should sit next to my 18-year-old buddies or next to this businessman who probably had more wisdom than the rest of the room put together?

There I was, an 18-year-old wearing sweatpants and a Walmart t-shirt, and I approached him, and said: "Hi, my name is Pedro, what's yours?" He told me his name was Frank Baxter and I asked if I could sit next to him and have breakfast. He said "yes" so I asked him how come he was there in the Golden Bear Café, which was really a freshman place and a hangout for students. He told me one of his board meetings had been canceled and he was hungry so being on campus he thought he'd stop by. Given my inquisitive nature I asked him what kind of board he sat on, and it turned out he was a Trustee at the University of California, Berkeley Foundation.

That's when I started getting super energized. Sometimes it's like I have antennae and I noticed that on his suit he had a ribbon, the US flag, but also the Uruguayan flag pins. I asked him about that, and he told me he used to be the US Ambassador to Uruguay under President Bush. Given my heritage we then started speaking in Spanish and our conversation completely evolved.

In that moment, Frank Baxter forgot he was 82 years old, forgot he was a Board Trustee at the university, and forgot that he was a successful businessman. Both of us just connected as humans and as friends. We bonded over Spanish.

Later in our conversation, I shared with him that I had founded a start-up, a fintech company, and he told me he used to be the CEO and Chairman of Jefferies and how he had started their global technology banking division in 2001. So suddenly, we've got all these things in common. He gave me his business card, and I did what many people don't do, and that was to follow up - I persisted.

I sent him newsletters of my start-up endeavors and classes and after three years of fostering that friendship and partnership, can you guess who was the first person to write a check to fund my technology company? It was Frank. Outstanding.

Later in my career, Frank connected me with other venture capitalists that also supported me and when I wrote my book, 'Differences That Make a Difference', Frank, was the first CEO I interviewed. That's how you close the loop and join the dots, by paying it forward and building relational bridges with people.

Most importantly, I am a firm believer in bilateral mentoring. As a 19-year-old entrepreneur, I asked "Frank how can I help you?". He replied, "I'm organizing this Seminar on Latin American Civics and would love to get more international students attending". I reacted "I will invite a lot of my buddies from Costa Rica, Chile, and Peru!". You don't need a title to be a leader.

You don't need to be a CEO to help another CEO. Can you imagine this 19-year-old kid helping this millionaire CEO and Ambassador? Yes! I did it. I brought my network of Latin American students to participate in the seminar hosted by Frank. Relationships are meant to be reciprocal. Not everything is to give, give, give or receive, receive, receive.

Pedro's is such an amazing journey. I completely get the idea of hanging out with people that are much older, much better versed in all things. That's how I spent most of my career - Many of my closest friends were 20 or 30 years older than me.

"I always remember my mom's Nugget of wisdom – Júntate con los mejores, which means surround yourself with the best."

"My parents really did a good job in fostering discipline and tenacity in me to be super laser-focused."

I asked Pedro if there was anything else he'd like to share about the people that have influenced him, maybe his parents?

My parents really influenced me on a soul, faith and personal level. My mom would always say, the three laws of the Incas "Ama Llulla, Ama Quella and Ama Sua", which is Quechua, a native language of the Incas in South America. It means: "Don't steal, don't be lazy, and don't lie,"

And my grandpa would always tell me "Solo hay que tener verguenza para robar, mentir y ser flojo", which means you should never be embarrassed or shameful, unless you're stealing, being lazy, or you're lying! And I really took that to heart because I'm never embarrassed. If anything, I literally dance in public. I don't have fear of what people think of my reputation or my name.

We have to be bold. We must be comfortable being uncomfortable. Growing up, I was not a popular kid; I was a nerd. And I think that was the key to success. In trying to make friends I found out so many ways that didn't work that by the time I turned 20 I was an expert! I discovered so much about how not to make friends that I actually realized I had learned how to make friends and get people to like me.

But really going back to the fundamentals, my family was instrumental in showing me how to share truth, family and Biblical values.

Who are the most influential people that have impacted your life? And how have they done so?

For sure, my mom has. She's an engineer, born and raised in

Pampas Grande, her hometown. She started coding in PHP many years ago and is now an entrepreneur and a published author. She really inspires me to give back, and to love the poor, and the underserved - not only of Peru, but the rest of the world.

My dad has a similar story. He's an entrepreneur, a visionary, hyper aggressive, and I learned so much from him in terms of negotiation.

My grandpa was mayor of Pampas Grande. He really emphasized his willpower. He was an orphan who didn't graduate from elementary school, but he had 10 kids, all of them became engineers, doctors or entrepreneurs.

Sadly, he died, but the life lesson he left me with was it doesn't really matter if you grew up in the 'hood', or if you grew up with a lot of money, what's really important is your willpower, your grit and your determination to succeed in business and in life.

But what was even more important to him than that was family - having that sense of community.

And then lastly, my two older sisters Deanna and Karina have been a major influence on my life. Deanna is spiritual and she always shared a truth with me, to uphold the values of being loving, forgiving, sharing, generous, and of course, always being resilient. Karina taught me the lesson of learning to say "no" and taught me the value of being laser-focused.

How did your upbringing and education influence who you are today?

It is extremely important. Growing up in Peru, it was natural to see a medical doctor or engineer who was Hispanic, but for people who are raised in the US they don't tend to see Hispanics that are decision makers in technology or engineering or health. So, coming from Peru really empowered me and that I could dream and aspire to be whoever I wanted to be. That really helped me dream big and as they say: "Aim for the stars and you'll end up at the moon."

In your first book *'Differences That Make a Difference'* what was your experience of interviewing these top CEOs?

The number one thing I learned from spending time with CEOs like Dan Schulman from PayPal, Reed Hastings from Netflix and Eric Schmidt from Google, was that top CEOs have self-awareness. They are extremely knowledgeable of their strengths and their weaknesses and are skilled at enabling and delegating.

Really, a CEO is like the Chief Emotional Officer. They are the cheerleaders of their team and of their companies. The CEO is a psychologist, a counselor, a coach and they have to love their team.

Number two, I would say is servant leadership - something I truly admire and respect. My good friend, Intel CEO Pat Gelsinger, taught me through reading his book and through his friendship, that when it comes to leaders "the last shall be first and the first shall be last."

You lead by serving, caring and nourishing your people. People run businesses, so it's important to really embrace that integrity and those ethics and with that humility in business, people will always remember you. Life goes in circles and cycles and if you don't treat someone the right way people will also remember that.

At the end of the day, people buy from people, so when you're raising capital for your tech company in San Francisco, you're selling equity. When you're hiring people, you're selling the vision of your company. When you're applying for a job, you're selling yourself and when you're dating, you're also selling yourself. Everything is sales. As a CEO of a company, it is really important to be a servant leader.

How and why did you get into technology?

My journey in technology started because I applied to the right schools. I went to Stanford and Berkeley and was exposed to technology and entrepreneurship. At any other school it would have been much harder, but when you're in Palo Alto, California, you're surrounded by so many technology companies and with my curiosity and intellectual vitality I really wanted to learn what HTML and JavaScript were and understand how venture capital worked.

As a child I always knew I wanted to be an entrepreneur to make things, build teams and launch products, that's what fuels me. I love working, for me it's fun, it's not work, and I'm well aware that's because my parents raised me that way.

No TV, no coffee, no dessert. Regardless of the time I go to bed I wake up every day at six by myself, no alarms; that's just the way I'm wired. My parents really did a good job in fostering discipline and tenacity in me to be super laser-focused.

What opportunities have you capitalized on since moving to the United States that perhaps others have missed?

Building relationships.

I was 18 when I moved to the US, but in a few short years I was able to build a world-class network of Fortune 500 CEOs that I was able leverage. Not only was this a network, but these people also became friends - I go to church with them, we socialize, meditate together, read the Bible, and we cook.

Building a network isn't about making connections on LinkedIn, it's about fostering real relationships with people. I am blessed to have an amazing support circle and tribe here in America.

What advice would you give other Hispanics on creating their own opportunities in whatever environment they're in?

Always be genuine and vulnerable. I believe it is important to make yourself memorable, because everyone is pitching themselves. For example, if you say: "I'm a college student studying STEM." Guess what? Everyone's studying STEM. So, building a personal brand and story is going to make it easier for people to be able to help you and buy into your story.

How can we get more Hispanics to understand the importance of building generational wealth? And how could they learn to build generational wealth?

It always starts with taking the initiative - you can't wait for others. In my opinion, you have to be entrepreneurial, take risks and innovate. And it's critical to be in the right places.

If you look at the largest companies in the world, most of the top 10 are technology companies. If we want to create generational wealth, we need to teach these kids entrepreneurship, STEM, and how to manage their personal finances. They need to learn how to lead people, hire people, fire people, and how to coach and mentor people.

That's far more important than learning Java. If I can be candid, you can learn Java on YouTube or Coursera, or Udacity, but to teach someone to be a CEO is way harder than teaching someone to do Math, or Calculus, or Physics, or JavaScript. It's much harder to teach someone emotional intelligence, and that's what I've been focused on.

How would you get Hispanics to invest in technology?

It starts with role models. I think we're doing a great job creating this book and showcasing powerful Hispanics that are crushing it in technology today.

It's about building a pipeline. We have to start promoting more STEM computer science, engineering technology, entrepreneurship classes, and not only in traditional colleges with a four-year degree. Students can take a three-month boot camp to get into technology and my advice is you don't require a Master's or an MBA to start a company. In my book, I talk about my experience that you learn by doing and failing forward. In Silicon Valley, we really cherish making a new mistake every day.

How can Hispanic men in tech encourage women to enter the field and what changes need to be made so that women can have a prominent role in tech organizations?

Us men need to be committed to supporting women. I'm a big believer in sponsorship, and mentor sponsors to be someone who vouches for and wears your t-shirt when you're not in the room. For example, with my company, Bamboo, we sponsor Latino women to help them get into entrepreneurship and STEM.

What advice would you give to millennials and other people your age about investing in themselves in order to shape the course of their future now?

Always make sacrifices and focus. I think, unfortunately, the vast majority of young people today are extremely distracted. They don't wake up early, they don't read the 'Wall Street Journal' and, probably, they are on Instagram and TikTok far too long. They should be focused on building their skills. It is so important to be intentional, but at the same time not only be focused on their career - you have to have balance.

It's important to work out, go for a swim or a run. Take care of your parents, I know so many young people here in the States, they talk to their parents once every five weeks, or they only see their siblings for Thanksgiving and Christmas. That's ridiculous. We are forgetting that family comes first. Those soft skills are the ones that will make you a CEO.

When you're a CTO, you're not coding every day, you're managing coders and you're managing developers. When you're a CEO of a tech company, you're building the vision of your company and nourishing people. So that's what I want to tell young people, really invest in yourself and focus on being relational over transactional and don't waste time. It's your most valuable asset.

*We have to be **bold**. We have to be comfortable being uncomfortable."*

My top three books:

Malcolm Gladwell - *Tipping Point*
Published by Abacus Books

Malcolm Gladwell - *Outliers*
Malcolm Gladwell - *David and Goliath*
Published by Penguin Books

My One Golden Nugget is - "Joy, Integrity, Truth, and
Perseverance."

*"Joy, Integrity, Truth,
and Perseverance."*

OGN INTERACTIVE
Pedro David Espinoza
Scan here
to visit my profile

Tayde Aburto

HISPANIC JOURNEY

Business Strategist, Entrepreneur & Speaker

When things are not going so well, Tayde Aburto is the kind of guy you need to have around. He specializes in driving growth by digital innovation to turn under-performing companies into more profitable ones, empowering small business owners to compete in wider markets.

The Founder of The Hispanic Chamber of E-Commerce and the United States Business Association of E-Commerce, through their work to date he has helped more than 14,000 small businesses. Tayde has also worked with major corporations including Meta, AT&T, Wells Fargo, GoDaddy, Univision, Sony and Kaiser Permanente to improve access to resources for small businesses.

Tayde, let me start with my favorite question. What makes your heart sing?

I'm sure this is going to sound like a common answer, but it's definitely my two children.

I was on a coaching session recently and we were discussing video content ideas. Everyone was talking about how they wanted to create content for entrepreneurs and getting very specific about the niche they were trying to serve. And I told them I just want to put out content that my great grandchildren are going to be able to appreciate. That would create a lasting legacy and hopefully inspire the future generations of my family.

That's beautiful, I feel the same. We do it for our children's children. That way it creates the ripple effect. There are so many different things we can do to lay that foundation. I've taught my son how to be 'unstoppable'.

Tell me about your journey, Tayde.

I was born and raised in Morelia, Michoacan, which is a city in the middle of Mexico, and I come from a family of entrepreneurs. Both my parents were entrepreneurs, and my dad was also a politician, committing 44 years of his life to serving the many.

In 1994, in a beautiful beach town in Mexico, I met a girl who would change my life. I was 18 and she was 16. We stayed in contact for almost 11 years, she had her relationships and I had mine, then in 2005 we decided that our destiny was to be together. I proposed and that took me to San Diego.

The first 18 months of living in San Diego were challenging because I didn't know anybody. I had to start building relationships, learn the system for immigrants, plus I didn't speak English. Not being born in the US you are challenged ten times more than people who are born here.

I started a business association and that was the one thing that helped me to open up a lot of doors in a shorter period of time.

Here in San Diego many people speak Spanish, so if you don't want to learn English you can still make a living just speaking Spanish, but I realized very early on that wasn't going to do it for me, just because of the things I wanted to accomplish.

I think it is important for anyone that moves to the US to understand what makes this country great. Speaking the language and understanding the system is key to advancing in both your professional and personal life. All the time I get Mexican immigrants reach out to me saying they want to start a business but feel uncomfortable

"Problems and progress go hand in hand."

conducting business in English. My answer is always the same - if you don't learn the language then it's going to be very difficult.

I have always believed in the importance of personal development.

'Master the basics.' That is a great One Golden Nugget Tayde. What makes you stand out as a Hispanic in the US?

I think it's my honest passion to serve the needs of the entrepreneurs that I care about.

I grew up seeing my grandma and aunt making a living out of their businesses and it's now that same demographic that I love to work with. It motivates me because these people start their business to be able to provide for their families and here in the States there are plenty of resources for immigrants, but often these resources are not in Spanish and it's difficult for them to understand.

The work we've been doing through the Hispanic Chamber of E-Commerce is something that is contributing to the growth and development of the people we are serving. For me, to see the positive results from the work that we're doing at a grassroots level is what motivates me to keep going. I find it elevates my internal frequency.

What opportunities did you see were missing when you came here to the United States?

There are many reports that showcase the economic power of the Latino community and how much we contribute to America on so many different levels, but we need more Hispanic leaders at the highest level that care for the overall health of the Hispanic community. By health, I mean economically, socially, and culturally, at all those levels. Right now, I feel like we have some leaders that know how to capitalize on those reports, but not for the benefit of the people that they're pretending to serve.

Of course, there are leaders who are doing positive things for the Hispanic business community, but we are about to become 65 million people strong in this country and that's a demographic that simply cannot be neglected anymore. I feel we need to be more proactive in terms of how we educate them to be more responsible when it comes about voting. For example, if we get more Latinos to vote, they are going to be electing people that are going to be more conscious about the needs of the community.

There is an organization called The Libre Initiative, a Latino-fronted non-profit run by Daniel Garza, and their mission is to increase economic freedom and prosperity by promoting free enterprise, responsibility and a more constitutional limited government. They invest a lot of time trying to get Latinos to vote by literally knocking on doors.

How do you feel that your cultural values have impacted your work here in the United States?

Everyone has their values based on how they grew up and how they were educated, but for me integrity and honesty are my two core values and ripple out into everything I do.

A lot of my deals never go sour because I like to create good expectations about what they can expect from what I do. When people join the Hispanic Business Association of E-Commerce I want them to understand the core values that drive us as an association.

One cultural thing that was very difficult for me when I moved to the States was that everyone wanted to sign NDAs and other agreements. Growing up in Mexico it's done on a handshake - our word is our bond. In Michoacán, you don't mess around with your word - go back on it, and it's tough to keep doing business in the State.

Your word is the most valuable asset that you have in a deal and if you say you're going to do something you have to deliver. Those are values I'm passing on to my children. Anyone who flip-flops around in business is not someone I want to be around. It's as simple as that.

What is your mindset in relation to failure?

Every New Year my wife makes fun of me asking how many new companies I'm going to incorporate this year! When you are an entrepreneur and have goals and a vision of what you want to create, you're going to face challenges and barriers. Problems and progress go hand in hand.

In 1996 my brother started a company building websites and that was my first taste of technology. I started to get more involved in the company and it was a roller coaster ride. Over the 12 years, we pivoted in many different directions, on one deal losing thousands of dollars, on others making a profit. Looking back, our failures were really dealing with the wrong people, or thinking the market was going to go in a certain direction and when we made an investment in technology, it didn't.

I remember we were developing this module that was going to be part of our platform and we invested $100k and 18 months in building it. It went sour.

When you are financing your dream and everything goes down the drain, it is not easy to assimilate, especially when you're married, but my wife is my foundation, my rock. She has handled a lot of mistakes that I have made on the professional side, but we always have the mindset that as long as we're healthy and our minds are working, which is really the engine that keeps us moving forward, sooner or later things always work out.

Failure is only temporary. What we must never do is play the victim card, then that failure will be permanent. I hear people saying the system doesn't work for them, they don't speak English, or they make fun of our language, but that mindset will get you nowhere.

How did your family mold you into the person that you have become? What specifically is it that your family did that led you to where you are now?

It was the role models I had growing up that shaped me into the person I am today.

My grandpa was an inspiration. He started a coffee plantation when he was only 15 years old. Then he opened the first movie theatre in his hometown. He never finished elementary school, but he taught himself how to read and how to manage his finances.

My grandparents always had successful businesses and I think that was where my mom learned to be an entrepreneur - modeling previous generations worked for us.

My dad was involved in politics and that was really his focus. He would invest all the money he was making from his business in the party, because at that time Mexican opposition parties didn't get any

"We are about to become 65 million people strong in this country and that's a demographic that simply cannot be neglected anymore."

"Failure is only temporary. What we must never do is play the victim card, then that failure will be permanent."

funding. I'm proud to say eventually, he became a Congressman, Assemblyman, State President of his Party, on Boards, and other positions where he was able to influence policy positively. So, after years of advocating for the well-being of the community, he accomplished a lot of his goals.

Seeing my parents working so hard was critical in my own development.

What was the most difficult thing that you've ever had to face? And how did you overcome it?

When my son Tayde was born, he had heart failure. I remember being in the room with my wife, she was having a cesarean and I was holding her hand. They took Tayde out of my wife and we couldn't hear him cry, everything was silent. I saw the doctors and nurses rushing around and start plugging things into my new-born son. An hour later he was having his first heart surgery.

That experience changed me forever, I certainly became humbler. Growing up in Mexico I felt I was unstoppable, I felt powerful, but this experience taught me how fragile life is. And anything can be taken away from you in an instant.

My son went through four heart surgeries in his first three years. We were at the hospital every two months but thankfully he made it through. Now, 13 years later, he's a strong young man playing soccer and we feel so blessed.

When you go through something like this, it obviously puts life into perspective. Now there isn't anything in business that ever makes me worry. The experience made me strong in terms of how I go about my life and my business. I don't take BS from anyone; life is just too short to be pleasing people I don't care about or taking on projects that don't interest me.

This experience helped me change the priorities in my life and I'm grateful for that.

Overnight success is a myth, so what steps did you take to get to where you are today?

When you have a mission in life, it's motivational. It's what gets me out of bed in the morning. That mission then helps to start connecting the dots, where people recognize your contribution. I believe in doing things from my heart, things I'm passionate about. In my case that's helping people to survive and thrive in business, and it's also helping people save money for their children to go to college and guiding entrepreneurs to buy their first home.

I have always been a firm believer in compounding, so my 'overnight success' is 20 years in the making!

How do we help Latino business owners grow to their true potential?

That's a beautiful question, Rocío. Hispanics are a very diverse community here in the USA and it's a very large country. I think in order for us to help more Latinos reach their full potential, we have to start developing regional strategies, they have to be segmented by region because for example Latinos in LA are not the same as Latinos in New York or Latinos in Miami, but they all have similar problems of course, 'for example', access to capital is one.

If you want to roll out a strategy that will help Latinos access that capital, you have to take the micro aspects of strategy into consideration in order for this to work. We need to acknowledge that a one-size-fits-all solution is not going to work, so we have to develop specific strategies that are going to be tailored to a specific community.

Here in California, we have 40 million people, and Latinos in the Central Valley are completely different to Latinos in the South. The Latinos in the Bay Area are thinking how they are going to raise $3 million for their start up; while Latinos in Central Valley are desperate for a $2,500 loan, so they can launch their home-based family business. But that person in Central Valley, if they can make it happen, they are going to move probably from the average $36,000 to $60,000 or $70,000, in an area where salaries are not above $36,000.

We need to empower Latinos to reach their full potential by teaching them financial literacy and how to invest in themselves by hanging out with the right people. In some respects, it's about going back to basics.

One thing that I love about this country is that if you respect the system and invest in yourself to become a more valuable asset to your community, you're going to get out what you put in. Why are Hispanics not being seen as vulnerable and asking for support? Because we paint that perfect picture, yet our reality is far-fetched.

I feel as a community we aren't being vulnerable enough when it comes to our work. For sure, we are one of the hardest working groups in America, but I'd like to see a shift in mindset. When people have enough to provide for their family, they sit in that comfort zone and I feel we could be more ambitious.

"I think it is important for anyone that moves to the US to understand what makes this country great. Speaking the language and understanding the system is key to advancing in both your professional and personal life."

"Integrity and honesty are my two core values and ripple out into everything I do."

I have had conversations with young Latina professionals, and they ask me how it is possible for me to do what I'm doing when I didn't grow up here and speak the language. I always tell them it's extremely important they create a vision of where they want to see themselves as an entrepreneur or professional, five to 10 years from now.

Make a list of the things that you need to do to reach to that goal. And then your dream becomes possible. I can see it now in my own children. They are doing things at their age I never dreamed of and are definitely going to be more competitive than I was when they reach 30 years old.

I think what we are seeing is a new generation of Latinos that are more ambitious, have bigger goals and understand that the sky really is the limit. And I love that.

Growing up in Mexico, I saw a lot of limiting beliefs in other people. I believe that's a cultural thing, but in our family, I was blessed to be told that I had the opportunity to become whatever I wanted.

OGN INTERACTIVE
Tayde Aburto
Scan here
to visit my profile

Ed Vargas

HISPANIC JOURNEY

President - Vargas and Associates LLC

I asked, what makes your heart sing, Ed?

I come alive leading or working with a team of people that share the same vision, goals, and objectives that contribute to the best of their abilities to achieve a win-win and make a positive impact. I communicate key tasks that need to be done and integrate team recommendations. If you express yourself with credibility, build trust with a stranger and give respect, you will get respect back. These are the key elements of a strong, successful working relationship.

I learned from my father, Philip Vargas, a WWII US Army Air Force radio operator veteran stationed in North Africa and Italy. When I was growing up, he started the first Hispanic post of the Regular Veterans Association in San Jose, CA. That bond you have with someone that 'has your back' makes you a great team player. I believe "we do what we do for our Familia."

My younger brother, Steve, was born with a cleft lip and cleft pallet. He had several operations before starting school and went to a speech class to learn to enunciate words. Since we went to the same elementary school, I saw some kids would make fun of the way he talked. I 'had his back' protecting him from these bullies. I did not hurt these other kids. I told them there will always be someone bigger than they are. They need to think about what it would feel like if they were bullied.

I enjoyed playing sports, especially football. Bellarmine College Preparatory was the all-boys Catholic high school I attended in San Jose, CA. I wanted to play quarterback but my freshman football coaches said with my size and strength, I would help the team more by becoming an offensive and defensive lineman.

I accepted these assignments to be a team player. When I was a freshman, the varsity football team was ranked the number one defense in the nation. They were not scored upon. There were four high school All-Americans. These high standards helped me always give my best effort.

Jesuit principles and teachings focus on personalized attention and concern for the whole person - mind, body and spirit. The emphasis was not only on academic excellence, but also ensuring we were strong in character and conviction as well.

I learned about the value and sense of self-worth of helping others. When I graduated, I went to Santa Clara University, another Jesuit school, where I got my business degree and later returned to get my law degree.

Success is not just about the 'bottom-line.' During my career at AT&T, in addition to working in marketing, operations, eCommerce metric analytics and other roles, I was active in five Employee Resource Groups and in leadership roles with the HACEMOS ERG. Each ERG helped local community organizations. I strive for work-life balance. Although traveling internationally on business was one of my life goals, I've turned down promotions requiring me to move to other states to stay near my family members. When my grandson was four years old he asked me to teach him how to play guitar like me. Those special moments help me balance priorities.

TIME TO THINK

I played football for four years at Bellarmine Prep. In my senior year I played first string offensive guard and first string defensive tackle, and was offered a full scholarship at St Mary's College in Moraga, CA. I was very happy my tuition was going to be covered for four years! First, I needed to get a knee operation to remove torn cartilage after football season ended. While recuperating at home, suddenly, I could not breathe properly. I was rushed to the hospital where I was placed in an oxygen tent to help me take a breath. They treated me as if I had pneumonia while they did tests. For 36 hours I struggled to take half breaths and could not sleep. I was only focused on taking my next breath.

The pulmonary embolism diagnosis confirmed that my knee operation had created blood clots that passed through my heart and had then attached to my lungs. They injected me four times a day with blood thinner to dissolve those clots. In that intense time, lying in a hospital bed, I did not know what the problem was or if I was ever going to recover. It was in those moments of 'life focus', that I thought to myself, if I ever get out of here, what do I want to do with my life?

During this deep contemplation I set three life goals for myself.

Firstly, whatever organization I worked for at the age of 30, I wanted to be a senior executive.

Secondly, I wanted to travel and conduct business internationally.

Thirdly, If I was to recover from this condition, I would 'pay it forward.'

My Jesuit education was then, and still is, my foundation, to help people that may be in difficult situations overcome the challenges that they face in life.

That was a very personal and truly life-changing moment for Ed. An adverse situation that gave him the focus to decide the path for the next stage of his life. I asked him what major lesson

he had learned from the situation.

For me, it's important to work toward 'win-win solutions', those actions that pay it forward with positive impacts. I turned down the St Mary's football scholarship. At Santa Clara University, I made the choice to work two part-time jobs, and played lead guitar and sang in a dance cover band to supplement my academic scholarship.

With two business school classmates I started a food co-op on campus for off campus students, faculty and staff. People paid a member's fee that gave us money to buy fruit and vegetables at the local farmer's market and bread from a local bakery. The 'Food Conspiracy' members would place their weekly orders in advance and take turns going to pick up the items that were ordered. We cut out the markups from the retail grocery stores and passed those savings on to our members. We even got academic credit from the Leavey School of Business as small business entrepreneurs!

I like to bring that kind of energy to all the projects I work on. I share my experience on how I have overcome challenges in the packaging industry, international B2B publishing, leading nonprofits and also the wisdom from my career at AT&T. I am President of Vargas and Associates LLC, a strategic planning, marketing & communications consulting group and Head of the Latinx and Employee Resource Group Practice at CTR Factor, Inc., a DEI Leadership consulting firm.

As an example, at AT&T I was a leader with the HACEMOS Employee Resource Group. I helped start 'High Tech Day'. These are Science, Technology, Engineering and Math, or 'STEM' workshops at AT&T facilities for local high school students. We showed them how to use code to create an app to upload to a mobile device, build Arduino engineering devices, and encourage them to think about a career in Tech.

In my sessions, I gave the students my 'strategic college-career plan' handout, so they could write down their responses. I asked them to visualize where they wanted to be in five years' time. To write down their vision, goals, objectives and much more. Once they completed their strategic college-career plan, I told them to discuss it with their parents and teachers.

High Tech Day is still the annual HACEMOS ERG flagship event. The last HTD I participated in before leaving AT&T was in 2017. We hosted 2,625 students from 87 schools in 35 AT&T facilities in cities across the USA, Puerto Rico and Mexico City. HACEMOS has given more than $3 million in scholarship funds to students.

Next, I wondered if there was a specific time in business when Ed had met somebody that proved pivotal. A time when suddenly everything changed.

From my experience in the hospital, my second life goal on the list was to conduct business internationally. Utilizing my business planning experience for Crown Zellerbach's packaging group, I was recruited to be the editor, publisher and conference director for a start-up B2B publishing unit highlighting the 'nonwovens industry'.

We published a magazine, newsletter and books, and hosted three technical conferences over a five-day period twice a year.

The then parent company, Miller Freeman Publications, bought a paper manufacturing trade show in Tokyo. My assignment was to create and host a nonwovens conference in Tokyo in the same week as the paper trade show.

I didn't speak Japanese and I didn't know anybody there. I introduced myself to Sato-san, the president of the Nonwovens

Japanese Trade Association who was at a nonwovens trade show in the US. Having learned the value of understanding cultural differences, I had my business card printed in Japanese on the reverse side and as he was the CEO of his company, I bowed lower when I introduced myself and presented my card. In my own Hispanic culture I give respect to my elders, and that helped develop a trust bond with Sato-san.

I discovered the reason many senior executives in Japan weren't coming to the US for our conferences to meet American businesspeople and individuals from other countries. I learned that if Japanese senior executives did not speak impeccable English, they would be 'embarrassed or lose face' which was not culturally acceptable.

Knowing this, I suggested that when we arranged our conference in Tokyo, we would bring simultaneous translators, just like at the United Nations. When Japanese business leaders spoke in Japanese the audience members, wearing headphones, could choose to listen in Japanese or in English. Likewise, when other executives spoke English, the audience members could select listening in Japanese or English.

My commitment to provide simultaneous translation resolved cultural concerns and supported three main cultural values in Japan, 'harmony, order and self-development'. Sato-san invited me to join him on a three-city tour in Japan. During this trip he translated my presentation and introduced me to C-Suite leaders of the top nonwovens companies in three different cities! This was something that would never have happened if we had not made the deeper connection based on credibility, trust and mutual respect.

Ed's answer pointed out that a basic cultural tradition, in this case not losing face because of language ability, had made such an important element of international trade difficult for the Japanese. It is something that I often wonder about - are there similar 'limiting' traditions in our own Hispanic culture? Many of those 'wonderings' are, thankfully, answered throughout the chapters of this book.

I asked Ed what specific experiences helped him to tap into his passion for music.

To help pay college expenses, I played in a dance party cover band that opened-up my creative side. My brother, Steve, was a gifted drummer in our band. Growing up in the San Francisco Bay Area, I was inspired to play guitar after seeing local artists like Carlos Santana, Neal Schoen with Journey and The Doobie Brothers. It was an opportunity to express myself - to take a song and modify it so our band played our own version or in a medley of great songs.

If we were playing a crowd's favorite songs the audience would just get up and dance. People enjoy getting together to dance, irrespective of their background, ethnicity or age. It always feels great to celebrate singing and dancing with other people!

I try to take the kind of positive energy that I feel seeing people dancing when I'm playing, into all the things that I do. Playing music was, and continues to be, a wonderful opportunity to express myself. I still get contacted by people to play because they remember those good feelings they had when they saw me with my band. Music is a very powerful connector.

What does success mean to you?

Throughout my career, I learned to work through any challenge, to become anything I wanted, or didn't want, to be. You don't have to have a corporate job to be a success to help others. My non-profit experience in the Bay Area includes Director of Communications & Media Relations, World Affairs Council of Northern CA, Chairperson of the Community Advisory Panel to the Board of Directors at KQED, President of Latinos in Communication and the President of the Hispanic Community Foundation, now known as the Latino Community Foundation.

My advice is simple; if you want to start your own business, focus on what motivates you, and what you really, truly want to do. When I talked to the students at the AT&T HACEMOS ERG High Tech Day, it was great to inspire them to develop a plan of what they wanted to be.

When I consult with ERGs, I recommend they align their activities with their corporation's objectives. e.g., AT&T needed to expand the number of towers for mobile devices in the Salinas Valley. I partnered with Ken McNeely, president of AT&T West, Arturo Rodriguez, president of the United Farmworkers Union, to launch AdelanTech, a 2-yeat program for the children of the UFW families attending college.

It provided leadership training from the Coro Foundation, Udacity courses and a certificate to become a web developer, business analyst or programmer. My role was to provide HACEMOS members to teach these AdelanTECH Fellows about business plans. They were assigned a business challenge that required them to research, conduct surveys and present their recommendations. Win-win! AT&T got community support to build towers in that rural region as a result.

Several of those students planned to get their tech certification and use the leadership training to return to their farmworker community and develop AgTech. This is now an emerging economic sector that has the potential to completely reshape global agriculture, dramatically

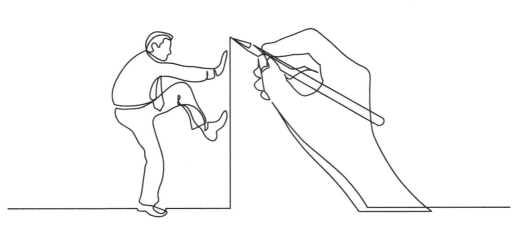

"If someone faces a huge obstacle, there is always a path forward. You can go over the wall, around the wall...with a plan that will keep you moving forward."

increasing the productivity of the agriculture system while reducing the environmental and social costs of current Ag production practices. This is currently a $15 billion business segment.

Similarly, the junior high teacher that recommended I apply to Bellarmine Prep changed my life. At the time I was not aware of that school, or what I could accomplish, or the possibilities it could bring. Because of that advice, and how it changed my life, I wanted to be that kind of person too.

As a mentor at the Miller Center for Social Entrepreneurship at Santa Clara University, I now work with entrepreneurs that want to improve the environment or address an area of poverty. With an assigned co-mentor, we help mentees assess their current business and develop a plan to scale up with impact investors. https://www.millersocent.org/

If someone faces a huge obstacle, there is always a path forward. Rather than banging your head against a wall, you can develop a plan to go over the wall, go around the wall, or even under the wall. If you have a plan, and something gets in the way, you can modify and change those strategies and objectives, so that you are still able to move forward. That way, you will not lose your dream. I enjoy helping and mentoring people to overcome what life puts in front of them.

One impact from COVID isolation on students, has been an increase in suicides in the US.

It shocked me to learn that three students at my alma mater committed suicide in the fall semester, 2021. (April 2022 CDC survey, Pew Research Center: 37% of US high school students report regular mental health struggles during COVID-19). When I learned

"If you want to start your own business, focus on what motivates you, and what you really, truly want to do."

"I would tell myself as a younger person to dream big, and have a vision, set goals and put a plan in place. If I did that, I would be able to achieve whatever I wanted to do, whenever I wanted to do it."

about these suicides, I contacted leaders at Santa Clara to share a report by 'Salesforce' on this trend and the value of providing a Center for Wellbeing for the students and faculty. It is now in place at SCU.

I wanted to know how Ed's international experience supported him on his leadership journey.

When I was a kid, I was inspired to think of international business travel. My mother would take us to visit my aunt where I would see a picture of one of my older cousins in the Air Force in Rome, Italy. In the background was the Roman Colosseum. That photograph lit a fire in me. I wanted to be in a position in my career to travel internationally. I wanted to learn how other people perceived me, and how I could also appreciate their culture by working in their country.

That is the dynamic I recommend to people in the US. We are so polarized right now. As we are all human beings, sharing one world, we need to focus more on what we have in common instead of getting hung up on differences. Developing relationships when meeting people and sharing experiences, broadens our understanding of different cultures.

I try to do this when I establish any relationship. I share my background openly, to build credibility, to develop that trust factor. The true strength of 62 million plus Hispanics, Latinx here in the US, is our collective strength from Mexico, South American, Central American and the Gulf Island countries. Don't get caught up on labels like 'Latinx' that divide us. Accept how people self-identify.

I wanted to know, specifically, how Ed had shown leadership, tenacity and grit when it was not popular.

I started my corporate career working in sales for Owens-Illinois, a major packaging company headquartered in Ohio, and I was doing well. They offered me promotions in New York and Ohio. However, at that time, I really wanted to stay in the Bay Area where my family and my fiancé, Christine's family, were located.

To stay true to myself, I resigned and went to work for a regional competitor of theirs, Poly-Vue Plastics, as manager for product development. I wanted to move up their corporate ladder, believing I could be an executive by the age of 30 and meet my first life goal. However, within a few months of being there, our largest single customer, Colgate-Palmolive, told us they were going to close their Berkeley, CA operation and relocate that production to the Midwest. They gave us a one-year advance notice. Our management was acutely aware that we were going to lose a third of our entire company's business.

The acquisition of new business became my whole mission. In those tough 'how do we get out of this situation' discussions, some of the senior executives indicated they were thinking of leaving. I worked closely with our president and manufacturing team to develop new business. I encouraged potential clients in California to use our facility for research and development on new packaging. We established really strong relationships.

In fact, we were so successful that we secured many new contracts and had to expand to a second facility in Southern California! Within eighteen months we not only replaced the lost client volume, but we had also transformed our operation, making it more profitable. All of that happened during, and despite, the global recession in the early 1980s. That challenge, and one of the biggest accomplishments in my career, was down to how we dealt with it as a team. We wanted to let the employees know we were really working hard to expand the business base so they would still have a job. The primary motivation for me, was to make sure that they were still able to work and take care of their families.

Given his success, I wondered what lessons Ed would wish to tell his younger self to learn at the beginning of his career?

I would tell myself as a younger person to dream big, and have a vision, to set goals and put a plan in place. If I did that, I would be able to achieve whatever I wanted to do, whenever I wanted to do it. Prioritizing your time and family is essential to keep life in balance. If you take that approach, anybody can be successful in what they truly want to do and not be pushed into what they are 'supposed to do.' Be ready to take advantage of opportunities. If it weren't for that one teacher recommending that I apply to Bellarmine College Prep, my life would be in a completely different place.

I had so much to ask Ed, and I wanted to get his thoughts on how important our humanity in business is, versus our business-only conversations.

That's a big focus for me. It goes beyond profitability and the global impacts we are seeing right now. I think it's important to look at long term problems, e.g., climate and health, to redefine what the problems are, and produce new solutions.

For me, technology has always been a tool. We've got a huge agricultural sector, and we've had a drought for the last several years in California. We need to redefine the problem, get more people working together and use technology in a positive way so we can be more efficient to manage water for the future. We need to get more leaders and groups involved to collaborate together. Here is an example. Seven of The Hispanic Journey contributing authors came to help me launch the first HLX+ West Coast Leadership Summit hosted by Bill.com in Silicon Valley on October 10, 2022. Rocío Pérez, Jazmin Diaz, Guillermo Diaz, Jr., Carlos Quezada, Gerardo Garcia-Jurado, Martha Niño and Andre Arbelaez. Going forward HLX+ core pillars of focus include Education, Health & Wellness, Entrepreneurship & Economic Progress, Culture, Representation, & Gender Equity and Media & Entertainment. As a result of that HLX+ Summit I am also now the Northwest Region President for HLX+.

One of my major motivations is working on behalf of people that 'do not have a voice.' I work with an organization called Ayudando Latinos A Soñar, a non-profit in Half Moon Bay, in the Bay Area, working with farm workers. www.alasdreams.com

I led a team at ALAS to collaborate with Mercy Housing of CA. Fall 2022, we were awarded an exclusive negotiation agreement with the City of Half Moon Bay to replace a dormant building with 40 units of affordable housing for farmworkers ($34M). The ALAS Farmworker Resource Center and a kitchen/pantry will be on the first floor for the local farmworker community.

It's so expensive to buy a home or rent an apartment in the Bay Area near agricultural work areas. We are helping them do that. I'm really pleased to assist in bringing a group of people together to handle some of these things, people that really look at the issues and then take a larger view about helping humanity.

Ed, what's your opinion on the greatest impact of the collective effort, as Hispanics all over the world come together?

After speaking at national Hispanic conferences as President of Vargas & Associates before joining Pacific Bell/SBC/AT&T, I was invited to participate in a round table discussion on diversity in the workplace at Harvard. The discussion became an article in the

Harvard Business Review: *"A Question of Color: A Debate on Race in the US Workplace"* by David A Thomas and Suzy Wetlaufer. The participants 'at the table' were all successful business leaders. The last two sentences of this article sum up where we are even today. "There have been too few successes and there has been too little change for the length of time that the struggle has been going on. We've been at this a long time."

When I was the AT&T HACEMOS ERG national EVP-Community Outreach, I launched HACEMOS Latino Diversity Stories on YouTube. The objective was to generate awareness of our members' volunteer activities with personal success stories across the USA, Puerto Rico and Mexico to address negative stereotypes.

The Gross Domestic Product, or GDP, of over 62 million Hispanics in the US from Mexican American, South American, and Central American heritage would be the fifth largest in the world, larger than the GDPs of the United Kingdom, India and France. (2022 Latino Donor Collaborative U.S. Latino GDP Report). Most Hispanics don't know this statistic and that our diversity is our collective strength. It's important to inform and bring all Hispanics together and lift each other up.

As a consultant and leader I mentor groups and speak at seminars and webinars to get that message out to Hispanics and allies to bring people together that can make a positive change.

I asked Ed if there is anything particular about the culture of Silicon Valley?

I am in my third year as a mentor for the Miller Center for Social Entrepreneurship at Santa Clara University. This group was started by Jeff Miller, a classmate that got his engineering degree when I got my business degree. After an amazing career in Tech, Jeff and his wife donated $25 million to launch the Miller Center. John Sobrato Sr. was the developer that built Apple's campus and many more tech campuses in Silicon Valley. John and his wife donated $100 million to launch the Sobrato Campus for Discovery and Innovation at SCU in 2021. These gentlemen are tremendous success stories. Wonderful people who have the compassion to help others.

The Silicon Valley Tech work environment was known for many years as a culture of "innovation, fast changes to gain a competitive edge." However, the COVID shutdown turned full offices into remote workers. The latest impacts for Tech companies are massive headcount reductions due to "hiring too many people during the pandemic and economic uncertainty." More than 68,000 global technology sector employees have been laid off from 229 Tech companies in the first few weeks of 2023, according to data compiled by the website Layoffs.fyi

There are also huge disparity gaps. Women doing the same work as white Caucasian males, would need to work until the following November to earn the same pay. Living here is a struggle for people that work for hourly wages. The median household income in Santa Clara County in 2022 for a family of four is $168.5K. Low income for a family of four is $94.5K as defined by Housing and Urban Development.

One way to address these gaps is to understand "Unconscious Bias, social stereotypes about certain groups of people that individuals form outside of their own conscious awareness. Everyone holds unconscious beliefs about various social and identity groups. These biases stem from one's tendency to organize social worlds by categorizing." At the Miller Center I'm also a member of the Unconscious Bias Working Group. We created a Toolkit for Mentors and Mentees to help Social Entrepreneurs scale up their business ideas more effectively. Rocío Pérez and I collaborated on an Imposter Syndrome article for the Miller Center to acknowledge the Unconscious Bias Toolkit on the cohort website. We will be publishing more articles to raise awareness.

California is also experiencing the worst drought in 1,200 years. The Bay Area has been in drought conditions since 2000. This is impacting agriculture production. California agricultural exports totaled $20 billion in 2020, a decrease of 2.8% from 2019. Governor Newsom and the Mayors and County Supervisors in the Bay Area are challenged to address affordable housing, transportation, the homeless and other key issues.

My intention for telling my experience growing up in Silicon Valley is to bring the energy I find in music as a strength to connect with all people. California is the state with the most diversity in the USA. Our cultural heritage is derived from over 300 indigenous tribal groups, explorers and immigrants from many continents. According to the 2020 Census 39% of Californians are Latino, 35% are white, 15% are Asian American or Pacific Islander, 5% are Black, 4% are multiracial, and fewer than 1% are Native American or Alaska Natives. I work to express ideas in ways people can relate to so they want to collaborate to make positive changes. If we can agree on a common vision we can set goals and objectives that can be measured over time to create win-win situations for our extended familia and future generations.

OGN INTERACTIVE
Ed Vargas
Scan here
to visit my profile

James Pérez Foster

HISPANIC JOURNEY

Venture Capital Entrepreneur

Having advised organizations including national banks, universities, NGOs, FinTech and start-ups, James Pérez Foster has a proven track record on Wall Street and far beyond in promoting investments for under-served communities, be they Hispanic, Black, Indigenous or people of color, women, veterans or rural markets.

In 2007 he founded Solera National Bank in Colorado, the first nationally-chartered bank in the state of Colorado in ten years, and the first national Hispanic markets focused bank in the US. He dedicated the bank to his Dominican-born grandmother, Patria Pérez.

I met James a number of years ago, networking, and I just saw this Latino who was absolutely on fire. I loved his energy, his mission, and he had a skill of connecting with people and making things happen.

As sometimes happens, we lost track for a while and then re-connected. He invited me to mentor at the Stanford Latino Entrepreneurship Initiative (SLEI) at Stanford University's Graduate School of Business. To this day, James has mentored every cohort for SLEI since the program's inception in 2015. It was amazing to be able to serve side-by-side with him and to help the program's cohort of entrepreneurs to implement the powerful tenets of scale as taught to them by some of the best business professors in the country. Ever since then James has mentored me, and I feel honored to be able to share time and space with him.

I started the interview by asking James what value he thinks he brings to his community.

It is an honor to be involved with The Hispanic Journey. You are relentless and, most importantly, respected. I'm glad to have you in my life, and now you have asked me a challenging question because the values I see in myself and what I can bring to others, especially within the communities I serve, have changed over time.

Growing up in New York City, I came up through the private school system, but I was an average student at best and had to deal with some learning disabilities when I was younger. It was something I had to work through as I matured and really sought to understand my place in the world both personally and professionally. I unfortunately put that pressure on myself when I was still young - perhaps feeling pressure that I had to have those answers by then.

I was a very curious kid, though, and this curiosity manifested a number of interests. I was always interested in music ahead of my time and age. I became obsessed with jazz, fusion and classical music which quickly piqued my interest towards jazz drumming. Imagine me with long hair playing gigs in New York and going to jazz clubs with my friends, watching these great musicians of the time.

Because showcasing my self-worth academically was never my strong suit, I commonly felt misunderstood. What I couldn't prove on a school exam score, I compensated my emotional frustrations with a personal "advantage" I believe I had. I knew I was a great communicator and that I expressed my thoughts through writing and art. I had rich and layered observations about the world around me. I journaled compulsively and, still to this day, have many of the journals I wrote back when I was a teenager.

When not performing music, some of my happiest times were by myself. Taking walks through Central Park in New York City, riding my bike, eating meals in restaurants alone with nothing but my journal and a newspaper. Deep down inside, my observations about people and culture felt relevant, they felt like a secret superpower of mine. This secret superpower carried me through the remainder of high school and college.

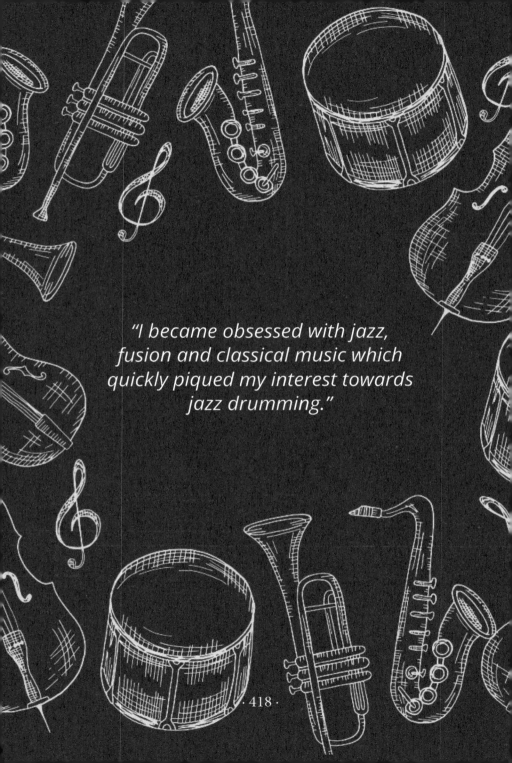

"I became obsessed with jazz, fusion and classical music which quickly piqued my interest towards jazz drumming."

When I think about who I am today, and the value I bring to communities, I'd like people to think of me in terms of my kindness. I value myself as a connector, a bridge, somebody who is selfless in terms of sharing both their personal and professional network; somebody who really leads with their heart on their sleeve.

Every single initiative I'm involved in, whether it's starting a company, scaling a company, or raising money for a company, I always represent those projects from a heart-felt and proactive-minded place. In terms of value, it's an unabashed sense of obligation, which comes from a very personal place.

James, you've been a success overnight! Now, all of a sudden, I see you rocking and rolling it. Tell me about that. Where did this come from?

That overnight success you perceive has actually taken decades of building a mindset of tenacity, grit and an unrelenting desire to see good things happen as fast as possible, but at the same time understanding they must arrive as realistically and authentically as possible.

This might sound funny, but I feel like I'm now at a place in my life where I don't need to be 'liked' anymore. I don't have some personal agenda that I need to put out there. What I do have are years of experience, aggregate anecdotes, and Golden Nuggets that I can put to work, pragmatically. I've had some great successes and, of course, failures and I find my motivation is to pull from those personal experiences to keep me or whomever I'm advising moving forward.

Why have you dedicated your career to making sure that people have access to capital and social advocacy?

Observationally, it started really early for me. My career began in New York City at Merrill Lynch and then I moved on to Smith Barney, which became Morgan Stanley shortly thereafter. Ahead of its time, I focused my buy-side equities portfolios on working exclusively with Latinx entrepreneurs and women founders in the New York City area.

The only reason that I elected to work with those different markets was because we were encouraged as young asset managers to specialize and work with groups that we felt comfortable with. And for me growing up in a fun, culturally diverse family with an inspiring Dominican mother and grandmother, choosing to focus my portfolios on working with Latinos and women-owned businesses in New York just felt normal to me. It felt like I was working with family and friends. Therefore, working as a asset manager in the early 1990s and focusing my portfolio clients and finding professional success on Wall Street with these markets, I knew unambiguously where my calling was.

I had a conversation that I'll never forget with a gentleman who owned a large company in the Bronx. By all sense of the definition, he was the example of the American dream. He originated from Puerto Rico and on paper was a deca-millionaire. I remember calling him from Merrill Lynch as this wide-eyed grasshopper asset manager and walking him through the value of why he needed to work with me.

I remember like it was yesterday how emotional he was on that call with me. Despite his high-net-worth and business success, he couldn't believe someone from Merrill Lynch wanted to talk to him. He showed such vulnerability and sincerity and quickly realized that others like him probably felt the same way.

There was another business owner who was from the Dominican Republic, who said he'd be happy to work with me but first I needed to meet his mother who was flying in and staying with him. For me that seemed so easy, but for the customer it was a big deal. And this and other similar occurrences helped me to understand the variable nuances and sensitivities in working with diverse markets.

What I saw in diverse markets was nothing but economic viability. I saw savvy Latinx and women business owners with highly sophisticated capital and investment requirements. I saw these business owners challenge themselves to grow smarter, to hire smarter and fire faster. I saw diverse business owners eschew the barriers of social definitions in order to thrive within competitive marketplaces.

Quickly erasing the academic challenges and stigma from my past, my calling became my ability to communicate and expedite cultural relatability. An understanding that diverse markets required nuanced and culturally specific approaches. Couple this with my communication skills and building a foundational emotional intelligence for diverse markets, I knew I was onto something very powerful. It really became my life's mission to make sure that my diverse clients understood it was safe to work with someone like me, who actually cared.

What is the biggest misconception in our Hispanic entrepreneurial community that limits our capacity for success?

Coming from the side of business consultancy and capital markets, the biggest and most frustrating misconception is that they don't possess the business sophistication for scaling a business to not only greater profitability but also to expansion and/or exit at some point.

This is a complete misunderstanding because the empirical data says otherwise. As somebody who has helped hundreds of these companies

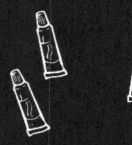

"*I knew I was a great communicator and I expressed my thoughts through writing and art.*"

in multi-industries, and throughout the different stages of their business life cycles, Latino and women-owned businesses specifically encompass some of the brightest, most tenacious, risk tolerant and risk-averse mindsets I have ever worked with. These businesses apply complex philosophies of scale, culture and team alignment behaviors to navigate through exceptionally volatile business cycles.

What risks are Hispanic entrepreneurs not taking?

Without question Hispanic entrepreneurs aren't taking on enough growth capital.

Culturally speaking, I can only make presumptions around some of the aspects of not asking for, or not wanting money. But I think, based on what I've seen, these entrepreneurs feel that they are not worthy of taking on smart capital, and that, someone like me on the capital side, is somehow going to uncover some huge mistake or knowledge gap the entrepreneur has. In truth, I would never see it that way and perhaps this is why I love the venture capital space so much. I would only see knowledge gaps as an opportunity to show them how much faster they could grow with a culturally competent financial partner like myself.

To show high-potential companies the tactical nature of taking on growth capital for opportunistic expansion, for deepening their human capital bench strength, to have the financial capability to develop and test new product offerings ahead of competitive peer groups, is essential for long-term sustainability.

I feel emotional about this because so many times I have sensed this unvocalized feeling from diverse founders and their teams. It's at times a perceived inability to embrace the opportunities of 'financial partnership' and becoming paralyzed with an unsubstantiated insecurity or mindset of 'Who am I? I'm just running a small $20-million business.'

A $20 million, business? That's incredible! They don't know how impressed I am, but somehow, they still think they're not worthy. I hear it so often, but from a personal perspective I have to anesthetize myself to stay the 'straight arrow' and focus the importance of my relatability to them. And to help foster a spirit of confidence in them while establishing a bridge of trust with me at the same time.

There is ample growth capital available. There are ample mentors and accelerators available to resource best-practices, to achieve venture capital readiness but first they must feel within their hearts that they deserve it. Thankfully, I now feel confidently that entrepreneurial mindsets and hearts are evolving. Worthiness is not cultural, it is an evolutionary step in the entrepreneurial journey, and now, more and more founder teams are starting to believe that their bold visions are possible through grit and by following the roadmaps around inevitable and tangible obstacles from fellow believers ahead of them. And I will be ready to fund them.

What do you wish the Hispanic community knew about you and your journey that sheds light on what's possible?

That "failure" is an asset. I have failed and made many mistakes in my career. Maybe it's the gray hair or beard that people see. They see age, they see experience and maybe even some wisdom. However, my hope is that people also see a pragmatic human being that learned from these mistakes along the way. I want people to say, there's James Pérez Foster - he got his shit together. And at the end of the day, that makes me a more potent, street-qualified executive leader.

I can offer every cliche there is - the mindset of 'fail your way forward', we all have different versions of it, but it's those life experiences I look for in companies I choose to invest in, I don't want a rosy picture, I want candor. It is a red flag for me when entrepreneurs present themselves with a pollyanna-ish 'Everything's perfect; look at my LinkedIn, my resume, my schooling, let me tell you about my successful bio and personal story'. The irony is that it's the exact opposite of what I'm looking for.

I choose to invest in individuals and teams who have been dragged through the mud, had their hair lit on fire and had doors slammed in their face because, ultimately, those are the entrepreneurs who are going to succeed and become the next generation of leaders. And the more they speak about those pitfalls, and those mistakes and "how" they persevered, the more impressed I am.

This is a tough world and I want to see realness because that shows me their character.

What was the hardest thing that you've had to face, and how did you overcome it?

That's such an easy one for me, Rocío: it was founding a national bank. I moved to Colorado because I had this big, hairy, audacious goal of starting the state's first national bank in 10 years. I had never done anything remotely close to something of that size and scope.

There was a statistic presented to me at the very beginning of that project - that "only 12% of bank concepts ever get to door open." To get a national bank approved by four federal regulatory agencies with a first-time founder, with a first-time organizational group, with a first-time management team, with a first-time Hispanic market focus

"Every single initiative I'm involved in, whether it's starting a company, scaling a company, or raising money for a company, I always represent those projects from a heart-felt and proactive-minded place."

that we intended to IPO? It must have sounded crazy to the regulators. However, we modeled our path to profitability, and we were approved.

In retrospect, I'll give my founding group a lot of credit for our gravitas. The task at hand was enormous and there were literally thousands of projects within the master project. There was also a tremendous sense of responsibility I placed on myself to work with Colorado's most prominent and respected Latino leaders, and to leverage their incredible experience and respect within the Denver community into an aligned and selfless joint mission to get the bank open.

Respecting their reputations and their 'need to be heard' with utmost sensitivity was my only priority yet sometimes lost upon them. Managing their expectation yet being unrelenting in my steadfastness to avoid mission creep for the greater good was one of the greatest executive learning moments in my career. However, in the end, it was the will and vision of all - a singular mission to open the first national Hispanic markets-focused bank in the country that became a grassroots oriented priority of an entire community. And I am forever humbled by this. Today, Solera National Bank is $1 billion in assets. I'm incredibly humbled to have brought this much economic activity to the region.

How has your familia shaped who you have become?

I mentioned earlier that I came from a vibrant Dominican family. It was a family that was always socially and issue-oriented and involved within the community - and so from an early age I was able to watch this - and this inspired me for a lifetime.

I watched my grandmother teach her students at her dining room table. I observed her laughter and her authentic interactions. I saw my mother teaching at New York University, I watched her late nights and weekends dedicated to authoring books on immigrant diaspora communities and cross-cultural immersion characteristics. I watched my father, a psychiatrist and researcher, originate theories about consciousness - and perhaps those precious moments inspired me to reach from deep within and to share my experiences with wider and willing audiences. Perhaps they were the rooted inspiration behind my passion towards mentoring high-potential, scalable companies. I was led, by example.

Learning and educating occurs in every aspect of my rich life. Now, my wife and two kids continue to shape me even further. I see the innocence in my kids' faces and I get to work and live and love every single day of my life to be a provider, a caring husband and present father.

This loving familia I have continues to evolve me as an executive who's doing things a little bit differently. I am a passionate and humble individual who is attempting to lead and inspire my teams every day with purpose and meaningful intent.

How are you preparing your children for success now?

By doing the same thing that my parents and family did for me - I make sure they know how strong they are. I needed more coddling as a kid because my confidence was so often affected by academic insecurities. My kids don't have that problem. They've got my wife's genes, thank goodness, but at the end of the day, grades don't define character. And this is what we talk about. I make sure they understand that their ideas matter and their perceptions of things are real and viable, but that they can also be incorrect as well. We discuss that 'ideas' must be tried and that failing is nothing but a learning opportunity.

What can Hispanic males do to support the women in their lives?

I don't want to get mixed up in the gender stereotypes of what men can do better because I believe ethics is the true north star within the relationship or family dynamic. Historically, maybe men had to be stronger within those dynamics, but that means nothing to me. The smartest thing men can do right now is to realize that women, as their partners in life or business, are just as viable as men, and perhaps more so in stewarding complex organizations and companies - and thankfully we are seeing near endless data supporting that women in leadership positions exponentially outperform their male counterparts. Wake up, dudes.

My wife, Lisa, is now the entrepreneur-in-residence in our home. She has a podcast called Real Life Momz and a branded Amazon store. Her podcast is focused on discussing tough, relevant and resourceful topics for parents. When she first came up with the idea, I quickly realized how brilliant it was and the importance of transitioning myself into her greatest champion and advocate.

James, to finish, I'm going ask you my favorite question - what makes your heart sing?

Let me state the obvious, it's my family and friends. They are the support system that makes my heart sing, but where I get my intellectual fire is actually something you mentioned at the start of the interview - it is the Stanford Latino Entrepreneurship Initiative at Stanford University's Graduate School of Business.

The Stanford program has kept me grounded and tethered to the Latinx community and the entrepreneurial market as a whole. I am the longest serving mentor since program inception. I'm a capital advisor and I lecture on engaging target communities for raising capital. I share grassroots-oriented strategies and anecdotes from my experience opening my bank in Denver, CO.

My heart also sings when meeting like-minded, wide-eyed entrepreneurs who have a desire to scale their companies with proven methodologies. Entrepreneurs who want to learn and embrace best practices. And for me to see that energy, that fire, that cadence and rhythm a founder team can synchronize together - reminds me of myself and the rhythms of my drums, playing jazz in my happy place.

OGN INTERACTIVE
James Pérez Foster
Scan here
to visit my profile

"That overnight success has taken decades of building a mindset of tenacity, grit and an unrelenting desire to see good things happen as fast as possible, but at the same time understanding they must arrive as realistically and authentically as possible."

Adrian Mendoza

HISPANIC JOURNEY

Founder – Mendoza Ventures

Adrian Mendoza is the Founder and General Partner of Mendoza Ventures, a company he started in order to address the funding gap for founders from under-represented communities at the earliest, pre-seed stage of their business ventures. Launched in 2016 and focusing on investments in AI, Fintech, and Cybersecurity, Mendoza Ventures is minority and women-led - the first VC firm on the East Coast founded by a Latino.

I first connected with Adrian online, I was 'cyber admiring' his work, particularly in FinTech, and when we finally met in person in 2021, it was clear my admiration was well founded - I was immediately inspired by his journey.

I started by asking Adrian my favorite question: what makes your heart sing?

Creating wealth for our communities. I've sat on both sides of the fence, firstly as a Founder and now as a Funder. I'm excited to take under-represented founders – both Latino and female founders - and help create wealth on both sides of the equation. I love giving our communities access to venture capital and creating an opportunity for them to participate in the wealth creation process.

I'm proud to say that 80% of our fund 2 is invested in immigrants, people of color and female founders.

As a company we've looked at how we could make venture capital accessible and I'm on a mission to create the next generation of Latino accredited investors to be able to take the next step in helping build wealth in America.

That's wonderful Adrian, can you tell me about your journey?

I am originally from Southern California where my mom was a bookkeeper, and my dad was a carpenter cabinet maker. They met in Tijuana, Mexico, and I was born in Los Angeles. I lived on a street where my fifth-grade teacher lived across from us, my godmother lived two doors down, and the kids I went to elementary school with me also lived on the same street.

My journey then took me east. Before that, the farthest east I had been was Nevada, but as Hispanics it's in our DNA to pick up, move and find the next opportunity. So, I applied to Harvard sight unseen and got in. This was a real opportunity, but luckily Harvard gave me a 50% grant and that was life changing. Because of that move to Boston, I was able to travel to Europe, Tokyo, and even Mexico City - Harvard paid for all those experiences.

I was fortunate to meet amazing people from around the world, from Latin America to Asia to Europe and classmates from all over US. This was literally the spark that changed the direction of my life.

I was also in Boston in the middle of the dot-com boom, and as soon as I graduated from Harvard, IBM hired me to be part of their e-commerce innovation lab. I was square in the middle of the Boston tech ecosystem, which was second only to what was going on in San Francisco at that time.

My father was an entrepreneur, he ran his woodworking business out of the house and like most entrepreneurs he worked on weekends, nights and holidays, the mindset of being able to start and run a business was ingrained in our family culture.

I had the wonderful opportunity to start my first company in 2008, when the market was losing 800 points a day. I was working for a

"I'm excited to take under-represented founders – both Latino and female founders - and help create wealth on both sides of the equation. I love giving our communities access to venture capital and creating an opportunity for them to participate in the wealth creation process."

start-up at the time and they let us all go. In the absence of any other opportunity, I made my own.

I started my first tech company out of my house with a co-founder. My wife joined us as our COO and is now my partner at Mendoza Ventures. The company was backed by some amazing investors who believed in us.

When you look at the tech culture of that time, no-one put a label on us. I was this ambitious brown guy, no one referred to me as the Latino founder; they had no idea who I was and the culture I grew up in. There were no Latinos in tech, finance, or VC at that time.

Five years later when the company went into acquisition mode, we looked at what our next steps would be. Instead of starting another company, we decided to start investing in other companies. We saw no-one that looked like us, there were no Latinos or women investors writing checks and that was the start of addressing how can we make change with the dollars that we had.

We started with a small pilot fund, just in the US. I remember thinking that I can't hide the fact I'm a short brown guy who speaks Spanish and that it was time to embrace who I was. We called the company Mendoza Ventures so that when people saw the name on a cap table they knew it was a firm run by a Latino.

I proudly remember, four years later, EY published a report on the state of FinTech in the North East. At the top of the list of Fintech investors were the usual suspects, but third on the list was Mendoza Ventures – the only diverse led firm that was on that list. That had the impact of telling everyone in the ecosystem that we were out there and there was no hiding it. At the same time, it did one amazing thing that I never expected - Latinos came out of the closet.

The Hispanic community heard what we were doing. Bolivians, Colombians and Peruvians, Founders, COOs and CTOs all started gravitating toward us knowing it was OK to be a Latino in finance. And we didn't know how special this was.

We were the first and only Latino-led VC fund on the East Coast and now when I looked back on this, it was a privilege. The question was, how do we mentor other Latinos to get jobs in VC and start other funds? How do we make sure that it perpetuates itself across the VC landscape?

An incredible fact is that Latinos represent 20% of US GDP. We need to be able to take that momentum and run with it.

Latinos are the fastest entrepreneurial demographic in the United States. What can a VC or other business owner do to help more Latinas get funding? And what would help Latinos prepare themselves to be in the position that you are today?

I think the issue is threefold.

Firstly, it's about education. I'm unique because I came from a family of entrepreneurs. My mom ran a business from home. She was always finding ways to make money for the family, doing little projects - there was always something she was cooking up. I think we have to educate our community that being an entrepreneur is a career choice. The reality is when you talk to someone first generation, or that's an immigrant, a lot of their family won't know what being an entrepreneur means.

It comes with the risk of leaving a full-time job with a retirement package to create a start-up. That's a mindset shift we must deal with

Adrian Mendoza

"Guide others and help them through their journey."

first. It will take more of us being out there to talk about what it means, sharing our own struggles of being Latino in business.

Secondly, how do Latinos create multi-generational family wealth? Creating that wealth isn't buying a new car or investing in real estate, but the type of wealth that is created through mergers and acquisitions, so the wealth gets passed down from generation to generation.

One of the things we've seen is the magic created in Boston and Silicon Valley. The wealth that was created by entrepreneurs and VCs was recycled back into communities, where it became angel investment that transferred back into philanthropy and was invested in other venture funds. That's very powerful.

It takes one to two generations of recycling that capital to build really amazing multi-generational wealth. Latinos are becoming accredited investors with some net worth. I educate them on investing in Latinos, not just in real estate but also in tech. It has to come from our own communities because no one else is going to do it.

Thirdly, it requires the large capital allocators, the pension funds, the retirement funds, and those institutions that manage millions to billions of dollars, to also make it a priority.

If the son of a carpenter cabinet maker can now be a general partner at a venture fund, I'd like to remind the Hispanic community that anyone can do this.

That's powerful, Adrian. When VCs and other minority investors are evaluating other Hispanic businesses, how important is it for the dominant culture, the white culture, to bring on board people of color, to evaluate others?

The first company we ever sold was a company called Good Dog Labs. It was a cyber security firm that was started in Boston and later moved to Austin, Texas. We sold it in five months and returned ten times back to us.

It was started by two Latino brothers. When you ask them about Mendoza Ventures, they will say two things. Firstly, everything I told them was going to happen, happened. Secondly, the reason they had this great connection with us was, we were the only investor that knew exactly where they came from. We understood their culture, their language and their background, so for them Mendoza Ventures being their investor was a magical experience and a fantastic outcome for their family. That event not only changed their trajectory, but that of their families as well. That is the power of venture capital.

What needs to happen in terms of our culture to change our mindset in order for us to invest?

I think from a culture perspective this is also a question of how we get more Latinos to start companies. It's this idea of safety, we do things in our culture that are safe even though we're one of the few cultures that have dropped everything and moved to another country with nothing. If you think about that, how unsafe is that?

The majority of Latinos have come to the US to start a new life and passed that idea of a safety net to their first generation of kids. But it's the first generation that really lives between two cultures. They have to be more aggressive by thinking not just in the short term, like their parents were thinking, but creating a vision for the future.

How do we create a light that's going to mirror that investment in white America? Is it important for us to continue to invest

our money in our own Hispanic communities, or should that be spread out through the general market?

Venture capital has always been localized. VC funds in Boston invest in Boston; New York funds invest in New York; and the Silicon Valley index invests in Silicon Valley. When we started Mendoza Ventures, we saw that as a missed opportunity.

We invest in the best founders regardless of where they are. Our fund has invested in Canada, UK, New York, and we talk with founders as far away as Hong Kong and Shanghai.

If you are a founder in the middle of nowhere at a certain point it is important for you to consider getting up and leaving. If there is no culture of venture capital where you are or a tech community, do like your parents did, pick up and go to the opportunity because that opportunity won't chase you.

A founder in Florida saw me speaking in Spanish while being interviewed on CNN's 'Money in Español' and reached out to me on LinkedIn. She didn't know anything about raising capital and wanted to know who to talk to, so I started connecting her with Latino investors in Miami.

That's the importance of breaking your network to find where the people are. As Latinos, we don't naturally go out of our circles to meet people, but it's so important to break that from our own cultural sensitivity and be more aggressive. You have to go out there and meet other people through LinkedIn, Facebook or whatever other media, because the opportunities are out there.

You describe yourself as a 'top dog'. Why is that?

"An incredible fact is that
Latinos represent 20% of US GDP.
*We need to be able to take that
momentum and run with it."*

It's an 'in-joke' really, but I will try to explain. When we sold Good Dog Labs, the acquirer wanted to change the name. Even though he was selling the company, the founder wasn't happy about this, so we made plush 'TOY' dogs with the company's name on them. The CEO and I went to meet the acquirer at their office and started to hand them out. They loved them so much they decided to keep the name. Three years later they sold the company again and the founders left the business at that point.

We were left with a pile of these dogs so we decided to make them our own. So, like any start-up founder, the dog failed up like an entrepreneur and now works at a VC firm. – The VC Puppy was born!

Years later, I would tell people that the reason we have the dog is because we are the underdogs. One day, a Latina investor stopped me to ask about the VC Puppy. She said, "You're not the underdog... You're the top dog!" That put a smile to my face.

What specific strengths do Hispanic women bring to business that most people overlook?

From my own experience, Latina women run the house and control the finances of the house. They are the matriarchs of the family and hold everything and everyone together. So as a community we should be encouraging them and reminding these strong women that it's part of their DNA to go out there and build something.

I think with regard to Mendoza Ventures, one day my daughter will succeed me. I want her to run the firm, like every Latina should be encouraged to do!

In which areas do you consistently see under investment in the Hispanic community?

It is mostly around tech-focused businesses. I think the easiest way to fix this is by finding Latinos that are building technology and being the ones that are writing the checks. We still don't have enough Latinos in cyber security or AI. We need more Latinos to be encouraged to not only find jobs in tech, but to also start these companies. This is how we can change the face of technology start-ups.

What was the most difficult experience you've had to overcome and how did you face it?

It was the same thing most Hispanics face and that was picking up and leaving.

Both my parents passed away a few years ago and they never really understood what we did. They always asked why I was doing this or that, why didn't I have a consistent job, all the usual things, because they didn't understand the work.

The pressure from family was always there even though both of my parents had been entrepreneurs. It wasn't until we moved our last start up onto the 17th floor of an office building in Boston - a gorgeous office that overlooked the entire city - and my mom showed up and said: "Mijo! You built something amazing!" She was very proud that day.

But even with that experience they both never really understood what we did in venture capital.

You cannot build a fund or a start-up and play it safe. That's something we teach founders and other new investors: that process of starting something and building a business is going to make you uncomfortable and is going to be risky.

"When people ask me what it's like to be an entrepreneur, I always tell them, "You haven't become an entrepreneur until your credit card has been declined buying milk!"

When people ask me what it's like to be an entrepreneur, I always tell them, "You haven't become an entrepreneur until your credit card has been declined buying milk!"

What specific steps did you take that allowed you to be in the position that you are in today?

Certainly, being in tech was critical in getting access to networks and people that were building the same things we were. It's important to be in a community where you're seeing what venture capital and private equity can do; you see what it means for other entrepreneurs to build businesses, raise capital, and sell businesses. That's the spark that lights the match when you can see it all tied together.

When Senofer and I started our first fund it was just our own money. We realized that to make the change and invest in diverse founders that we would have to take that risk. So instead of putting that money away, we pushed forward, invested it, and risked it all to make that difference. We knew someone had to do it so why not us?

We had been in venture capital for seven years when one investor told me that we were Boston's best-kept secret. At the same time, we had an investor that looked at the performance of the first fund and told me if he had those numbers he'd be screaming them from the mountain top! We decided it was time to tell the world about what we build and no longer be a secret. Since that first conversation, we have been covered in Yahoo Finance, CNN Money, Forbes, American Banker, The Boston Globe and even had an appearance on CNBC.

We quickly realized the importance that our story could resonate to others in our community, especially when they see stories with brown faces on the media. I am always proud when I receive notes

"*Guide others* and
HELP OTHERS
through their *Journey*".

Adrian Mendoza

"As you're helping others have
one hand pulling yourself up
and have another hand pulling
the next person up behind you."

from other Latinos about being proud to see a Latino on television talking about business.

As Latinos we were terrible at telling our own story. Ironically, the thing I always tell Latinos is that we should ask for help and share our journey. I am glad I took my own advice.

What is one piece of technology product that changed your life?

The mobile phone. We developed an app for the Prudential that was the first financial mobile app to go through FINRA approval. That was the genesis of the tech companies we built and without that app and mobile tech, there would have been no Adrian Mendoza and no Mendoza Ventures and no VC Puppy.

"As you're helping others have one hand pulling yourself up and have another hand pulling the next person up behind you."

My One Golden Nugget for tenacity is:

"Never stop."

OGN INTERACTIVE
Adrian Mendoza
Scan here
to visit my profile

Andre Arbelaez

HISPANIC JOURNEY

Hispanic National Leader

I want to introduce Andre Arbelaez, an extraordinary individual. I was looking at top leaders around the nation and I came across Andre. I was fascinated by the work that he was doing and the impact that he was making in the Latino community, and I thought: 'That is a man that I want to get to know.'

A global technology executive, Andre is President and CEO of the non-profit Hispanic C-Suite Corporate Council and is a sought-after speaker on Technology, Diversity and Inclusion, and Globalization issues including Smart Cities and Smart Grid technologies. He has had global technology executive roles with Globant, Argentina's Digital and Cognitive Transformation Leader, and previously with Softtek USA, Mexico's largest private near-shore firm as their SVP and Chief Strategy Officer. He also has served leadership roles in Global Business Development with T-Systems and Covisint LLC, the automotive global portal owned by General Motors, Ford, DaimlerChrysler, PSA and Renault.

In 2018 Andre received the Maestro Award in Leadership and was also named one of the 101 Most Influential Latino Leaders in 2017 by Latino Leaders Magazine.

I am honored Andre has joined me as a co-author in creating this book. On our call I first asked him to introduce himself and outline his journey.

As we grow as Hispanics in the United States of America, I am amazed at the unification of our community, the assimilation, that brings us all together. Our common dreams and goals - because of our heritage, our background, our families, and our efforts - are to find the great opportunities available in the United States.

As a community, we can achieve success faster when we work towards a common goal and help each other: "pushing up and pulling up".

That was one of the first incredible journeys that you and I kicked off with. And here we are today.

I asked Andre my number one question: What makes your heart sing?

One of the things I enjoy the most is watching Hispanics that have traditionally taken a backseat role step up to the front. My heart sings when I see them evolve and grow into that frontline leader. I'm literally watching that transition right now with an incredible lady named Marcela Escobar.

Most of you might not know who she is, she is the Special Assistant to the President of the United States, and deputy CIO of the White House. She has been in a role that is perhaps a little bit behind the scenes. Hispanics, as a community, need to celebrate her and make sure that she is seen nationally, as it's a very important role, being involved in policy. Marcela performs administrative and technical functions to support very famous people at, probably, the most important address in the world.

It's those kinds of individuals in our community that we need to constantly push up and get seen - not only for now, but in their next role, and then the role after that, and so on, going potentially to board memberships.

That is what makes my heart sing, seeing that evolution and doing it in a way that is very assimilated, making sure we get things done in an incredible way where we celebrate Latinos.

In my conversation with Andre, I asked him about his remarkable story. I wanted to go back to where he came from and how he grew up, to be where he is now. His reply was as passionate as any I have interviewed and began with his childhood.

I know I'm very fortunate. I come from two great parents – my father was a computer programmer for the national airline, Avianca, and my mom was a teacher. They emigrated from Colombia to the United States for the unique opportunity to improve their lives and those of their children.

Very fortunately, I was born here during that time, and I watched my parents work hard, and do things that were out of their scope - my father was a good computer programmer, but that wasn't the reason he came to the United States. He came here to be a tool die machine operator doing midnight shifts. He did what he had to do to create the opportunity. My mother sold Avon, even though she was a teacher, and as young kids, we helped fill the bags and fill inventory.

So, right away I was involved in business, and it was that engagement of working hard, taking individual responsibility, and making sure we did it without taking money from the government that really established guiding principles for myself and my sister. And now I do that with my children - I want to drive that mentality and I'm honored to say we have done that very successfully.

My mother really has been a great guiding light to me as an entrepreneur. She is a shameless marketer and of course, the blood, sweat and tears that come with it. That is something that has been a great American family journey that I'm so proud of. I definitely follow in her footsteps - that perspective of always leading.

"As a community, we can achieve success faster when we work towards a common goal and **help each other***: pushing up and pulling up."*

Fantastic! There are really so many amazing Latino professionals - I remember meeting a doctor who was also a janitor. He was doing whatever it took to be in this country, to learn, to move forward, and be able to contribute and lift himself back up to where he belonged.

Andre is a very active member of the Latino community; he is clearly on a mission to help others. I asked him, what was his path?

I will go back and say it all starts in the home, it's that guidance from your parents, the work hard responsibility, the 'do I have what it takes to make it on my own? mentally'. I was very fortunate, that through my mother's business and her 'help fund', my parents financed college for me and my sister, but I knew, for sure, that I had to give it back and engage with our community.

After college, I spent time helping with my mother's business, I gave it back. I spent four and a half years with her and simultaneously got involved in the community engaging in something called the Hispanic Business Alliance. Straight away I knew that as a board member I needed to make many changes and within six months I became President.

We really helped transform a small business community in Michigan into a mainstream business community. We became engaged with corporations and did something to bring the whole community together by starting an initiative with the Detroit Tigers, our Major League Baseball team.

We, at the HBA started something called Fiesta Tigres, where the Detroit Tigers - the entire team and the coach, who were not all Latino - engaged with us. We staged off-site events, celebrating the Hispanics who were playing on the team, and really brought the community together, so much so that it came to the point where now once a year they change their uniforms from the Detroit Tigers to Detroit Tigres.

We have bands and music in a really wonderful celebration of culture and an exposure of the knowledge that there are people in the community that can do everything that everyone else does.

We just wanted a fair opportunity. I think that's the American Dream - don't treat us differently, treat us equally. I know we have driven things forward from that perspective, in an incredible way that has kept growing.

Next, I became involved in different organizations and pursued a career in technology. A small group of us young men in Detroit decided to start the Hispanic IT Executive Council. We were very ambitious and followed a model of an African American group called Information Technology Senior Management Forum (ITSMF), a guiding light on what an incredible job a community of hard-working individuals can do - chief information officers, chief technology officers and chief security officers.

When we first met with them it was a little bit of a West Side Story kind of a situation! It was the Jets and the Sharks coming together and I was very doubtful because I thought we were both fighting for corporate sponsors, but we found ITSMF very embracing, and they guided us. They said there's money for everyone and we can all work together if you let us show you how to avoid the pitfalls that happen when you run an organization like this. It was such an incredible start to the journey.

This was back in 2007 and just a month ago, I was at their big summit gala in Atlanta and it was hugs and welcomes and a celebration of us reaching corporate levels that you would not have thought possible 30 years ago.

The African-American Community protested in Detroit in 1967 and many cities across America for better treatment from the government, so they have come a long way, and these African American IT Leaders have done it the right way.

Seeing that coming together of individuals is what really drives inspiration for the next generation.

That is why I call it the 'push up, pull up' because those who have gotten here today, have a direct responsibility to make sure the path is set for the next generation, for our children, and their children's children. It is not an easy path. It's a path of doing the right things - go to college, study, use your network, that's a big thing.

Use that expression, 'it's not who you are, but who you know'. Leverage that network. That is why people need to make sure they are engaged in their local community, their business community, and the community they're connected to in the world of technology.

Tying all that together creates opportunities - companies don't do business with companies, people do business with people. If we strive towards those goals, I believe we're going to be on a great journey following the path of American exceptionalism that I'm a big fan of and helping lead the way to a peaceful society. We can solve all these struggles that we have in the world today by working together.

I asked Andre on his journey, what has shaped him to become the man he is today?

The journey is never a straight line and it's been hard work, and hard philosophy, throughout the process. When I was 12 years old, I was delivering newspapers. I worked hard and had two or three streets as my customers. In fact, I worked so hard, 365 days a year, that I earned enough money to buy a motor scooter. Then I was able to do 10 streets!

It was always that mentality of: set this better, do more, set again, and do more. That was something that working for the *Detroit News* really taught me because I had to get up at 4.30 in the morning to get the job done. It was that self-responsibility, knowing I had an assignment, that I had a task, and I had to deliver the newspapers at people's front doors by 7 am, that taught me at a very early age that level of discipline.

When I was 15, I started working at McDonalds. By age fifteen-and-a-half, I was promoted to assistant floor manager. One other buddy of mine started at McDonald's at the same time. He is now a professor at Tufts University in Boston. We mirrored our career paths. He is African American, and I'm Latino, but we immediately bonded the first day because we knew we were on a journey together.

Within six months, at 16, we were both promoted to assistant managers, and we were managing teenagers, and senior citizens, just doing something for fun to keep busy.

It was an incredible experience learning how to deal with different types of people in that process, really an eye-opening experience that gave me the foundation of who I am.

When they offered me a chance to go to 'Hamburger University', in Oak Brook, Illinois, I think that's where I drew the line. I had to go to college and that is where I found myself - Northwood University, which promoted the 'free enterprise market philosophy'. It promoted individual responsibility with Judeo-Christian values. It was a private business school, and it really drove the mentality of 'you can do things, and here's how'.

I took full advantage of it while I was a freshman and joined a fraternity. Within six months, I was elected president of ALL the fraternities - as a freshman! It was an incredible experience managing and dealing with 600 fraternity guys, some of them liked you and some of them hated you just because you had that title. We had to deal with underage campus drinking and decided to promote a philosophy of doing it responsibly by creating an alcohol policy and befriending the administration really closely, as well as the town and its leadership, to make sure we were a part of the community.

That leadership process really engaged us. I started the college newspaper, '*The Entrepreneur*', and because I was the All-state college hockey goalie and President of the fraternities, I made sure I wrote an opinion in each of the bi-weekly newspaper sections about something controversial to get readership. The paper quickly became known as *'The Andrepreneurship!'*

The school was so thankful for what I had done they awarded me an MBA program, without qualification. They just said it is because I had done so much, it was incredible.

After graduating from college, I discovered a contradiction between the theory taught and the hard work philosophy of a family business. It really teaches you a lot. Sometimes the reality of people management and psychology that you have to do in corporate America is super overwhelming. However, you learn, and I think that's why the

"The journey is never a straight line and it's been hard work."

expression 'the blood, sweat, and tears' is so pervasive because you just can't sleep. You're thinking about payroll, you're thinking about employees leaving, you're thinking about challenges with business opportunities, you're thinking about legal issues, accounting - you know, you have to fully understand a P&L, what is the balance sheet really telling you?

All these elements you learn along your journey. I was very thankful to my mother who gave me that opportunity and drove me, my father who guided me and was a steady hand in this process, as I started my climb into corporate America, realizing that the journey would take me into the technology sector.

The reason I was hired in the technology sector was that being involved in the Hispanic community, I was fortunate to receive press, so when I went to a company that was a start-up funded by automotive companies back in the year 2000, I walked in with a newspaper clipping that detailed how I had been a speaker at the wake of a famous baseball player for the Detroit Tigers and, it had nothing to do with technology.

That showed them that I was able to present, I was somebody in the community, and the hiring director looked at my background, and said they wanted me because they needed me to bring it in. Before I knew it, I had taken the job and my salary jumped over $125,000 from Friday to Monday from the manufacturing company that I was working for, to joining a technology company.

I am a big believer in the concept of positioning based on four key elements - say the right things, be with the right people, be at the right place, and at the right time. Combining those elements together really creates opportunities. It is not luck. That expression, 'luck', in my opinion, is when skill meets opportunity. I inherently positioned myself so when the career move opportunity came, I was ready, and that allowed me to start traveling the world. I was traveling to Europe and then Asia, and South America, representing this technology company.

The challenge that appeared for me was that the Hispanic community thought I had abandoned them for money. They started calling me a 'coconut'. I didn't know how to take this. It was strange to me because one moment I was an advocate for the community, the next I was being chastised as a coconut – 'brown on the outside and white on the inside'. I took that as something of a compliment because from my perspective considering that I'm living on a lake with both my boats in the water, a back yard that I don't have to put locks on, and my keys are in the ignition eight months of the year without even having to think twice about it. I have a beautiful home, and a beautiful family, "led by my wife, Susan", and for that I can be called a coconut all day long. Instead of it being a negative, I took it as a positive. Something that as businesspeople, you have to deal with.

There is always some of that adversity because people will look at me and say I'm just climbing. But yeah, that's what we're supposed to do!

Sometimes we need to deal with challenges from within our community where the mindset between the Central Americans and the South Americans comes into play. Of course, those are broad strokes, but that journey of continuing to climb and going to companies and being an advocate for excelling no matter what your background, is something we must all strive for.

Along that journey, I was asked to become a sponsor and help start an organization called HITEC, the Hispanic IT Executive Council. I focused on the 'push up, pull up' mentality that we all need to foster within our community. In a couple of years, I was asked to become President. It was a tremendous honor. I called it HITEC 2.0, Ditto. When I came in, I focused on that 'push up, pull up' mentality, and really helped drive the mentality that we all need to do that within our community.

By my desk, I have a statue of one man lifting another up a mountain, awarded to me by a professor from Duke University. It's all focused on a mindset of making sure we were driving not only the top executives, but the younger executives coming out of college and giving them a guiding path.

I call it the "If you can see it, you can be it" mentality.

After I became President of HITEC, I hunted down top executives from around the country, male and female, getting them involved and encouraging them to be part of it. When I was in front of the CIO of AT&T, I had to beg and plead with him to join because I knew he was essential to that process.

He told me he'd join if Ramon Baez the CIO of Hewlett Packard joined. So, I flew from Dallas to Palo Alto, California, to show Ramon what we could accomplish with the power when we all worked together. It was literally down to a text between them. They were texting each other in front of me, and they each said yes, they'd join. When put those two executives together, great things happen... and they did!.

Then, of course, it's an amazing domino effect. The CIO of Hewlett Packard says to me: 'Do you know Tim Campos?' "No, I don't," I

"There are many opportunities in the tech industry that do not require a college degree. Certifications for programmers and developers allow entry into corporate America into fast-paced and, more importantly, high-paying roles that have a huge elasticity of income over non-traditional technology roles."

said. 'Because', he continued, 'he is the CIO of Facebook, you should really reach out to him. He's Dominican.'

I jumped on a place, we met, we connected! When executives see that they're in the right room, they want to be in that room all day long because now they can share stories and experiences with each other. And that has continued and grown.

I was President of that organization for eight years and it keeps growing to this day, led by an incredible group of executives. That's been a wonderful part of my journey and now I have started taking that journey to the next level, to move on to something called HC3, which is about Hispanic corporate executives in the C-Suite. So, it's not just technology, but right across the board – legal, accounting and general administration. Uniting these executives to keep focusing on that 'push up, pull up story, with tons of support from corporate executives across America, because they want to take that to the next level.

With that background, I have been fortunate enough to bring 75 Hispanics to the White House, and the CIO of the United States of America, Tony Scott hosted us. He was tremendous in the process and continues to be one of my good close friends. He was the CIO of Walt Disney and Microsoft until President Obama tapped him on his shoulder he took on a service role to unite the federal government under one key technology platform and brought us in with open arms.

And how did I connect with him? On LinkedIn. I just sent him a note. I believe that happened by following my core philosophies of integrity and character - that your history will follow you. The integrity that I laid before, through what I have done, has opened up a lot of doors. It was a 'this is the real deal' moment - an individual coming through my door in corporate America. I was very proud, I would take my business card, as President of HITEC and say this card gets me in any door in corporate America.

That journey of establishing credibility and integrity for our Hispanic community is something that I hold with the utmost respect, but I also make sure my community is also held to that level of respect. I make sure I call out when I see something wrong and say it with authority directly to them. It happened just this week in Dallas, at a summit, when people moved away from the direction that we were going, I made it very clear that that's not the direction that speaks to our community. I'm very fortunate to have that role, one I take with a great deal of seriousness.

That journey keeps going as I take things to the next level, and it's a great honor when I can pick up the phone and call somebody inside the White House and say, "I want you to speak", "I want you to be engaged". The answer has never been "no", It's always been "when and where".

That's the kind of engagement that we bring to the table. I'm very honored by it whether I'm here in Detroit, in the automotive community, or whether I'm in Dallas with an incredible, diverse business community, there's always the next major event we're going to be doing all around the country. If you deliver great American values that just happen to be matching Hispanic values, everybody is on board. I think that's what we have celebrated and why we continue to grow.

One of the key things that we need is to hold ourselves accountable. Not only as Hispanic leaders, but also in the 'pull up' area as parents. A lot of us who are in you know, who are raising second and third-generation children, when we send them away to college, or in their early teen years, we need to have a responsibility to guide them.

I know way too many parents, particularly in the Hispanic community, that say they just want their kids to be happy and they'll figure it out, but I think there is a lot more that we can do than just sit back and let that happen. I think it's our role to give them guidelines, to engage with them and use our network to push them into specific areas.

We see a lot of women move into social care, physical care, and health care and we want to make sure we show them all the options. I think that's too easy, because they may have had the role of the older sister taking care of the younger sister, maybe we need to be encouraging them to move into STEM fields?

Engaging and guiding our children is very important. That is why I joined the board of an organization called The Latino Career Assessment that creates curated programs for kids to really engage, by taking an assessment, to be self-aware, so they can make smart decisions. It's not only good for them, it is also good for the parents that are paying for college, or university as well.

Student debt is a big topic and what an overwhelming burden it is for them, they just can't get out of it. So, having these assessments, engaging parents, would be very helpful. That is a passion of mine, not to let parents sit back. Let's all get parents engaged in guiding our future leaders.

What would be the word Andre would wish to be remembered by?

SELFLESS.

Pushing our community is my passion, making sure that we are living the American Dream.

What can Latinos do to stand out in the tech space? And what are their opportunities and challenges?

Latinos can stand up in the tech space by making sure they're getting involved, researching, getting certified in certain technologies, but the key thing is making sure they're involved in their ERG groups and looking for mentorships at levels above them.

Considering the economic limitations of Latino American countries, what opportunities do you believe are in the tech industries for Latinos outside of the US, in their own countries?

There are many opportunities for Latinos outside the United States to be involved in technology projects, the concept of 'nearshoring'. The same time zone, same culture, and excellent English language skills, really give Latin America an incredible opportunity to get involved in projects over the United States, let alone all around the world. The schooling is excellent. The jobs and companies are growing rapidly, and you'll see more nearshoring companies growing faster in Latin America than in the United States.

In your professional experience, what are the challenges of Latinos in the tech space right now?

The challenge for Latinos in the tech space is to make sure they evolve from their nature of being humble and quiet to being more assertive, visible and engaged. Those are traits of leadership and faster growing faster career-paced individuals.

What opportunities are leaders not taking advantage of in bringing Latinos into the C-Suite?

The challenge is to overcome the belief that if I'm the only one in the room that looks like me, maybe I'm the only one that should be in the room.

We need to encourage Latinos already in the C-Suite to foster the 'push up, pull up' mentality, to open the doors for others.

Andre, technology is one of those industries where education is a necessity. What would you say to individuals that don't have that educational path, that may not be able to afford college, what would you say to them to get into the tech industry?

There are many opportunities in the tech industry that do not require a college degree. Certifications for programmers and developers allow entry into corporate America into fast-paced and, more importantly, high-paying roles that have a huge elasticity of income over non-traditional technology roles.

What questions do you wish Latinos were asking to advance their careers?

The question that Latinos are not asking is how do I negotiate better? How do I get that sponsor within my company? Don't be afraid to ask, be more open and be more engaged with that process.

Beautiful, any closing remarks?

In closing, it is very important for all of us to make sure we join the journey, but not alone. Bring others with you. It's a constant effort. Look around. Who do you see? Make sure you bring them with you. That is the greatest story that this country allows you to do.

Is there one book and author you recommend?

I recommend the book *'12 Rules for Life'* by Dr Jordan Peterson. Published by Allen Lane. I believe concepts of common sense really helped drive excellence in corporate America.

My One Golden Nugget is

"The concept of pushing up and pulling up, being engaged in your community. Help your friends reach the next level while knowing the responsibility of turning around and helping that next executive. Come up and follow your footsteps. So, the journey is fuller and deeper. They help the Hispanic community."

OGN INTERACTIVE
Andre Arbelaez
Scan here
to visit my profile

In Rocío's Words

Throughout the book there are uncomfortable stories of strife and the ability to overcome it. I've been asking people to shout about their successes and must I put myself in there as well. I too felt uncomfortable sharing this.

Yet here goes:

We have developed the world's first self-coaching system, allowing anyone to coach themselves to success.' Our product is called '*The MindShift Game*', a physical board game that assists people on their own journey.

Players discover exactly what is important for them to do in order to achieve success.

We also have *The MindShift Guild* which provides opportunities for players to come on board five days a week, to have conversations, to get inspired, to interact with other leaders, to learn what it is to take courageous actions, and to develop other skills.

This book is here to serve as a tool to inspire people. My book, "*Unstoppable*", which is also inspirational. We have many different products that will be coming out on a global scale.

As a team, we have dedicated the rest of our life journeys' to making this world a better place through our products, and we have realized that we cannot do it by being meek. We must be at the top of the mountain, shouting out that we have something that will help people achieve the level of success that they are seeking for themselves.

Rocío Pérez

OGN INTERACTIVE
Rocío Pérez
Scan here
to visit my profile

Gratitude

Mil Gracias and a huge thank you to each of our co-authors for generously sharing their stories to touch, move and inspire people to find ways to achieve their dreams.

I am forever grateful to Angélica Killion, Joanne Siracusa and Gerardo Garcia Jurado for their insights, love and compassion during this beautiful work and the countless hours invested.

Thank you to Maxwell Preece, Steven Foster, David Torres Mora for your support and guidance throughout this process.

We express our gratitude to people from all walks of life who saw what was possible, shifted their beliefs, took bold actions and achieved what others thought was beyond their reach. Thank you for creating the life you powerfully chose to create.

And to all the extraordinary dreamers out there who are investing in their dreams and consciously inspiring themselves, their families and communities, may the ripples of your extraordinary impact bear fruit for generations to come.

Enjoy connecting with these touching and insightful life stories from our amazing co-authors.

Let's create our own empowering narrative!

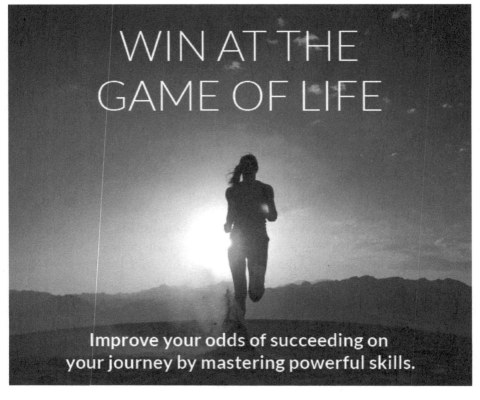

WIN AT THE GAME OF LIFE

Improve your odds of succeeding on your journey by mastering powerful skills.

The MindShift Game is a board game based on proven processes of effective visualizations, affirmations and bold actions. Play to bring your dreams into fruition.

The MindShift Game teaches you how to create empowering habits which support you in achieving your desires. Increase your COURAGE, VISION, CONFIDENCE, POWER, and ENERGY by playing this game. As you make your way around the game board, everyone wins.

This is your journey, you powerfully choose how to play it, we give you the tools to arrive where you want to go.

VISIT TheMindShiftGame.com

What is your
One Golden Nugget?

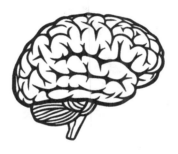

www.onegoldennugget.com